Illustrator
Agi Palinay

Editor
Walter Kelly, M.A.

Editorial Project Manager
Ina Massler Levin, M.A.

Editor-in-Chief
Sharon Coan, M.S. Ed.

Art Director
Elayne Roberts

Associate Designer
Denise Bauer

Art Coordinator
Cheri Macoubrie Wilson

Cover Artist
Denise Bauer

Product Manager
Phil Garcia

Imaging
Alfred Lau
James Edward Grace

Publishers
Rachelle Cracchiolo, M.S. Ed.
Mary Dupuy Smith, M.S. Ed.

Thematic Activities and Patterns

for the
Early Childhood Classroom

Author

Beverly Ann Beckmann, M.S. Ed.

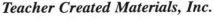

Teacher Created Materials, Inc.
6421 Industry Way
Westminster, CA 92683
www.teachercreated.com
ISBN-1-57690-470-9

©1999 Teacher Created Materials, Inc.
Reprinted, 2002
Made in U.S.A.

Table of Contents

Introduction

This book represents years of collecting ideas and trying them out. It is based on traditional philosophy and developmentally appropriate material. Each unit is structured as follows:

Lesson Plans

Daily lesson plans are given for each theme. Use the ideas according to the teacher's plan for the day. There may be specific things that are in the school's schedule but not in this material. Everyone has a different plan for the day. Regardless of the particular teacher's plan, it is hoped that he or she remembers to be "structured to be unstructured." Every day has a "teachable moment." That time is when a child brings up a problem. An answer to the problem will last with the child for a long time. Even though the teacher has something scheduled for that time, it is often best to drop that and make full use of the teachable moment.

Room Preparation

Room preparation includes creating bulletin boards, puppet stages, mobiles, and patterns. Suggestions are given for needed materials and literature for the week. Suggestions are also given for famous paintings, reproductions of which can be obtained from some libraries and museums, plus classical music to use for background listening.

Individual Activities

Activities can be selected per day, or they can be used according to the plan at the beginning of each unit. There may be too many activities for the class to use in one day. It is possible to spread the plan over more than the suggested days, using some suggestions in both the children's activities and the group activities on the next day.

Always allow the children to select and do their own activities. This can be achieved by refraining from showing what a finished picture or product should look like. Rather, show the process of doing it. When the child takes a project home and it is posted on the refrigerator, the child should be able to think "I did it myself" rather than thinking the teacher did part of it. That means that the teacher should not use one finger, brush, or glue bottle in helping the child finish the item. But always use encouragement!

Group Activities

Group activities, though listed in sequence for the week, can be used any given day of the week. They contain an introduction to the story, presentation of the story or activity, and a follow-up. In some cases, the introduction or follow-up can be used without the story, depending on the age level of the children.

Introduction *(cont.)*

Group Activities *(cont.)*

When reading orally to the class, pique the children's interest with an introduction and follow with the story. Afterward, use a follow-up activity that involves the story. This activity can incorporate language arts, science, and hands-on math. Then use a transition-time activity to lead to the next time frame.

Games

Games are suggested per day. They, too, can be rotated daily.

Songs, Action Poems, and Fingerplay

In some cases the suggested songs go with the book for the day. In order for children to learn them, of course, songs, action poems, and fingerplay should be used for more than one day.

Transition activities are suggested per week or in some cases per day. They will lead the children from one activity to another if needed.

General Instructions

Patterns are given at the end of the unit. As they are needed in the individual activity, group activity, or game time, the title and page number of the pattern will appear. To make a pattern larger for the bulletin board, door, or mobile, reproduce the page on a transparency. Place the transparency on an overhead projector and focus the outline on larger paper taped to the wall. Draw the outline with pencil and then take it down and complete it with markers, crayons, or paint. If you are drawing an item taped to the wall, do not use markers. They will bleed onto the wall and sometimes stay permanently. Prepare your material to last. If possible, laminate or cover it with clear plastic. It can be used again.

Rather than restricting them to a special unit, include nursery rhymes with all themes. Rhythm and rhyme are a good basis for reading skills.

Inquire at local libraries or museums for loans of famous painting reproductions. Keep them in view of children and frequently bring them into casual conversation. Suggestions are given for artwork which children can identify with and associate with the theme.

Background music may include children's songs but should also include soothing pieces by well-known classical composers. Suggestions are given where appropriate.

It is hoped that the ideas in this book can be used according to the needs of each school and teacher. Have fun moving from theme to theme, watching the children grow in confidence, competence, independence, and cooperation.

Handy Hints

- ❏ Leaving the family for the first week of school may be difficult for some children. Here are some ideas to cope with that.

- • Take pictures of each child and tape them to the cubbie areas. They will help the child identify his or her own area.

- • Have the child carry a photo of mom, dad, or a special person.

- • Draw a circle on the blackboard to represent a clock. Show where the clock hands are now and where the hands will be when the child goes home.

- • Have the child bring a favorite stuffed toy or blanket. As the day or week progresses, suggest that the item can be kept in the cubbie and the child can get it when needed.

- • Have ready to read a copy of *The Kissing Hand,* published by the Child Welfare League of America, 440 First Street Northwest, Suite 310, Washington, D.C. 20001. The story deals with Mother Raccoon giving Chester a special secret dealing with leaving home and going to school.

- ❏ Always place the child's name in the upper left-hand corner of a page or object. This establishes the format for reading. Also, starting on the left edge sometimes prevents the child from writing backwards, although this is a common pattern in early childhood.

- ❏ Some children use both hands at a young age. To determine the dominant hand, place a crayon in front of the child. See which hand the child uses to pick it up. *This has to be done many, many times in order to be sure which hand is dominant. Do not force a child to use a certain hand.*

- ❏ Young children have a difficult time with scissors. Begin by having them tear paper rather than cut it. When children are ready to cut, try to have them use the thumb in the smaller hole and the third finger or both the second and third fingers in the larger space. Always use child-size blunt scissors. It is common for the beginner to twist the thumb down. To cope with this problem, draw a smiley face on the child's thumb. Tell the child that he or she should always be able to see the smiley face.

Handy Hints *(cont.)*

❏ Easels may be a handicap for beginners. Tables may be better to begin with.

❏ Use washable school glue and non-toxic paints and materials.

❏ Orange tempera rarely washes out of clothes. Make sure that children wear smocks. When purchasing tempera paint, order wide-mouth containers with twist-off lids. The squeeze bottles are difficult to empty when you get to the bottom of the bottle, which means that you may not get your money's worth.

❏ Use plastic, stackable cylindrical containers. Commercially made containers have lids and funnel pieces to push brushes through when painting. If you do not have a paint rack with holes, fill the paint containers half full. That will avoid spills.

❏ Use firm, wide-bristle brushes for large tempera painting and not watercolor brushes. Young children are not developed enough to wash their brushes before going to another color. It may be necessary at first to place a separate brush in each container. Explain to them that each time a color is changed, the brush in the new color is used. Older children can be taught to wash the brush before placing it in another container.

❏ If you are using several colors, place the lighter colors beginning on the right side of the rack closer to the right hand. Or place them on the left if the child is left-handed. Tempera paint has to be placed on paper with the light color first, but a small child does not understand this. The child cannot lighten a dark tempera color. Therefore, strategic placing of the paint is necessary. If the darker color is placed first, it will be used first.

The opposite is true of chalk. If a dark shade is placed on the paper first, it can be lightened with yellow, etc.

❏ If you do not want to buy newsprint paper, use the classified section from the newspaper. Or use grocery bags, cut and spread flat.

Here are some ideas for easel use.

• Put garbage bags or plastic bags over the surfaces of easels. Remove them at the end of the week and avoid scrubbing paint from the easels.

• Put plastic lunch-size bags in paint containers at the easel. During the week, keep the containers covered when not in use. Remove the plastic bags at the end of the week and avoid scrubbing out the paint containers.

Handy Hints *(cont.)*

❑ Using finger paint requires strategy. Place newspapers on the table. Place the glossy side of finger-paint paper on the newspaper, right side up. Cover the paper with a light coating of water, using a wide painter's brush. Place about two tablespoons of finger paint on the paper if it is about 18" x 24" (46 cm x 60 cm) or larger-sized paper. Watch the children blend, swirl, and create!

❑ Accept any product as the work of the child. Avoid praise such as "Great!" and "It's beautiful." Instead, be specific. Say, "The red looks nice in the center of the circle." Praise what you see.

Put creative projects in other areas besides the "art corner." That will encourage some children who do not want to do "arty" things.

❑ If the teacher displays the children's work, display all the children's work. Do not center only on what the teacher considers well done.

❑ Keep several all-purpose large-motor and small-motor activities nearby to use when necessary. Such activities might include these:

• Parachute

Record/Cassette: *Rhythmic Parachute Play.* Children love to toss wiffle balls in the parachute.

• Beanbags

Record/Cassette: *Beanbag Activities and Coordination Skills*

• Rhythm Band Instruments

Record/Cassette: *Play Your Instruments and Make a Pretty Sound* by Ella Jenkins

❑ When using string or yarn, put tape around the ends so that it resembles a shoestring.

❑ To prevent glitter from dropping to the floor and making a mess, mix with corn syrup. Make sure that it is completely dry before sending it home.

❑ Laminate or cover with clear plastic anything you may wish to use in future years of teaching.

❑ Use heavy-duty noniron Pellon for name tags. This material will not tear so easily as paper. Draw on it with permanent markers.

Handy Hints (cont.)

❏ To make a basket for Easter or any occasion, dip a nine-inch (23 cm) paper plate in water. Make sure that the water has dripped off. Select a metal can that is the size of the basket you want to create and center the paper plate on top of the can. Press down the sides of the plate and overlap the circular sections. Secure with a rubber band until dry (about an hour). Take off the rubber bands, and the basket will retain its shape. Punch holes in the sides and place a pipe cleaner through the holes to make a handle. Since the basket is paper, the child can use markers, crayons, stickers, etc., to decorate.

❏ Standing in front of a window when talking to children causes them to look at a glare rather than at the teacher.

❏ If a certain child gets unruly, merely stand next to him or her and continue talking. If the teacher stops talking and tells the child to behave, it interrupts the instruction and gives attention to the unruly child.

❏ Use a standard fingerplay to capture the children's attention when things get out of control. Try the following:

"Open, Shut Them"

(traditional)

Open, shut them; open, shut them; (*Open and close fists.*)
Give a little clap. (*Clap hands.*)
Open, shut them; open, shut them; (*Open and close fists.*)
Lay them in your lap. (*Place hands in lap.*)
Open, shut them; open, shut them; (*Open and close fists.*)
To your shoulders fly. (*Place both hands on shoulders.*)
Then like little birdies,
Let them flutter to the sky. (*Wiggle all fingers and have them rise skyward.*)
Falling, falling, falling, falling almost to the ground. (*Have fingers move slowly to the ground.*)
Pick them up and make them twirl round and round. (*Rotate arms round and round.*)
Faster, faster, faster; (*Rotate rapidly.*)
Slower, slower, slower; (*Rotate slowly.*)
Put them to sleep. (*Say rapidly and place hands in prayer fashion next to face.*)

After saying the fingerplay, go immediately into the activity without allowing the children to take control of the class again.

Five Plans for Introduction to School

	Day One	Day Two	Day Three	Day Four	Day Five
Individual Activities	• Bears Activity for Children and Parents • Cook Cereal	• Gingerbread Dough • Gingerbread Cookies	• Blocks • Ice Cubes	• Sink/Float • Water Table	• Store • Dress-Up Hats
Group Activities	Bears Porridge	Gingerbread Person	*Who Wants Arthur?*	*Elephant Fell in a Well*	*Caps for Sale*
Games	Hot Potato and Doggie, Doggie, Where's Your Bone? (according to animal for the particular day)	Ball Roll	Beanbag Pass		
Songs, Action Poems, Fingerplay	(Select from suggested items.)	"Head, Shoulders, Knees, and Toes"	"Good Morning to You"	"I Clap My Hands"	"Monkey See, Monkey Do"
Transitions			Walk like a dog, cat, snake, mouse, or fish.	Move to next area, pretending arms are trunks.	Say, "Caps for sale," walking to next area.

Room Preparation for Introduction to School

Bulletin Board

See the pattern for the bulletin board the first week of school on pages 21–27. The school building is in the center, and the bears, gingerbread, dogs, elephants, and monkeys are placed on a path leading to the school. Have children's names on the animals or gingerbread. These patterns can be used for name tags also.

Name Tags

Name tags for bears, gingerbread, dogs, elephant, and monkey are found on pages 22–26.

Dramatic Play Area

Set up a store in the dramatic play area and have many hats in the housekeeping area.

Suggested Literature for Introduction to School

Ets, Marie Hall. *Elephant Fell in a Well.* Viking Press, 1972.

Galdone, Paul. *Goldilocks and the Three Bears.* Houghton Mifflin, 1972.

Graham, Amanda. *Who Wants Arthur?* G. Stevens Publishers, 1987.

Schmidt, Karen Lee. *The Gingerbread Man.* Scholastic, Inc., 1967.

Slobodkina, Esphyr. *Caps for Sale.* Young Scott Books, 1940.

Materials

- cooking ingredients for three-bears porridge
- cooking ingredients for gingerbread
- tempera paint, craft sticks, one sheet each of green and red construction paper, water table, blocks

Planning Information

The plans for introduction to school are set for Monday, Tuesday, and so on. However, the teacher may want to begin with one of the other stories and choose follow-up stories from a unit consistent with that day's story. If the bears' first day is used, for example, choose either bear stories for the rest of the week or use the remaining stories in the Introduction to School.

Patterns for before-school material for each day, plus material for parents and activities, are given for every day. For countdown until school, name tags, and parents' first day, it is necessary to use the first-day patterns for only one of the following: bears, gingerbread, dogs, elephants, or monkeys. Save the rest for the following year.

Also make sure that each day the children go around the school building. By the end of the week, they should feel confident in their surroundings.

Activities for Introduction to School

Meeting Children Before School Begins

Schedule children at half-hour intervals to visit school and teacher before school begins. Parents can be sent a letter informing them of an opportunity to see the room and teacher without having to share that time with other children. Have them visit the room, playground, toys, and the teacher. When they leave, inform them that they will receive a postcard about the first day of school. Also give them a sheet of paper with a countdown until the start of school. Countdown patterns are found on pages 28–32.

In the days that follow, send out postcards to children informing them of the first day of school and asking them to bring a parent, guardian, babysitter, or adult on the first day. A postcard pattern appears on page 20.

First Day of School

Greet parents and give them name tags. Patterns for name tags are on pages 22–26. The teacher should bend down to greet children face to face and give them their name tags. Some children may not want name tags but will be happy if they are pinned to their backs.

Have assignment sheets for things that the parent and child are to find in the room. Patterns for each topic are given on pages 40–42. Remember that this activity is to be used on the first day only. After everyone has completed the assignment, gather them on chairs or rugs and ask about things they found by using the prepared sheet. The teacher may then use any of the activities for the specific day and have the parents join in.

Individual Activities

Choose which unit you will begin with and prepare for that.

Bears

Have the following charts around the room and have parents put the names of children in the appropriate spots. Make sure that there is a jar of gummy bears available for the children to guess the number contained. Have them write their estimates on the chart for the gummy bears. Arrange the charts in separate areas such as *block, housekeeping, science, library,* etc. Charts may be made of poster board, laminated, and kept for the following year. Use patterns on pages 33–39. They would include the following questions:

- How old is your teddy bear?
- Are you a morning bear or a nighttime bear?
- Which bear paw do you write with?

- How many gummy bears are in the jar?
- How many buttons are you wearing?
- What does your bear cave look like?

Give parents the Teddy Bears Welcome You handout. The pattern is on page 33. After it is completed, discuss as a group.

Activities for Introduction to School *(cont.)*

Individual Activities *(cont.)*

Cookies

Instruct children that the gingerbread man has been running all over the room. In some places he has left cookies, and in other places he has left raisins and, sometimes, footsteps on the floor. Find all the places in the room that the gingerbread man has been. Then find out why he spent so much time in that area.

Place boxes of raisins, packages of cookies, and cookie footprints in various areas of the room. Instruct parents to take children around the room. When they find the items, decide why the gingerbread man would spend time there. Write the answers on Gingerbread Welcomes You. The pattern is on page 40.

Dogs

The teacher places pictures of dogs around the room. The bulletin board pattern or name tag pattern on page 24 can be used.

Parents and children follow the dog prints around the room. Locate pictures of dogs at various areas of the room, such as housekeeping, art, science, block, manipulative, library, etc. Parents write down what the children see in the areas on Dog's First Day of School pattern on page 41.

After all the dog prints are followed and all areas of the room explored, find the bone or doghouse placed in the group activity area. Children, parents, and teacher discuss all the things in the room.

Elephants

Place pictures of elephants in various areas of the room. Use the bulletin board or name tag pattern on page 25. Use the block area, play apparatus, story area, art area, etc.

Housekeeping: Put two bowls out. Have plastic food in one bowl and peanuts in another bowl. Have two more sets of bowls. One should have a picture of a boy and girl and the other a picture of the elephant. Put food that a child would like in the bowls that have the children's picture and put in the other bowls something an elephant would like.

Give parent and child a copy of Elephant's First Day of School on page 42. When all have completed the sheet, have them come together in a central area and discuss what they have found.

Monkeys

Cut bananas from construction paper, using the pattern on page 27. Place them around the room in areas for blocks, manipulatives, story, science, housekeeping, motor activities, art, etc. Then explain to the children and the parents that a pretend monkey is going to visit the room. When he comes, he is going to look for something to eat. While we are waiting for him to come, look around the room and see if you can see any bananas there for the monkey. When you have found all the banana areas, return to a central area. The teacher will then go around the room and count how many bananas there were. Write the numeral on a large sheet of paper.

Activities for Introduction to School *(cont.)*

Individual Activities *(cont.)*

Monkeys *(cont.)*

Bring out either a sock monkey or any commercially made monkey and have him say he is hungry. Explain to the monkey that we have only so many bananas. Show the monkey the written numeral. Then have the monkey walk around the room in the teacher's hand and pretend to eat the bananas. Children and parents should follow and talk about what happens in each part of the room.

Cook Cereal (Bears)

Make cooked cereal using standard oatmeal with added raisins and cut-up apples. When the oatmeal is cooked, show it to children and parents.

Gingerbread Dough (Cookies)

Make sure that children put the items in the mixing bowl. Help them read from the rebus recipe (page 43). Allow them to break the eggs, measure all ingredients, stir, and form the figure. Form into one large gingerbread man/boy/girl so that it can run away. When it returns, it can be broken into pieces so that each child can try it. The following recipe, also found in rebus form on page 43, is for softer gingerbread (not the crunchy kind.)

    1 cup (240 mL) butter

    1 cup (240 mL) sugar

    $^1/_3$ (80 mL) cup light molasses

    1 egg

    5 cups (1,200 mL) sifted all-purpose flour

    1 teaspoon (5 mL) baking soda

    1 teaspoon (5 mL) salt

    1 teaspoon (5 mL) nutmeg

    3 teaspoons (15 mL) ginger

Use soft butter and mix in sugar, molasses, and egg. Combine the remaining dry ingredients separately. Stir in four cups of the dry ingredients. On floured surface, knead in remaining flour mixture until soft and pliable. Use a lightly greased cookie sheet.

Have children form the head, arms, body, and legs. Press down in pan so that it is about the size of the cookie sheet. It should be about $^1/_4$ inch (64 mm) thick. Try to even out the entire cookie so that the baking is even. Decorate with red-hots and raisins.

Bake at 375° F (190° C) for about 15 to 20 minutes. Test with a toothpick after 10 minutes to see if the gingerbread is baked. Allow to cool in pan. Do not try to take it off the pan until it is cooled.

Activities for Introduction to School (cont.)

Individual Activities (cont.)

Blocks (Dogs)

With all types of blocks (including Lincoln Logs), build many doghouses.

Ice Cubes (Dogs)

Mix water with a small amount of liquid tempera paint and pour into ice trays. Place in the freezer. Prop a craft stick in each cube so that it can be used as a handle for the children. When the cubes are frozen, remove from the freezer and place in a plastic bag. Return to the freezer until ready for use. Use 9" x 12" (23 cm x 30 cm) manila paper for the children to color pictures of their favorite dogs, using the ice cubes as paintbrushes.

Sink/Float (Elephants)

Place a pan of water on the table. Find items that you think will float and sink in water. Have children try out the items. If they float, place them on a piece of green paper. If they sink, place them on a piece of red paper.

Water Table (Elephants)

Have a water table with boats and other water toys.

Store (Monkeys)

Set up a store with items for sale. Have prices on the items, pretend money in the cash register, a shopping basket, and a cashier to ring up the items. Paper bags for the "sold" items will also be needed.

Dress-Up Hats (Monkeys)

Make sure that there are plenty of hats in the dress-up area. Look in resale shops for hats that are washable and prepare them ahead of time.

Group Activities

Bears Porridge

After making the cooked cereal, bring a pot of cereal out to show to the children. Ask if anyone knows of a story that talks about cereal that was too hot. Wait until someone mentions the story of *Goldilocks and the Three Bears*. Tell the story. Test the cereal and inform the children that the cereal is too hot to eat. Say, "I guess that we will have to take a walk around the building just as the three bears did while the cereal is cooling off." Walk to the various places in the building the children should be aware of. Introduce them to people like the secretary and others who will be in their lives during the school year. Have the children tell the secretary that they are waiting until the cereal cools down, just as the three bears did. Return to the room and find that the cereal has cooled and that it is ready to eat. Add brown sugar and milk to make the cereal especially tasty!

Activities for Introduction to School *(cont.)*

Group Activities *(cont.)*

Gingerbread Person (Cookies)

After the gingerbread figure has been formed, have children watch while you put it in the oven. Have them return to play. When the gingerbread is baked, take it out of the oven, and set it in a safe spot to cool (out of children's reach). Do not tell the children that the gingerbread is out of the oven.

When the children are not watching, hide the gingerbread and announce, "The gingerbread man ran away. He left this note.

> 'Dear boys and girls,
>
> I got tired of waiting for you to finish playing,
>
> so I went down to the office to visit the secretary.'"

This gives the children a chance to see the school building. When you arrive at the secretary's office, have her explain what she does all day and how important she is to the school. Then have the secretary explain that the gingerbread person was there, got tired of waiting, left a note, and went to whatever section of the building you want the children to see. (Prior to going to the office, you will need to have given the note to the secretary, who will now read it to the children. It will tell what other part of the building the gingerbread man went to.)

If you are fortunate enough to be in a day care operated by a high school which has an auto class or if you have access to a junkyard car, have an adult inside the empty engine area. Gather the children around the empty engine and say "Mr. Car, have you seen the gingerbread person?" Encourage the children to ask questions of Mr. Car. Conclude with "Did the gingerbread person leave a note?"

Read:

> "'Dear Children, I decided to go back to the classroom. See you there.'"

Return to the room and act shocked that the gingerbread person has beaten everyone back to the room. Snack on the gingerbread which can be broken into small pieces.

Who Wants Arthur? (Dogs)

Show pictures of different pets (rabbit, snake, fish, cat). What sounds do they make? Was a pet missed? Oh, yes, a dog. Here is a story about a dog named Arthur. Show the picture from the cover of the book. Arthur lives in a pet store. Who do you think will want to buy Arthur?

Read *Who Wants Arthur?* to the bottom of page 24. Then say, "Poor Arthur. I wonder if he will ever find a home? Let's ask the secretary if she has a home for Arthur."

Proceed around the school building and ask anyone who will interact with the children if he or she has a home for Arthur. (*Always inform any adults that you will be coming with the children and what answers you want them to give.*) Inform the children that "We cannot find a home for Arthur. Maybe we can find an answer at the end of the book." Return to the room and read the book to the end.

Activities for Introduction to School *(cont.)*

Group Activities *(cont.)*

Who Wants Arthur? *(cont.)*

Say, "Arthur thought that nobody wanted an ordinary dog. So he tried to be like the other popular pets in the store. Let's see if we can be like those pets too."

- Rabbits eat what? Carrots. Let's try to be rabbits and eat carrots. *(Pretend to push a carrot in your mouth and chew.)*
- Snakes like to hiss. Can you hiss like a snake?
- Fish swim and blow bubbles. Can you pretend to swim and blow bubbles?
- Cats like to purr. Can you purr like a cat?
- Mice like to squeak and nibble cheese. Can you do that?
- Frogs like to say "Ribbit." Can you do that?
- What was the thing that Arthur liked to do most? *(Chew on an old pair of slippers.)*
- Then walk to the next area like a dog, cat, frog, snake, mouse, or fish.

Elephant Fell in a Well (Elephants)

Prior to the story, make hand puppets using the patterns on pages 44–52. Duplicate and cut out animal faces. Glue each onto the face portion of a hand puppet which has been folded with construction paper. Faces can be colored with markers or crayons.

Show the picture of a well in the book. Talk about how people used wells long ago to get water. That was before they had faucets, and a lot of people had wells on their farms. Show pictures of wells. Notice how easy it would be for someone to fall into the elephant well.

Read *Elephant Fell in a Well*. Stop after the elephant fell in the well. Have children walk through the school and ask the secretary, maintenance people, etc., if they have any ideas of how to get the elephant out of the well. *(Make sure that you tell the adults beforehand that you are coming, at what time, and what the children are going to ask them.)* Bring children back to the room and read the rest of the story to them.

Act out the story. Use a Hula-Hoop to represent the well. Give each child a folded hand puppet of an animal. Use a rope and have the elephant stand in the Hula-Hoop, which is on the floor. Have the elephant child hold one end of the rope with his or her puppet hand. Then have each child come up with an animal puppet, grasp the rope with the puppet hand, and pretend to pull the elephant out of the well. Make sure that the children just pretend to pull. Finally, at the end of the long rope with all the animals holding on, have the mouse gently pull the elephant out of the well. Children may want to do this once again.

Move to the next area with everyone pretending to be an elephant with their arms extended and serving as trunks.

Activities for Introduction to School *(cont.)*

Group Activities *(cont.)*

Caps for Sale (Monkeys)

The teacher should be prepared to tell and act out the story rather than reading it. Ask the children if they wore anything on their heads that day. What was it? Describe it.

(The teacher puts a stack of hats on her head.)

Once there was a peddler who sold caps. But he was different—he kept those hats on his head while he was selling them. He did not have a store.

(Keep track of hats on head.)

Walk around saying, "Caps for sale. Fifty cents a cap."

(Repeat as you walk among the children.)

"I am so tired, I think I will take a nap under the tree."

(Pretend to take a nap under the tree. Snore at the same time. While you are sleeping take hats off the head and hide them behind you. But keep one on your head.)

Wake up and say, "Where are my caps? We better find them. Maybe the secretary in the office knows where they are."

Go to the office and ask the secretary if she has seen your caps. *(Make sure you have told her that you are coming and why.)* Go to other sections of the building, pretending to look for caps. Go back to the room, make sure the children are seated, and look up at a pretend tree.

"You monkeys have my hats!" *(Teacher shakes fist at monkeys up in the tree.)*

Then the teacher changes positions and becomes the monkey while shaking a fist and saying "Tzz, tzz."

Teacher reverses roles and again becomes the peddler who says, "Give me back my hats!" while stamping on the floor.

Again the teacher becomes the monkey and says, "Tzz, tzz," while stamping her feet.

Now as the peddler salesman, the teacher pretends to get very angry and throw the one remaining hat from her head to the ground.

Have all the children pretend they are the monkeys and throw the one remaining hat from their heads to the ground, imitating the peddler. Then use "Monkey See, Monkey Do" in the song section (page 19).

Pile all the hats on the peddler's (teacher's) head and call out, "Caps for sale! Fifty cents a cap!" Then have all the children continue saying "Caps for sale" as they walk to next area.

Games

Ball Roll

Have all the children sit in a circle. Go around the circle and have each child say his or her name. Use a large ball and have one child roll it to another child. The child who receives the ball then says his or her name. Keep on having the children roll the ball until all children have said their names.

Beanbag Pass

Using one beanbag, have the children pass it around the circle. Have music playing and periodically stop the music. Children (whoever is holding the beanbag when the music stops) then introduce themselves to each other. Mix up children in the circle and pass the beanbag and begin music again.

Activities for Introduction to School *(cont.)*

Games *(cont.)*

Hot Potato

Use this game according to the theme for the day. If it is bears, use a honey jar. If it is dogs, use a dog bone. If it is elephants, use a peanut, and if it is monkeys, use a banana. In all cases, have the children sit on the floor and pass the item as if it is hot, not to be held any longer than necessary. Music may be used, or the teacher can just clap hands to stop the passing of the object. The person who has the object puts it down, blows on his or her hands pretending to cool them, and the game continues.

Doggie, Doggie, Where's Your Bone?

Have one child seated on a chair with his or her eyes closed. This child has his or her back to the rest of the class. Under the chair, place the object to be stolen. The rest of the class sits in a line at least three yards (three meters) away. One child tries to sneak up and remove the item without the seated child hearing the theft. If the seated child does hear, he or she cries, "I caught you," and the culprit then sits on the seat. If the child is able to steal the item, he or she returns to the spot he or she was in and places hands behind the back. In order to confuse the child on the chair, all children place their hands behind their backs. The seated child then has three guesses to catch the culprit. The child who stole the object then sits on the chair to detect the next thief. Variations for the theme are the following:

- Teddy Bear, Teddy Bear, Where's Your Button?
- Gingerbread Man, Gingerbread Man, Where's Your Cookie?
- Elephant, Elephant, Where's Your Peanut?
- Monkey, Monkey, Where's Your Banana?

Songs, Action Poems, and Fingerplay

"Head, Shoulders, Knees, and Toes"
(traditional)

Head, shoulders, knees, and toes,
(Touch body parts as you sing or say the words.)
Knees and toes.
Head, shoulders, knees, and toes,
Knees and toes,
Eyes and ears,
And mouth and nose.
Head, shoulders, knees, and toes,
Knees and toes.

"Good Morning to You"
(traditional)

Good morning to you,
Good morning to you,
We're all in our places,
With sunshiny faces.
And this is the way,
We start a new day.

Activities for Introduction to School (cont.)

Songs, Action Poems, and Fingerplay (cont.)

"I Clap My Hands"

(Suit actions to words.)

I clap my hands,
I touch my nose,
I jump up from the ground.
I clap my hands,
I touch my toes,
And turn myself around.

"Monkey See, Monkey Do"

(traditional, altered to fit "Caps for Sale")

Oh, when you clap, clap, clap your hands,
(Use motions indicated by words.)
The monkey clap, clap, claps his hands.

— Chorus —

Monkey see, monkey do,
The monkey does the same as you.

And when you put hats on your head.
The monkey puts hats on his head.
(Chorus)
And when you shake, shake, shake your fists,
The monkey shakes, shakes, shakes his fists.
(Chorus)
And when you stamp, stamp, stamp your feet,
The monkey stamps, stamps, stamps his feet.
(Chorus)
And when you throw your hat right down,
The monkey throws his hat right down.
(Chorus)

References

Hap Palmer. *Learning Basic Skills Through Music, Volume I.* "What Is Your Name?"

Mr. Al and Stephens Fete. *Back to School.*

"Back to School Bop"   "Cool to Be in School"
"Teacher Says" (Simon Says)   "First Day of School"
"Introduce Yourself"   "I Gotta Move"

Records, Cassettes, and CDs

Mr. Al and Stephen Fete. *Back to School.* Melody House, 1992.

Palmer, Hap. *Learning Basic Skills Through Music, Volume I.* Educational Activities, Inc., 1971.

Video

Caps for Sale. Children's Circle. Weston Woods, 1989.

Patterns for Introduction to School

Postcard for First Day of School

Dear _____,
                   child's name

Please bring your mother, father, or babysitter with you on the first day of school, _____, _____, at _____ A.M.

_____
                  Teacher

(Use a stamp or sticker appropriate for the first day's story.)

Patterns for Introduction to School *(cont.)*

Bulletin Board for Introduction to School

If five different animals or cookies are to be used during a week, show all types walking into school. If you have decided to use just the bears, have only the bears walking into school.

Patterns for Introduction to School *(cont.)*

Bear for Bulletin Board and Name Tag

22

Patterns for Introduction to School (cont.)

Gingerbread for Bulletin Board and Name Tag

Patterns for Introduction to School *(cont.)*

Dog for Bulletin Board, Name Tag, and Room Area Identification

Patterns for Introduction to School (cont.)

Elephant for Bulletin Board, Name Tag, and Room Area Identification

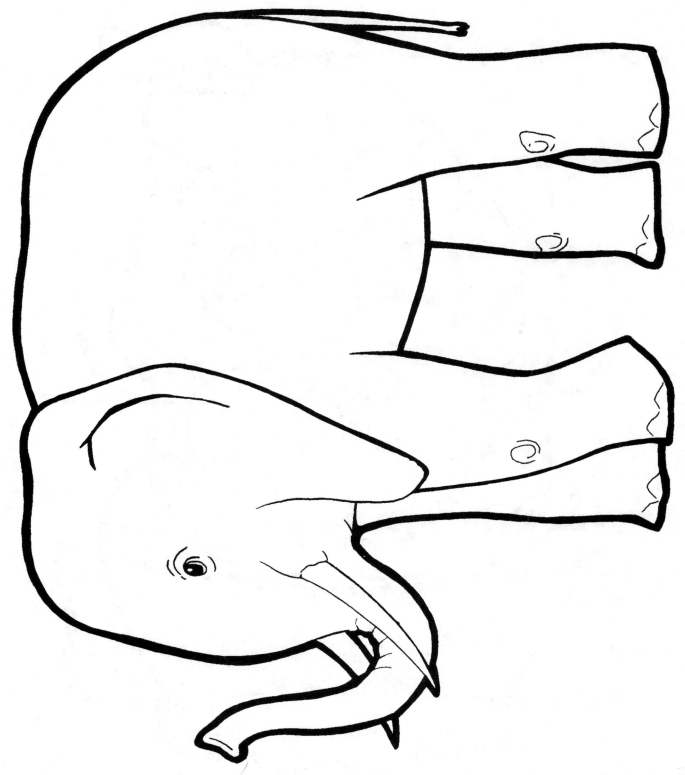

Patterns for Introduction to School *(cont.)*

Monkey for Bulletin Board and Name Tag

Patterns for Introduction to School *(cont.)*

Banana for Bulletin Board and Identification of Room Areas

Patterns for Introduction to School *(cont.)*

Countdown for Bear's First Day at School

Instructions: Put the number of the days remaining until school starts on the ribbon. The highest number should be near the duck and the lowest number near the bear.

Patterns for Introduction to School *(cont.)*

Countdown for Gingerbread's First Day at School

Instructions: Put the numbers of the days remaining until school starts on the center of gingerbread. The highest number should be near bottom and the lowest number near the smile.

Patterns for Introduction to School *(cont.)*

Countdown for Dog's First Day at School

Instructions: Put the number of days remaining until school starts in the maze path. The highest number should be near the dog and lowest number near the schoolhouse and bone.

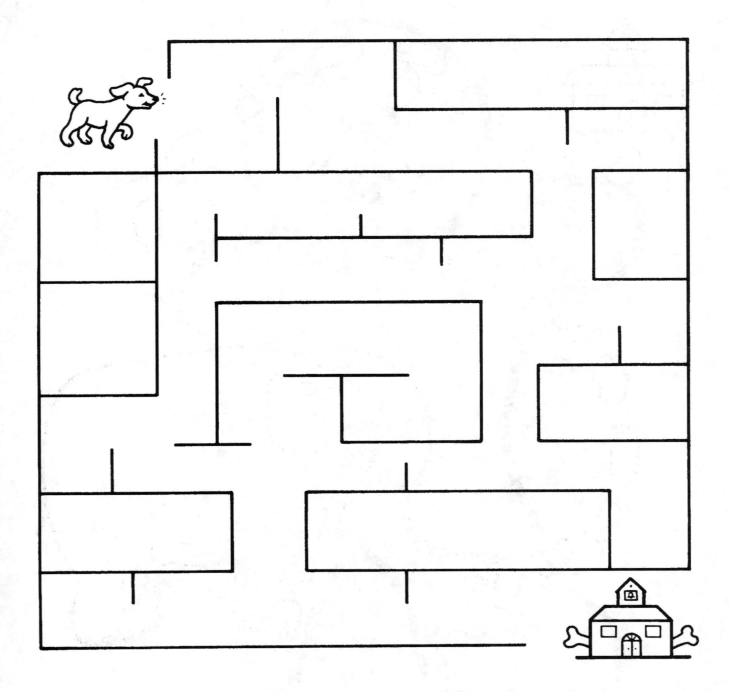

Patterns for Introduction to School *(cont.)*

Countdown for Elephant's First Day at School

Instructions: Have the elephant follow the peanuts to school. The highest number should be near the elephant and lowest number near the school.

Patterns for Introduction to School *(cont.)*

Countdown for Monkey's First Day at School

Instructions: Put the number of days remaining until school starts on the bananas with number one on the banana nearest the monkey's face.

Patterns for Introduction to School *(cont.)*

Teddy Bears Welcome You

To Parents

There are six charts in the room. Use a marker to put your child's name on each chart. Then write your child's answers on this paper.

◆ How old is your teddy bear? _____

◆ Guess how many gummy bears are in the jar._____

◆ Are you a morning bear or a night bear?_____

◆ How many buttons are you wearing? _____

◆ Which bear paw do you write with? _____

◆ What does your bear cave look like?_____

When you have completed this sheet, keep it with you so we can see what kinds of "bears" we have in our class.

Name_____

Patterns for Introduction to School *(cont.)*

How Old Is Your Teddy Bear?

Directions: Put an X under the correct numeral in the same line as your name.

Name	1	2	3	4	5	10	20

Patterns for Introduction to School *(cont.)*

Guess How Many Gummy Bears Are in the Jar

Directions: Write the numeral in the jar.

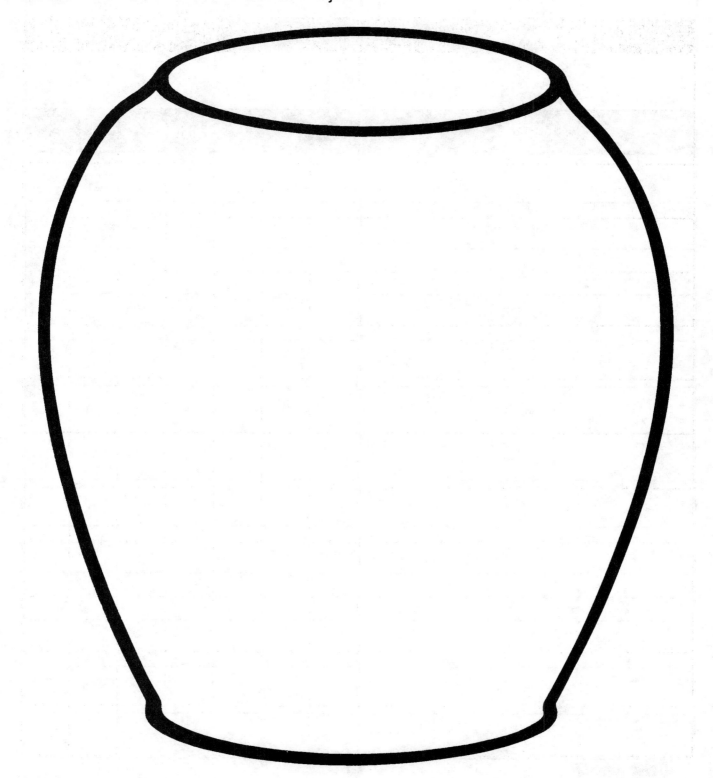

Patterns for Introduction to School *(cont.)*

Are You a Morning Bear or a Night Bear?

Night	Morning
Name	**Name**

Patterns for Introduction to School *(cont.)*

How Many Buttons Are You Wearing?

Directions: Put an X under the numeral in the same line as your name.

Name	0	1	2	3	4	5

Patterns for Introduction to School *(cont.)*

Which Paw Do You Write With?

Directions: Put your name under the hand used.

Left			Right

Patterns for Introduction to School *(cont.)*

What Does Your Cave Look Like?

Directions: Put your name under the appropriate "cave."

house	apartment	farm	trailer

Patterns for Introduction to School *(cont.)*

Gingerbread Welcomes You

To Children:

The gingerbread man has been running all over the room. In some places he has left cookies, in other places he has left raisins, and sometimes he just left his footprints on the floor. Find all the places in the room that the gingerbread man has been. Then find out why he spent so much time in that area.

To Parents:

Find a box of raisins, a package of cookies, and cookie footprints on the floor. When you find them, have your child explore the area so that he or she can decide why the gingerbread person would like to spend time there; then, write down your child's answer. When you are finished, move to the next area.

Write your child's answers to the following:

◆ In the art area I found _____.

◆ In the science area I tried _____.

◆ In the block area I built_____.

◆ In the housekeeping area I used _____.

◆ In the manipulative area (small toys) I did_____.

◆ In the large-muscle area I did _____.

◆ In the small-muscle area I did _____.

Name_____

Patterns for Introduction to School *(cont.)*

Dog's First Day of School

Parents and Children:

Follow the dog prints around the room. Locate pictures of dogs at various areas of the room. Then write down what you see.

- ◆ **Housekeeping** _____

- ◆ **Art** _____

- ◆ **Science** _____

- ◆ **Blocks** _____

- ◆ **Manipulatives** (small toys) _____

- ◆ **Library** _____

- ◆ **Large motor** _____

- ◆ **Small motor** _____

- ◆ **Books** _____

After all dog prints are found, find the doghouse in the circle area. Everyone find a place to sit on the carpet.

Name_____

Patterns for Introduction to School *(cont.)*

Elephant's First Day of School

Parents and Children:

Look for elephant pictures in different parts of the room. The locations follow:

♦ **Housekeeping**—There are two bowls out. One has a picture of a boy and a girl on it. The other has a picture of an elephant on it. There are plastic pieces of food next to it. In the bowl that has the children's picture, put any plastic food that your child likes. In the other bowl put something that an elephant would like.

♦ **Block Area**—Elephants like to pick up very heavy things. Can you stack the blocks and pick up a very heavy one?

♦ **Play Apparatus**—Go down the slide (or any other piece of play equipment you have) and wave at the elephant nearby.

♦ **Story Area**—Find an elephant book and look at the pictures.

♦ **Art Area**—Play with the edible play dough made of peanut butter.

When finished, come to the central area with the other parents and children.

Name _____

Patterns for Introduction to School *(cont.)*

Rebus Recipe for Gingerbread

A

B

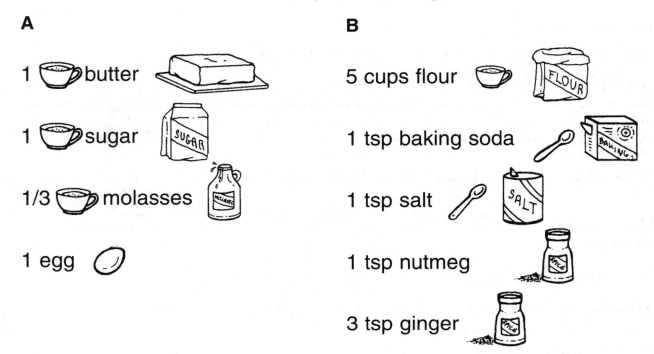

Mix ___, ___, ___, and ___.

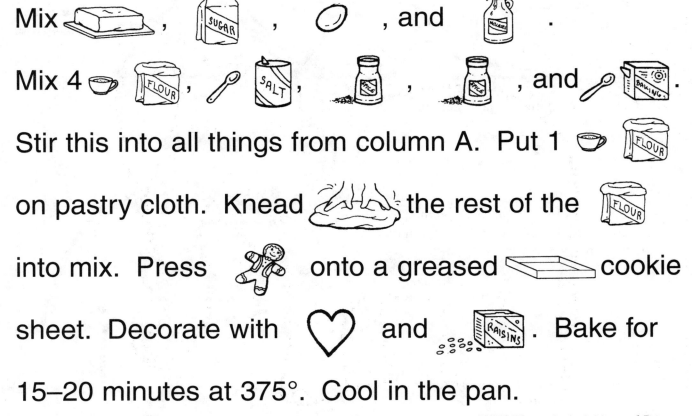

15–20 minutes at 375°. Cool in the pan.

Patterns for Introduction to School *(cont.)*

Puppet Pattern for *Elephant Fell in a Well*

1. Fold 12" x 18" (30 cm x 46 cm) construction paper into thirds. To make it exact, put four-inch (10 cm) marks on paper and fold at that point.

2. Fold paper accordion-style as shown below. Place hand with four fingers in face section.

face section ⟶  ⟵ **bottom jaw section**

3. Place thumb in bottom jaw section.

4. Use patterns for animal faces on the next pages to complete the animal. Glue pattern on the face section.

Patterns for Introduction to School (cont.)

Elephant Puppet Pattern for *Elephant Fell in a Well*

Patterns for Introduction to School *(cont.)*

Horse Puppet Pattern for *Elephant Fell in a Well*

Patterns for Introduction to School *(cont.)*

Pig Puppet Pattern for *Elephant Fell in a Well*

Patterns for Introduction to School *(cont.)*

Cow Puppet Pattern for *Elephant Fell in a Well*

Patterns for Introduction to School (cont.)

Goat Puppet Pattern for *Elephant Fell in a Well*

Patterns for Introduction to School *(cont.)*

Lamb Puppet Pattern for *Elephant Fell in a Well*

Cut thin pieces of white construction paper. Wrap them around a pencil to make curls. Attach to the top and sides of the lamb's face.

Patterns for Introduction to School *(cont.)*

Dog Puppet Pattern for *Elephant Fell in a Well*

Patterns for Introduction to School *(cont.)*

Mouse Puppet Pattern for *Elephant Fell in a Well*

Attach pipe cleaners to the nose to make whiskers.

Five Plans for Bears

	Day One	Day Two	Day Three	Day Four	Day Five
Individual Activities	• Three Bears Stick Puppets • String Cereal • Teddy Bear Tea Party • Bears in the Den	• Chalk Drawings • File Folder Game • Lacing Bear • Dictating a Letter	• Finger Painting with Chocolate Pudding • Bear Stencil • Classifying Bears • Coloring Bear Balloons	• Special Bear Drawing • Button Collage • Sewing Buttons	• Hanging Clothes on a Line • Sewing Pockets • Finger Painting with Shaving Cream
Group Activities	*Goldilocks and the Three Bears*	*Ask Mr. Bear*	*Brown Bear, Brown Bear, What Do You See?*	*Corduroy*	*A Pocket for Corduroy*
Games	• Obstacle Course • "Sometimes I'm a Small Bear"	• Bear Says . . .	• Parade to "Bear Went over the Mountain"	• Go on a Bear Hunt • Teddy Bear Toss • Ball Roll	• Tumble Like a Clothes Dryer • Match Clothes Relay • "Who Is Wearing Red Right Now?"
Songs, Action Poems, Fingerplay	"Teddy Bear Song" (Traditional)	"Teddy Bear Song" (Old American Rhyme)	"The Bear Went over the Mountain"	"Hello, My Name Is Joe"	Song Review for the Week
Transitions	Crawl like a bear.	Hop like a bear.	Jump on two paws (feet).	Wave paws.	Walk slowly like a bear.

Room Preparation for Bears

Bulletin Board

See the pattern on page 65. Make hills of construction paper. The brown bears in the cave and the white polar bear sliding down the hill can also be made of construction paper. The children at the bottom can be made of any colors of construction paper with names written on the figures. Portions of the bulletin board can be covered with thin cotton or quilt batting. Remove a portion each day and say, "Some of the snow melted last night."

The pattern can be cut from butcher paper, oak tagboard, or construction paper. To enlarge, make a transparency of the pattern and place it on an overhead projector. Focus on a larger sheet of paper. If you intend to use it in future years, laminate pieces or cover with clear plastic.

Puppet Stage

If your room does not have a puppet stage or store area, use a large cardboard box. Have children crouch behind it and raise stick puppets above the box. Use the three bears stick-puppet patterns on page 66.

Door

See the pattern for a door on page 64. Make of oak tagboard. If you want to keep it for future use, laminate or cover with clear plastic.

Suggested Literature for the Week

Flack, Marjorie. *Ask Mr. Bear.* Macmillan, 1971.
Freeman, Don. *Corduroy.* Viking Children's Books, 1968.
Freeman, Don. *A Pocket for Corduroy.* Puffin Books, 1980.
Galdone, Paul. *The Three Bears.* Clarion Books, 1985.
Martin, Bill, Jr. *Brown Bear, Brown Bear, What Do You See?* Henry Holt & Co., 1983.

Materials

- colored construction paper
- craft sticks
- buttermilk
- yarn
- colored burlap fabric
- typing paper
- brown and white balloons
- manila paper
- string
- colored chalk
- chocolate pudding mix
- clamp clothespins
- envelopes
- felt-tip markers
- finger-paint paper
- circle cereal
- file folder
- blunt needles
- shaving cream
- stamps

Extended Activity for the Year

Have a stuffed bear which is the classroom pet. Every weekend have a child take home the teddy bear for a sleepover. When the child brings the bear back after the weekend, let the child share with the class all the things done with the teddy bear. On chart paper, write down all the events as the class participates in the sharing. Keep a journal of the weekends throughout the whole school year. This journal may be collected into a big book for all to read. For health reasons, you may want to have a washable bear to be cleaned after it returns from each sleepover.

Activities for Bears

Individual Activities

Three Bears Stick Puppets

Have the children cut out the three bears from construction paper, using the pattern on page 66. Tape or glue craft sticks or tongue depressors on the back of each. Have the children act out the story in the puppet stage area.

String Cereal

Place tape around one end of a string and tie a piece of circle cereal at the other end. Have children place the string through the center of the cereal and make a necklace. If you do not want to cook cereal for the story of the Three Bears, use this type of cereal, but not the ones you have strung!

Teddy Bear Tea Party

Have a teddy bear tea party in the housekeeping area. Encourage children to use special dresses, vests, hats, and even gloves if you have them in the dress-up area. Place a tablecloth on the table and set out dishes. Have the children count how many cups and then decide how many saucers are needed. Count the utensils needed. Pretend with them at first and then fade out of the picture. You will be surprised at what they create.

Bears in the Den

Read stories to "bears" in the bear den. Place a sheet or blanket over a small table to create a bear den. Use a flashlight to see the printed page and read the story to one or two children.

Chalk Drawings

Cover a page of manila paper with buttermilk. This can be done with a wide painter's brush. Have children draw with colored chalk on the paper. The wetness of the buttermilk on the paper will make the colors more vibrant and will prevent the chalk from coming off.

File Folder Game

Use the pattern on pages 68 and 69 and a standard file folder. Use plastic bears and numbered dice or a numbered spinner. Move the number of spaces indicated on the dice or by the spinner. To make the game more challenging, write the following on some spaces.

Stepped on a bee hive. Go back 2 spaces.	**Helped wash dishes.** Go ahead 1 space.
Forgot to wash paws after supper. Go back 2 spaces.	**Ate supper as a good bear should.** Go ahead 3 spaces.
Climbed the wrong tree. Go back 1 space.	**Took out the trash.** Go ahead 2 spaces.

Activities for Bears *(cont.)*

Individual Activities *(cont.)*

Lacing Bear

Use the pattern on page 67. Reproduce the pattern, glue it to tagboard, laminate, and punch holes. Use a piece of yarn to do the stringing. Place a piece of tape around one end so that it resembles a shoelace. This makes it easier to lace through the holes. The more advanced children will push the yarn in from the top and pull it out on the underside of the bear. They will then go to the top and pull it out at the bottom again. Others will choose their own style of lacing the bear.

Finger Painting with Chocolate Pudding

Use glossy finger-paint paper. Use a very wide painter-style brush and dip it in water to coat the paper. Use instant chocolate pudding and mix with one cup of water. Whip. Place two tablespoonfuls on each sheet and have the children use their fingertips, sides of the hand, knuckles, and whole hand to create the beautiful swirls in the bear's brown fur coat.

Bear Stencil

Using the pattern on page 67, have children draw around it on manila paper or construction paper. Have them complete the activity by filling in the bear with crayons or markers. Draw other objects around the bear, such as its cave, trees, bushes, sun, etc.

Classifying Bears According to Color and Size

Cut three sizes of bears, using the patterns on page 66. Use colored construction paper and make sure there are three sizes of each color. (You can also find commercially made bears in colors and various sizes.) Put out containers with the colors taped on and let the children sort bears according to color. Have other containers with duplicates of the different sizes of bears taped on them. Have children sort the bears according to size. If you do not have containers, place pieces of colored construction paper on the table or floor and have the children place the matching bears on the properly colored and/or sized construction paper.

Special Bear Drawing

On Teddy Bear Day have the child draw a picture of a special bear or animal. Use crayons or markers on manila or white construction paper. Make sure to write the child's name in the upper left-hand corner to begin reading skills.

Button Collage

Have assorted buttons on the table. Have children glue them onto pieces of small cardboard. The children can be encouraged to make designs, flowers, or anything else they want. **Note:** This should not be used with very young children because they could swallow the buttons.

Activities for Bears *(cont.)*

Individual Activities *(cont.)*

Sewing Buttons

Regular buttons or buttons made from cardboard with two holes punched in them can be used. Use burlap as the fabric and sew with blunt-end needles. Pre-thread the needles with yarn and then tie both ends of the yarn together. This will prevent the yarn from coming off the needle. Each child should sew on the button according to his or her developmental level. Regardless of how the button is sewn on, encourage the child.

Hanging Clothes on a Line

Have the children use their small pincer muscles in the fingers to place clamp clothespins over garments or towels on the line. Or have clothes for them to place on the clothesline with regular push-on clothespins.

Sewing Pockets *(A Pocket for Corduroy)*

Use colored burlap fabric and blunt-end yarn needles. Pre-cut pockets and pieces of burlap on which they are to be sewn. Find things to put in the pockets, such as buttons, acorns, hankies, bottle caps, etc.

Finger Painting with Shaving Cream *(A Pocket for Corduroy)*

Use an unsectioned cafeteria tray or large Styrofoam tray and spray on some shaving cream. Pretend it is laundry soap. Have children finger-paint with all parts of their hands. When they are done, place a sheet of dark blue or other dark-colored paper on the shaving cream. Press the paper gently over the tray so the child's design will be printed on the dark paper. Lift the paper carefully and make sure it is dry before sending it home.

Dictating a Letter

Have the child dictate a letter to a parent, guardian, or friend. As the child talks, the teacher writes and then re-reads, pointing to the words. Place the letter in an envelope and use a stamp pad and rubber bear stamp (or a real stamp if you intend to send it). Set up a pretend post office and have children mail the letters.

Coloring Bear Balloons

Inflate brown or white (polar bear) balloons prior to class. Have children use markers to paint eyes, nose, and mouth on each balloon to make a bear face. You may want to show where the eyes are and then point out how the eyes and mouth are positioned.

Activities for Bears *(cont.)*

Group Activities

Goldilocks and the Three Bears

Here is a practical way to have children repeat lines after the teacher. Make a paddle with a teacher's picture on one side and a group of children on the other. Tell the children they are going on a bear hunt. Say that when the teacher talks, the picture of the teacher will show on the paddle and when they are to talk, their picture will show. Go through the entire bear hunt, and as the children grasp the concept, stop using the paddle.

"Bear Hunt"

Children repeat every line after the teacher. Keep the rhythm going while slapping thighs.

Goin' on a bear hunt. *(Slap thighs.)*

Gonna catch a bear,

A great big bear.

Came to a wheat field.

Can't go over it,

Can't go under it,

Have to go through it.

Swish, swish, swish! *(Rub hands from body outward.)*

Goin' on a bear hunt.

Gonna catch a bear,

A great big bear.

Came to a river.

Can't go over it,

Can't go under it,

Have to swim through it. *(Pretend to swim through the river.)*

Goin' on a bear hunt.

Gonna catch a bear,

A great big bear.

Came to a tree.

Can't go over it,

Can't go under it,

Gonna have to climb it. *(Pretend to climb a tree by raising hands alternately and slowly above head.)*

Goin' on a bear hunt.

Gonna catch a bear,

A great big bear.

Came to a cave.

Can't go over it,

Can't go under it,

Have to go in it. *(Put hand above eyes and pretend to look around.)*

I see eyes. I see fur.

IT'S A BEAR! *(Shout this line.)*

Run, run, run. *(Slap thighs.)*

Climb the tree. *(Pretend to climb tree.)*

Swim the river. *(Pretend to swim river.)*

Run through the wheat field. *(Swish, swish, swish with hands.)*

Run, run, run. *(Slap thighs.)*
 (Pretend to open the door of the house.)

SLAM! *(Pretend to slam door.)*

Whew! *(Pretend to wipe sweat from brow.)*

Activities for Bears *(cont.)*

Group Activities *(cont.)*

Goldilocks and the Three Bears *(cont.)*

Say "Let's read the story of *Goldilocks and the Three Bears* and see what kind of bears they are." After reading the story, have the children dictate another ending to you. Write it down on a large sheet of paper in view of the children. Read the new ending back to the children and point to the words.

Brown Bear, Brown Bear, What Do You See?

Use the chant of "Bear Hunt" described in *Goldilocks and the Three Bears*. Use this many times so that the children learn the words and the rhythm. Have them try saying the whole poem together without repeating after the teacher. Try slapping thighs through the whole "Bear Hunt" to get the rhythm going. Of course, you will have to stop slapping thighs when doing the actions.

Read *Brown Bear, Brown Bear, What Do You See?* After reading the story, place clear water in a glass container or an empty plastic honey bear container. Add food coloring to mix colors. You may start with red and blue and have children guess what color it will become. Add yellow to this, and it will form brown like the bear. Use an eyedropper and always add the same amount of food coloring. Start again with clear water and put yellow in and add blue. What color will it become? Continue with fresh water to form colors.

Colored plastic used to protect food can also be used to obtain colors. This can be held up to the light to see what colors are needed to form other colors. Have the children experiment.

Ask Mr. Bear

Use the bear puppet pattern on page 73 to talk to the children. It is not necessary to change your voice because the children will always feel that the puppet is talking, even though they know that you are speaking. Ask if they have ever talked to a bear before. Use *who*, *what*, *where* questions as you talk to the children. Then say, "We are going to read a book called *Ask Mr. Bear*. I wonder what we could ask Mr. Bear?"

Read *Ask Mr. Bear*. Before the end of the story, have the children walk around the building and ask various people (secretary, custodian, principal, etc.) what a good gift for Mom would be. Return and read the end of the story. Then give everyone a big bear hug or blow a kiss to each child as he or she is named.

Corduroy

Use a cloth or paper bag and place a button in it. Have children guess what is in the bag by touching or shaking. When they have guessed the item, take it out of the bag and ask if they ever lost a button off some type of clothing. Say, "We are going to read a story about someone who lost a button."

Read *Corduroy*. When finished with the story, have a tray of buttons in different colors and sizes along with scissors and thread. Point out the different items to the children and then cover them with a towel or piece of cloth. Have all the children close their eyes. Remove one item from the tray. Children open their eyes and try to remember which item is missing. Return the item to the tray and rearrange the items. Cover and guess again.

Activities for Bears *(cont.)*

Group Activities *(cont.)*

A Pocket for Corduroy

Wear a garment with pockets. In it store a feather, a whistle, a nut, a letter that has been mailed, or any other item. Ask children, "What can you do with a pocket? (*Take out the feather.*) What could I be with a feather? (*bird*) What could I be with the whistle? (*policeman*) What could I be with a nut? (*squirrel*) What could I be with a letter? (*mail carrier*) Sometimes pockets are very necessary. Listen while I read a story, and then we will decide if pockets make a difference."

Read *A Pocket for Corduroy*. Ask, "How many have a pocket in what you are wearing? (Count how many have pockets.) Why are they important? Why is a pocket important for Corduroy?"

Showing Teddy Bears

The day before this activity, send home a note using the pattern on page 71. If they have no teddy bear, ask them to bring in any stuffed animal as the guest for the day.

Have children show their bears or stuffed animals and describe them. Let them tell how they got their animals. Guess how many total bears there are. How many other animals? Then count all of them. If teacher has a bear from childhood, bring that one to school. Measure how big it is with a piece of string. Have each child measure his or her bear or animal with the string. Cut off at the height of the animal. Place double-sided tape on a counter edge in three spots. Place a string the height of the teacher's bear in the middle. Have each child bring up string the height of his or her bear or animal and decide if it is longer or shorter than the teacher's bear. If it is shorter, place it on the double sided tape to the left of the teacher's string. If it is longer, place it to the right of the teacher's tape. After all children have done this, count how many are shorter and how many are taller than the teacher's bear.

Have each child show his or her bear or animal. Sing "Do You Know the Little Bear?" and have each child pretend to be in a circus ring and have the bear do a trick. It can stand on its head, swing around, jump up and down, or do anything. If the child would rather do the trick, that is fine too.

"Do You Know the Little Bear?"

(Tune: "Do You Know the Muffin Man?")

> Do you know the little bear, little bear, little bear?
> Do you know the little bear climbing on the stair?
> He can do so many things, many things, many things.
> He can do one special thing in the circus ring.
> *(Have bear, animal, or child do a special trick.)*

Go on a bear hunt. Pile all the bears and animals in a big pile in the center of the room. Walk around the room pretending to be looking for a bear cave. Instead, come to the pile of bears and animals and have the children find their own animals or bears.

Transitions for Bears

To move from the story area to another, talk about how bears crawl on all fours. Have children do this one day and the next day have them hop, jump on two feet, wave arms, walk slowly, etc.

Activities for Bears *(cont.)*

Games

Obstacle Course

Tape paper bear feet on the floor. Follow the feet and have children go over chairs, under tables, over large blocks, and end in a "cave." The cave can be made of a table with a sheet placed over it or a large refrigerator box. Make sure that the bear feet are pointed in the direction of the next obstacle and also lead to it.

"Sometimes I'm a Small Bear"

Talk about the heights of the three bears. Papa Bear was very tall, Mama Bear was a little bit shorter, but Baby Bear was very low to the ground. Have children pretend that they are either the Papa or the Baby Bear. Make a circle and have one child in the center. All other children close their eyes. Everyone chants the "Sometimes I'm a Small Bear" verse as they bend over and touch the ground. They reach up to the ceiling as they chant "Sometimes I'm a Tall Bear." Repeat the actions several times. The child in the middle decides if he or she is to remain tall or small. Children in the circle guess if the child is tall or small. Make sure that no one opens his or her eyes before the guess is made.

> Sometimes I'm a small bear,
> *(Touch the ground.)*
> Sometimes I'm a tall bear.
> *(Reach high.)*
> *(Repeat twice.)*
> Guess what I am now?

Bear Says . . .

Play Simon Says but change to "Bear Says." Have children stand in line facing the teacher. Teacher gives commands such as "Bear says: scratch your head, growl, hop on back paws, crawl on all four paws, take two steps forward," etc.

Go on a Bear Hunt

Have the children pile all their bears in a big pile on Teddy Bear Day. If anyone brings another stuffed animal, include that in the pile. (You may want to have some spare bears on hand in case anyone forgets his or her bear.) Walk around the room pretending to try to find the bear cave. When you reach the pile of bears, have each child try to find his or her bear.

Teddy Bear Toss

Have a large blanket or sheet. One child holds two corners on one end of the sheet. Another child holds the other end. Place a bear in the center of the blanket or sheet as the children try to toss the bear up in the air.

Activities for Bears *(cont.)*

Games *(cont.)*

Ball Roll

Have all children sit in a circle. Have some children place their bears in their laps. Others will place bears behind them. Have children roll the ball only to those who have bears in front of them. Rotate so that bears that are behind children are placed in front while those that are in front are placed behind.

Parade

Practice singing the song several times. Talk about what a parade is. Children follow one behind the other as they walk around the room. Say, "Where would be a good place to go with the parade? Do we walk slowly or rapidly? Do we raise our knees up high?"

"The Bear Went over the Mountain"

(Traditional)

The bear went over the mountain

(Repeat twice.)

To see what he could see.

He saw a yellow tulip

(Repeat twice.)

And that is what he saw.

Replace "yellow tulip" with anything else the children think the bear saw as they parade around the room.

Tumble Like a Clothes Dryer (*A Pocket for Corduroy*)

Have children roll on their sides as if they are in a dryer.

Match Clothes Relay

Make two lines of children. Have a pile of clothes at the end of each line. It could contain a coat, jacket, or sweater belonging to each child in the line. A child runs to the end, picks up one item of his or her clothing, puts it on, and runs back. The next child then runs down and gets his or her item of clothing, puts it on, and runs back. When using relays with young children, make sure that everyone is told "Job well done!" even if they make an error. Young children cannot cope with not being winners.

Cutout Match Relay

Have cutouts of a shirt and pants that match for each child in the class. Give one shirt pattern or color to each child in the line. Have a pile of matching pants in a pile. One child runs to the pile and matches the shirt to the pants and then runs back to the group. The next child then takes his or her turn, runs to the pile, finds matching pants, and returns to the line. The relay is completed when all have matched their shirts and pants.

Activities for Bears (cont.)

Songs, Action Poems, and Fingerplay

"Who Is Wearing Red Right Now?"
(Tune: "Mary Had a Little Lamb")

Who is wearing red right now, red right now, red right now?
Who is wearing red right now?
Stand up, WOW!

Repeat using different colors and make sure all colors are mentioned so that all get a turn to stand up.

"Teddy Bear Song" *(Traditional)*

Teddy bear, teddy bear, turn around.
Teddy bear, teddy bear, touch the ground.
Teddy bear, teddy bear, reach up high.
Teddy bear, teddy bear, touch the sky.
Teddy bear, teddy bear, bend down low.
Teddy bear, teddy bear, touch your toe.
(Have children do the actions described in each line.)

"Hello, My Name Is Joe"

He *(pause)* lo, my name is Joe *(accent on "lo" and "Joe")*
I *(pause)* work in a button factory *(accent on "work" and "button")*
One *(pause)* day my boss said, *(accent on "day")*
"Hey, *(pause)* are you busy, Joe?" *(accent on "Hey" and "Joe")*
I said, "No." *(accent on "No")*
"Turn *(pause)* the button with your left hand."

Continue with the same chant but replace left hand with right hand, left foot, right foot, and head. As each part of the body is named, keep moving all parts named. After all parts are named, conclude with the last verse ending:

> "Hey, are you busy Joe?"
> I said, "Yes." *(Shout "Yes.")*

Additional Literature

Berenstain, Stan and Jan. *He Bear, She Bear*. Random Books, 1977.

Cartlidge, Michelle. *Dressing Teddy*. Puffin Books, 1986. (A cutout model book available in museum stores.)

Cooper, Helen. *The Bear Under the Stairs*. Dial Books for Young Readers, 1993.

Dale, Penny. *Ten in the Bed*. Discovery Toys, 1988.

Degen, Bruce. *Jamberry*. Harper Children's Books, 1983.

Patterns for Bears

Bear Pattern for Door

So Many Teddies to See

Patterns for Bears (cont.)

Bear Bulletin Board

Patterns for Bears *(cont.)*

Stick Puppet Patterns for Goldilocks and the Three Bears

Use for puppet stage, children's stick puppets, stencil of bear, and classifying bears according to size and color.

Patterns for Bears *(cont.)*

Lacing Bear

Patterns for Bears *(cont.)*

Bear File Folder Game

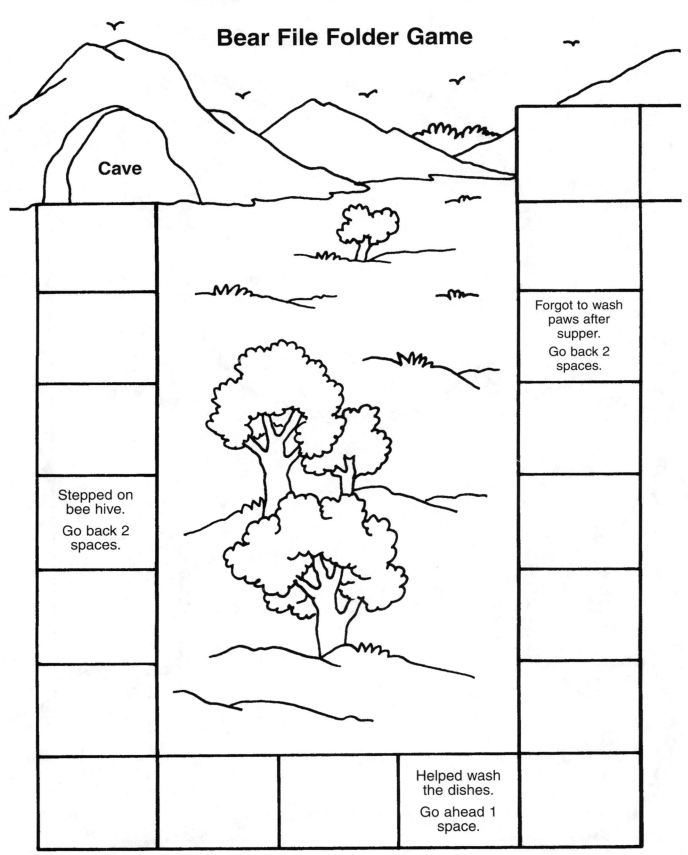

Cave

Stepped on bee hive.

Go back 2 spaces.

Forgot to wash paws after supper.

Go back 2 spaces.

Helped wash the dishes.

Go ahead 1 space.

Patterns for Bears *(cont.)*

Bear File Folder Game *(cont.)*

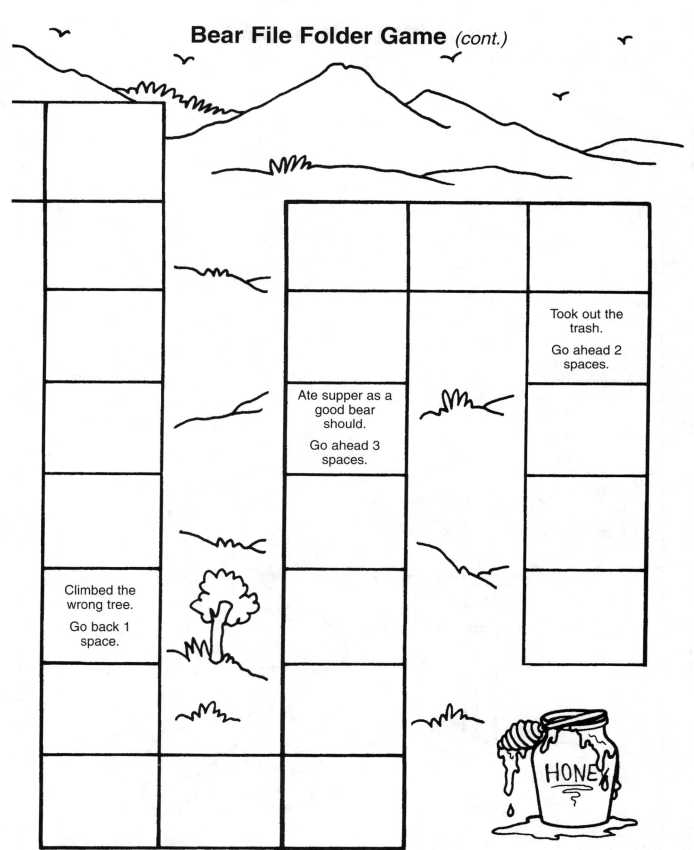

Took out the
trash.

Go ahead 2
spaces.

Ate supper as a
good bear
should.

Go ahead 3
spaces.

Climbed the
wrong tree.

Go back 1
space.

HONEY

Patterns for Bears (cont.)

Invitation to Bear Day

fold

70   © *Teacher Created Materials, Inc.*

Patterns for Bears *(cont.)*

fold

Teddy bears are invited to our school on Teddy Bear Day

_____.

Sometimes bears don't live at our house, but stuffed dogs or other animals or dolls do. Anything stuffed is welcome to our special day.

Patterns for Bears *(cont.)*

Shirt and Pants for Relay

Patterns for Bears *(cont.)*

Ask Mr. Bear Puppet

(See next page for directions.)

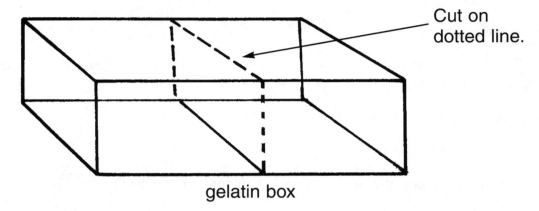

Cut on dotted line.

gelatin box

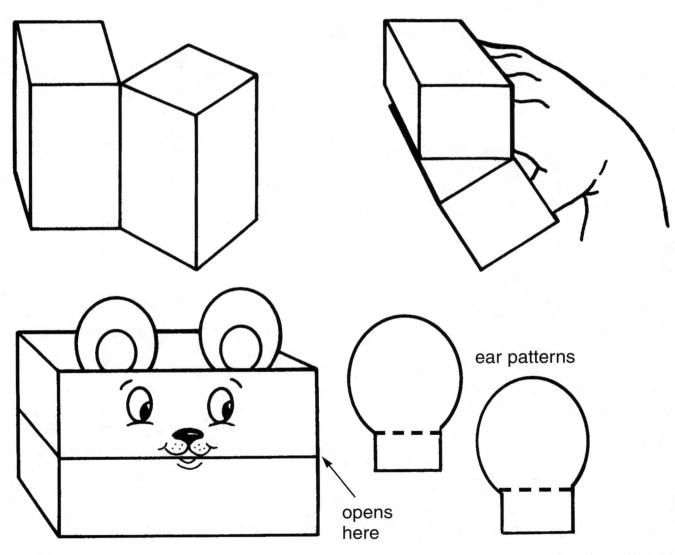

ear patterns

opens here

Patterns for Bears *(cont.)*

Directions for Mr. Bear Puppet

1. Cut a gelatin box in half on three sides, leaving one long side uncut. A single-edge razor blade or utility knife works well.

2. Fold the box in middle so it forms a mouth.

3. Cover the top and bottom, using the standard gelatin box cover pattern below (cut two of these patterns.) Use construction paper, fake fur, or felt to cover the box.

4. Put glue completely around the cut edges.

5. Glue down the one-inch rectangle first.

6. Looking at the inner mouth, glue the sides so there is a smooth fold on the mouth edge.

7. Draw a mouth and add any features necessary.

Standard Gelatin Box Cover

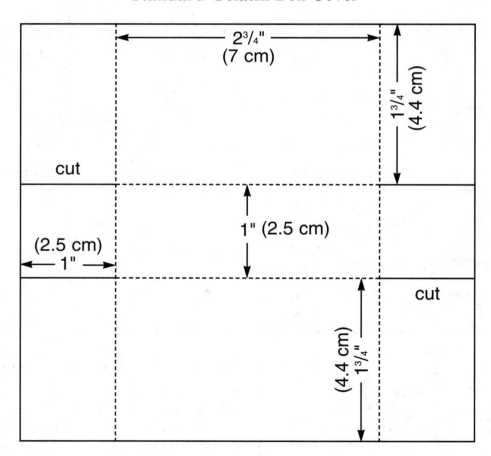

Six Plans for Clothing

	Day One	Day Two	Day Three
Individual Activities	• Make a Quilt • Fabric Quilt • Quilt Pieces	• Sheep Stencil • Weave • Sheep in Barn • Explore Yarn and Cotton • Dye Coffee Liners	• Hat Match • Easel Paint • Parquetry Blocks • Dramatic Play
Group Activities	*The Quilt*	*Charlie Needs a Cloak*	*Anthony's Hat*
Games	What Are You Wearing?	Freeze Tag	Hat Action
Songs, Action Poems, Fingerplay	(Sing "Miss Mary Mack" all week, using Ella Jenkins record and the book *Miss Mary Mack* by Mary Ann Hoberman. Little Brown & Co., 1998.)	"Baa, Baa, Black Sheep"	"My Snow Suit"
Transitions	Walk to next area with clothes color matched to a friend.	Walk around saying "Baa, baa."	Stand up straight with a pretend hat.

Six Plans for Clothing (cont.)

	Day Four	Day Five	Day Six
Individual Activities	• Clothes Concentration • Place for Clothes • Dress-Up	• Sort Clothes • Mittens and Clothespins • String Macaroni	• Frozen Paper Paint • Winter Dress-Up • File Folder Clothing Game
Group Activities	*Oh, Lewis!*	*The Jacket I Wear in the Snow*	*The Hat*
Games	Boot Pile	Freeze Tag	Hat Pile
Songs, Action Poems, Fingerplay	• "The Three Little Kittens" • (Sing "Miss Mary Mack" all week using Ella Jenkins record and the book *Miss Mary Mack* by Mary Ann Hoberman.)	"My Snow Suit"	"My Hat, It Has Three Corners"
Transitions	Clomp as if wearing boots.	Shiver and act cold.	Lisa leads "animals" to next area.

Room Preparation for Clothing

Bulletin Board

Have heavy string hang from one side of the bulletin board to the other. Place clothes using the patterns on pages 87 and 90. For longer bulletin boards, it may be necessary to enlarge the pattern by using an overhead projector. Attach clothing to the string, using small clamp-on clips. The teacher may want to put children's names on the shirts.

Mobile

Use a clothes hanger as the basis for the mobile. Cut clothes using the patterns on page 90 and hang from crisscrossed hangers.

Extended Activity

Have parents come in daily to share their sewing, spinning, quilting, or weaving skills. If the teacher cannot find anyone in these categories, have them bring in old items such as quilts, old clothes that grandmother wore, or baby clothes that the children in the class wore. Or maybe a grandmother would like to show how she knits, crochets, or sews.

Suggested Literature for Clothes

Brett, Jan. *The Hat.* G.P. Putnam's Sons, 1997.
dePaola, Tomie. *Charlie Needs a Cloak.* Simon & Schuster, 1973.
Hoberman, Mary Ann. *Miss Mary Mack.* Little, Brown & Co., 1998.
Jonas, Ann. *The Quilt.* Greenwillow Books, 1984.
Neitzel, Shirley. *The Jacket I Wear in the Snow.* Greenwillow Books, 1989.
Rice, Eve. *Oh, Lewis!* Macmillan Publishing Co., Inc., 1974.
Robinson, Deborah. *Anthony's Hat.* Scholastic Book Service, 1976.

Materials

- old magazines
- glue gun
- two dowel rods for width of quilts
- shower curtain rings
- crayons
- manila paper
- construction paper
- cotton balls
- Concord grapes or food coloring
- newsprint
- macaroni
- zip-lock bags
- glue sticks
- string
- cotton fabric
- sample wallpaper book
- dinner-size paper plates
- yarn
- coffee liners
- frozen white construction paper
- primary and secondary colors of tempera paint
- yarn needles

Dress-Up Area

In the dress-up area have many different types of clothes. Make sure there are both boy and girl dress-up items. The boys need sport coats (even if it is a dad size), and girls need fancy dresses. Make sure that there are baby clothes and dolls ready to be dressed. Thrift shops usually have plenty of clothes at inexpensive prices.

Activities for Clothing

Individual Activities

Make a Quilt

Have the children cut out pictures of clothing from magazines. Place each picture flat in a zip-lock bag. Tell the children that we are going to glue the pictures all together and make a quilt. Have children arrange the bags in a pattern that they like. Tell them that the teacher will use a glue gun to attach them after school, and they are to watch the wall the next day to see the quilt. After school, glue the sides of each row together. Then glue the horizontal rows together. Glue the top row to a dowel or punch holes in the bags and put shower curtain rings through the holes. Put the dowel through the shower curtain rings. Attach string on the ends and hang. Sometimes a notch cut out at the end of the rod prevents the string from creeping towards the middle.

Fabric Quilt

Cut out 12" x 12" (30 cm x 30 cm) squares from 100% white cotton. Have each child draw on the square a picture of the favorite thing he or she does with the family or friends. Find an energetic mother who loves to sew and see if she will sew them together. It really does not matter how they are sewn together. They may be zigzag sewn together, or they may be sewn together with a strip of fabric between each block. The children will not care since it is their quilt. Hang from a dowel on the wall.

Quilt Pieces

Obtain old wallpaper books from paint stores. Cut pieces of the wallpaper in various geometric shapes. Have children pretend they are making a quilt and are arranging the pieces. When one child or group of children is finished, take a picture. Then put the pieces in a pile again and have others make their quilt.

Sheep Stencil *(Charlie Needs a Cloak)*

Cut a sheep stencil (page 97) from cardboard or plastic coffee lids. Have children place the stencil on manila paper and draw around it. Color with crayons or colored markers. Complete the picture with trees, fences, etc.

Activities for Clothing *(cont.)*

Individual Activities *(cont.)*

Weave

Cut a large paper plate with lines about one inch (2.5 cm) apart in the center section. Also cut strips of construction paper about one inch wide. Have children weave the strips in and out of the paper plate. Younger children may need help doing this, but older children need only to be shown, and then they will be able to do it themselves. Trim off the ends of strips that show on the edge of the plate.

Sheep in Barn *(Charlie Needs a Cloak)*

Use commercially made barns and fences. Use the film canister sheep and Charlie the Shepherd cut from the pattern on page 96. Have children pretend that the sheep want to get out of the fence, and Charlie has to keep them inside the fence.

Explore Yarn and Cotton

Place balls of different colors of yarn and cotton on a table. Have scissors, glue, and construction paper placed nearby. Have the children explore the items and make their own projects.

Dye Coffee Liners *(Charlie Needs a Cloak)*

Try to obtain Concord grapes. If found, boil in water and drain water from the grapes before the children arrive. If grapes are not available, use red or purple food coloring thinned with water. Fold the liner into a triangle shape and dip into the color. Dry flat.

Hat Match

Cut hats using the pattern on page 93. Two hats of each texture or color must be made. They can be colored with markers or crayons to make them more interesting. Have children match the shape, texture, or color.

Easel Paint

Set up an easel with primary colors. If another easel is available, set it up with secondary colors.

Parquetry Blocks

Put out commercially made parquetry blocks and have the children follow the commercially made patterns for the blocks.

Dramatic Play

Put out as many hats as available for the children to try on and pretend. Wigs can add interest. Put out curlers, pretend hair dryers, hair clips, and barrettes.

File Folder Clothing Game *(The Hat)*

The pattern for the file folder game is on pages 88 and 89. Use dice or a numbered spinner to determine spaces to move from Lisa to Hedgie.

Activities for Clothing *(cont.)*

Individual Activities *(cont.)*

Clothes Concentration

Use the patterns on pages 91 and 92 and cut out cards. They can be glued on tagboard and then cut if the activity is to be used again. Have about three children play the game at once. First, one child flips the card and then another card. If the cards do not match, the child flips them back down, and the next person tries to find a match. Continue until all the cards are turned up.

Place for Clothes

Use the pattern on page 94 to make a figure with marked spaces for the clothes. Use the patterns on the next page to cut out the matching clothes. Have the children place the clothes on the correct spaces on the figure.

Dress-Up *(Oh, Lewis!)*

Place winter clothes such as jackets, scarves, mittens, hats, and boots in the dress-up area. Make sure that children have clothes to practice zipping and buttoning.

Sort Clothes

In the housekeeping area, have the children sort the clothes according to baby and big-people clothes, cold or warm clothes, mommy or daddy clothes, and colors.

Mittens and Clothespins

Have children use clamp clothespins and attach the mittens to a string or rope line. Talk about the color of each, hang them in pairs with the thumbs facing each other, or hang them by alternating colors (patterning).

String Macaroni

Use the straight macaroni tinted with food coloring and rubbing alcohol. (See tinted macaroni on page 198 in the food unit.) Use a yarn needle and thread with double string. Tie a piece of macaroni on the end so that the string will not fall off. Tie and make a necklace to wear with the clothes.

Frozen Paper Paint

Place the easel paper in a freezer or outside if the weather is cold enough. Bring in as it is needed and have the children paint on the paper with tempera paint. Is there a difference between this paper and paper that is room temperature?

Winter Dress-Up

Put out winter coats, mittens, scarves, hats, etc., in the dramatic play or housekeeping area.

Activities for Clothing *(cont.)*

Group Activities

The Quilt

Try to find a handmade or machine-made quilt. Show it to the children and if there is an explanation about the quilt, share it with them. Sometimes, children still have quilts from their baby years. Have them bring the quilts in and share with the class. If these cannot be located, show the cover of the book *The Quilt* to the children. Say, "The quilt is something that keeps us warm in the winter. This story is about a quilt very important to the little girl on the cover. Let's listen to her story."

Read *The Quilt*. After reading the story, point out to the children that, "All the fabric in the quilt came from some clothing or curtains that were from the little girl's younger time. Sally, her dog, was made from some fabric, too. And the leftovers are also in the quilt. Look closely at Sally. She is light blue. Can you find the fabric that was used to make Sally?"

Bring in pre-cut squares of wallpaper samples. Cut them in half. See if the children can match one side of a specific pattern to the other side of the pattern.

Say, "Colors and patterns match when they are cut in two like the wallpaper we matched. Can you find someone in the class with clothes that match the colors in your clothes? Take that person's hand and walk around the room with him or her."

Charlie Needs a Cloak (available in big book)

Show puppets of Charlie and his sheep. Show Charlie's cloak of red. If puppets were not made, show the picture of Charlie on the cover of the book. Ask "What is a cloak?" Explain to the children that a cloak is like a cape or shawl with no arms. Use a sheet and drape it around the shoulders of the teacher or a child volunteer to look like a cloak. Say, "Look at the first page of the book. Does Charlie need a new cloak? Why?" (Notice the bite out of the cloak on the Charlie puppet.)

Read *Charlie Needs a Cloak*. Explain each process to the children.

- *"Charlie sheared his sheep."* In spring the sheep has so much wool which kept him warm during the winter. So the wool has to be shaved from the sheep. It does not hurt the sheep anymore than it hurts a man to shave his face in the morning. In fact, it will make the sheep feel cooler during the warm weather.
- *"He washed the wool."* During the winter the wool gets dirty, and washing is needed to get it clean. Sometimes people don't wash the wool because the oil or lanolin in the wool makes it waterproof.
- *"And carded the wool to straighten it out."* The cards used to comb the wool are like a dog's comb.

Activities for Clothing *(cont.)*

Group Activities *(cont.)*

Charlie Needs a Cloak (cont.)

- *"Then Charlie spun the wool into yarn."* If possible, have someone who spins come to demonstrate the process. If a spinner is not available, show ready-made yarn. Show how the threads are twisted together. Then show two-ply wool. Explain that the two spun threads of wool are twisted together to make a heavier piece of wool. Long ago this was done on a spinning wheel that is seen in the picture.

- *"Then Charlie dyed the yarn red in the berry juice."* Long ago, Charlie did not have a store to buy dye for the wool. He had to find berries and boil them. The color was red, and when he put the wool in the berry juice, the wool became red.

- *"Charlie put the strands on the loom."* A loom is kind of like the paper plate that we wove. Look at the picture in the book. It is much bigger than the paper plate, and Charlie was able to make a big piece of fabric.

- *"Then Charlie cut the fabric and sewed it together by hand."* He did not use a sewing machine because he did not have one.

Read the last page. *"Charlie had a beautiful new red cloak."* Ask the children, "But what is happening to his beautiful new cloak? Who is nibbling at it? Why do you think that Charlie needed a new cloak in the first place?"

Walk to the next area, saying "Baa-baa" like the sheep.

Anthony's Hat

Teacher places a hat on his or her head. Ask what color it is. Then place a towel over the hat. Ask, "What color is it now?" Place a colored scarf over the towel. "What color is it now? Can things change color simply by another item being placed over the first thing? Let's listen to a story where just that thing happened."

Read *Anthony's Hat*. Did Anthony's hat change color? What really happened to Anthony's hat? (Have a pile of dress-up clothes at hand.) Can we change the color of clothes that we have on now? How could we do it? Then have the children put a dress-up item over their parent clothes. Have each child say what color they have on now.

Walk around the room, standing up very straight and pretending to have a very beautiful hat.

Activities for Clothing *(cont.)*

Group Activities *(cont.)*

Oh, Lewis!

Put out several pairs of boots. See how many of the children can close the boots. Help them if needed. Most boots use Velcro, but some children may have buckle boots. Tell children that "Lots of people have trouble closing boots and have trouble putting on other things too. One little boy named Lewis had a very difficult time. This is his story."

Read *Oh, Lewis!* After reading the story, have the children practice putting on coats, zipping them up, and putting on mittens.

Walk to the next area, pretending to have heavy boots on. The children will have to step very high.

The Jacket I Wear in the Snow

Explain to the children that, "Most stories have words which we read so we know what is happening. But some stories have pictures instead of words. We read the pictures instead of the words. We have some recipes that are like that. We read the picture which means *cup*. Sometimes the teacher needs help reading a story that is like that. Can you help with the story today?"

Read *The Jacket I Wear in the Snow*. Hold the book up so everyone can see. The story is written so that the item is pictured large first, and then it is placed in the word sequence as a small picture representing the word. The children should be able to figure out the word from the picture. Read it again because it is so much fun!

Walk to the next area, shivering and acting cold.

The Hat

Have the teacher wear a winter hat to the group activity. Take the hat off and talk about the hat's color(s), size, and shape. Ask children if they have ever hung a hat someplace and found that it was gone when they went back to get it. "Did you ever find it? We are going to read a story about a hat hung on the clothesline and the wind blew it off."

Read *The Hat*. Have children make the sounds of the animals as Hedgie explains to each that he has a new hat. At the end of the story, talk about how each animal has a hat. What does each animal actually have on his or her head?

Then have the children act out the last part of the story. Decide who will be Hedgie, Hen, Gander, Barn Cat, Farm Dog, Pig, and Pony. Have a pile of clothes, mittens, and hats from which to choose. Once all the children have their "hats" on, have them make the animal sound individually. Then make them all at once for an animal chorus. Have one child be Lisa as she retrieves all the clothes that were on the line. Then have Lisa lead all the "animals" to the next area.

Activities for Clothing *(cont.)*

Games

Freeze Tag

Have children walk around the room. When the teacher says "Freeze," the children pretend that they are frozen and stay in the same position until the teacher says "Walk." If the game is played outdoors, have the children run until the teacher says "Freeze."

Hat Action

Have the children line up in two lines. Give a hat to the first one in each line. When the teacher says "Pass the hat," the children pass the hat over their shoulders. Next, have them pass the hat between their legs. The activities will depend on the developmental level of the children in the class.

Boot Pile

Have all the children get their boots. Place the boots in a pile (and hope they all are labeled with the owners' names). Have the children find their boots, put them on, and walk around the room saying "My big boots are so much fun, but they tell me, 'Please don't run.'"

Hat Pile

Have each child get his or her hat and put it in a pile on the floor. The teacher mixes them up, and the children have to find their hats. Have them put the hats on and sing "My Hat, It Has Three Corners." (Hap Palmer, *Learning Basic Skills Through Music,* Volume 1, "What Are You Wearing?")

Activities for Clothing *(cont.)*

Songs, Action Poems, and Fingerplay

"Miss Mary Mack"

(Ella Jenkins. *You'll Sing a Song and I'll Sing a Song.*) Children slap thighs, clap hands, slap hands of partner across from child. Continue same pattern until end of song. This is one of the best songs to teach children patterning.

"The Three Little Kittens"

(Nursery Rhyme)

Three little kittens lost their mittens,
and they began to cry,
"Oh mother dear, we sadly fear
Our mittens we have lost."
"What! lost your mittens,
you naughty kittens!
Then you shall have no pie!"
"Meow, meow, meow!"
The three little kittens found their mittens,
and they began to cry,
"Oh! mother dear, see here, see here,
Our mittens we have found."
"What! found your mittens,
You good little kittens,
Then you shall have some pie!
"Purr, purr, purr."
The three little kittens put on their
mittens and soon ate up the pie.
"Oh, mother dear, we greatly fear
Our mittens we have soiled."
"What! Soiled your mittens,
You naughty kittens!"
Then they began to sigh,
"Meow, meow, meow!"
The three little kittens washed their mittens,
and hung them up to dry.
"Oh Mother dear, look here, look here,
Our mittens we have washed."
"What! Washed your mittens,
you darling kittens!
But I smell a rat close by!
"Hush, hush, hush!"

Activities for Clothing (cont.)

Songs, Action Poems, Fingerplay *(cont.)*

"Baa-Baa Black Sheep"

(Nursery Rhyme)

Baa, baa, black sheep,
Have you any wool?
Yes, sir, yes, sir, three bags full:
One for my master, one for my dame,
And one for the little boy
Who lives in the lane.

"My Snow Suit"

My snow suit is a darker brown.
(*Pull hands up to zip up.*)
The coat zips up, and the legs zip down.
(*Pull hands down to zip down.*)
My dad brought it from downtown.
Zip it up, and zip it down.

"My Hat, It Has Three Corners"

(Traditional)

My hat, it has three corners.
Three corners has my hat.
And had it not three corners,
It would not be my hat.
(*Join thumbs to thumbs and index fingers to index
fingers in a triangle shape and place on top of head.*)

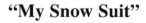

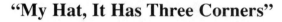

Additional Literature

Andersen, Hans Christian. *The Emperor's New Clothes.* Houghton Mifflin, 1986.

Carlstrom, Nancy White. *Jessie Bear, Jessie Bear, What Will You Wear?* Macmillan, 1986.

Hoberman, Mary Ann. *Miss Mary Mack.* Little, Brown & Co., 1998.

Monsell, Mary Elise. *Underwear!* Albert Whitman & Co., 1988.

Munsch, Robert. *Thomas' Snowsuit.* Annick Press, 1985.

Seuss, Dr. *The Cat in the Hat.* Random House, 1987.

Records, Cassettes, and CDs

Jenkins, Ella. *You'll Sing a Song and I'll Sing a Song.* Folkway Records, 1966.

Palmer, Hap. *Learning Basic Skills Through Music, Volume 1.* Educational Activities, Inc., 1971.

Video

Charlie Needs a Cloak. Children's Circle. Weston Woods, 1989.

Patterns for Clothing

Bulletin Board for Clothing

Patterns for Clothing *(cont.)*

Clothing File Folder Game

Follow footprints in snow.

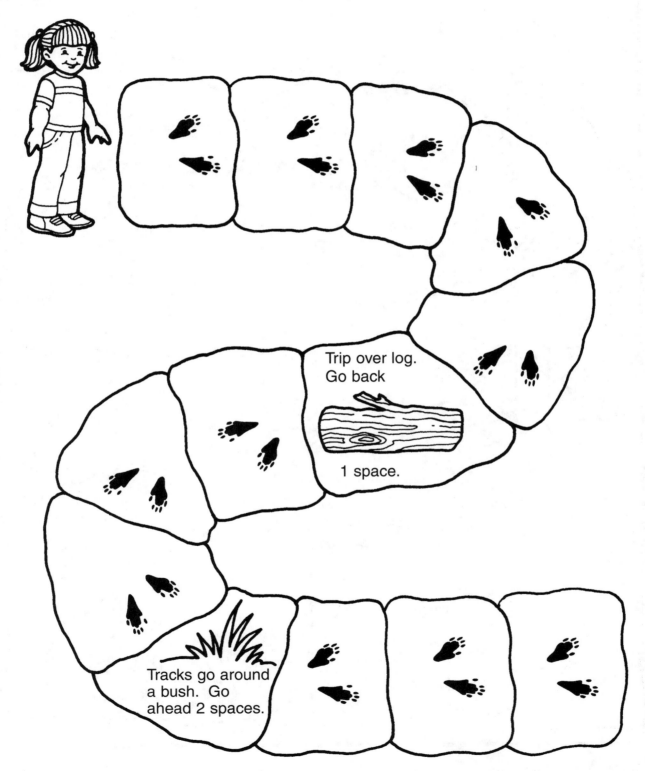

Trip over log.
Go back

1 space.

Tracks go around
a bush. Go
ahead 2 spaces.

Patterns for Clothing *(cont.)*

Clothing File Folder Game *(cont.)*

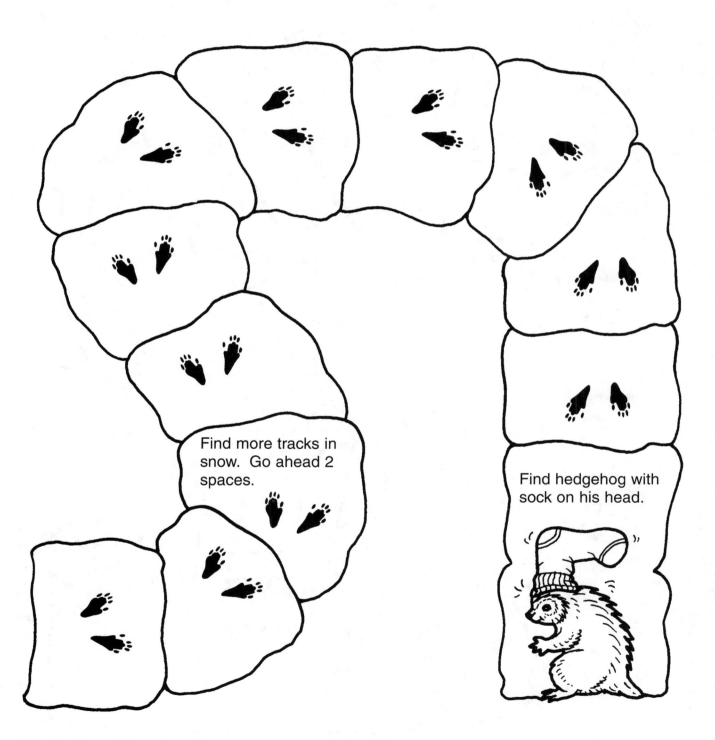

Find more tracks in snow. Go ahead 2 spaces.

Find hedgehog with sock on his head.

Patterns for Clothing *(cont.)*

Clothing for Bulletin Board and Mobile

Patterns for Clothing *(cont.)*

Clothes Concentration

hat	hat	T-shirt
T-shirt	short pants	short pants
boots	boots	mitten

Patterns for Clothing *(cont.)*

Clothes Concentration *(cont.)*

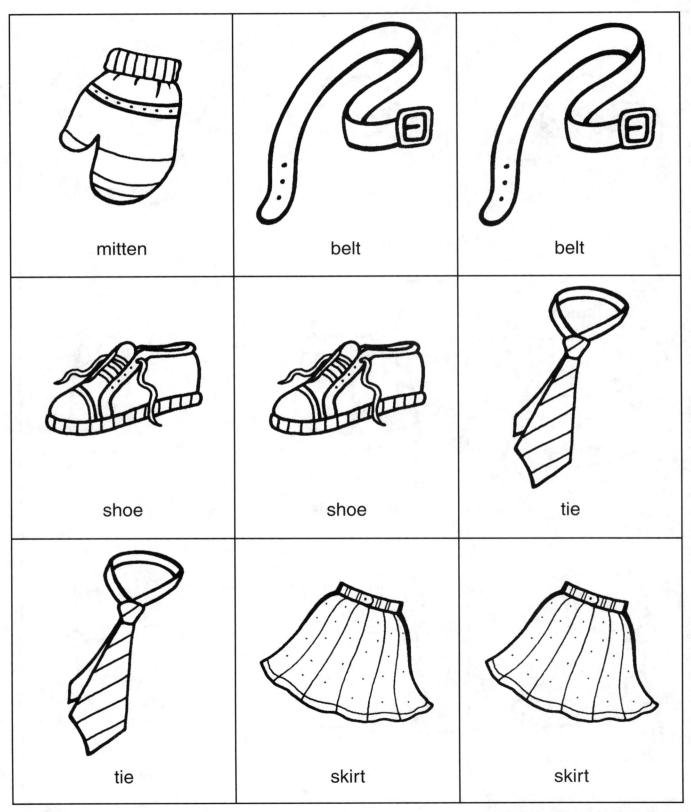

mitten	belt	belt
shoe	shoe	tie
tie	skirt	skirt

Patterns for Clothing *(cont.)*

Hat Match

Patterns for Clothing *(cont.)*

Figure for Clothes

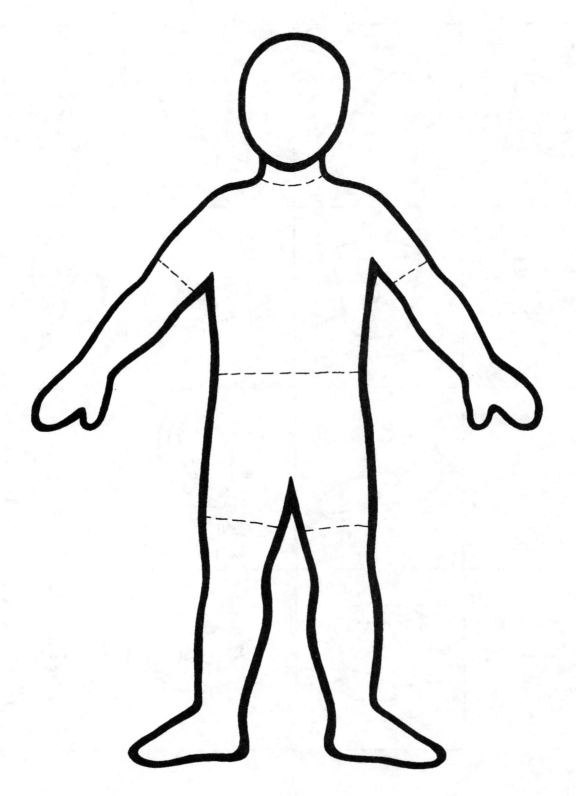

Patterns for Clothing *(cont.)*

Clothes for Figure

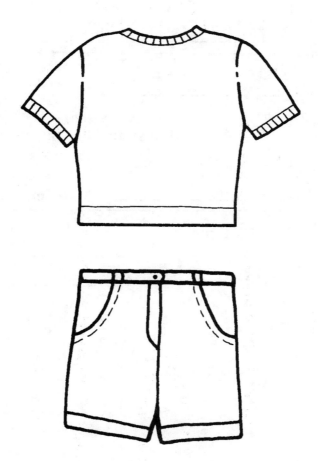

Patterns for Clothing (cont.)

Film Canister Puppet for Charlie and His Sheep

Step 1

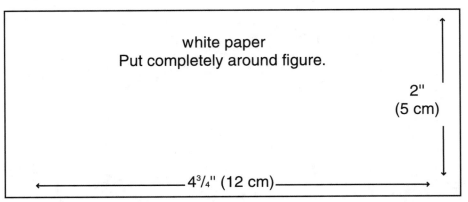

white paper
Put completely around figure.

2"
(5 cm)

4³/₄" (12 cm)

Step 2

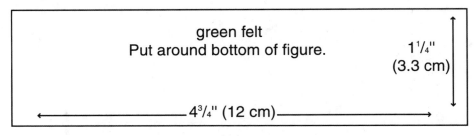

green felt
Put around bottom of figure.

1¹/₄"
(3.3 cm)

4³/₄" (12 cm)

Make shepherd's staff
from pipe cleaner.
(Use marker for eyes
and nose.)

Step 3

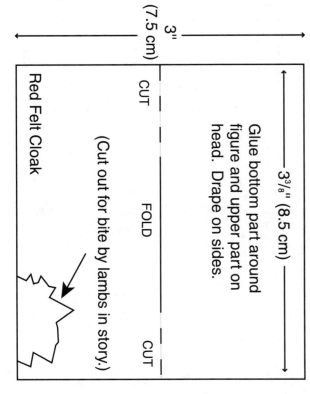

3"
(7.5 cm)

Red Felt Cloak

CUT   FOLD   CUT

Glue bottom part around
figure and upper part on
head. Drape on sides.

3³/₈" (8.5 cm)

(Cut out for bite by lambs in story.)

Step 4

Arms—Make two.

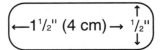

←1¹/₂" (4 cm) → ¹/₂"

Step 5

Lamb—Cut container in half. Cover
with cotton or yarn center.

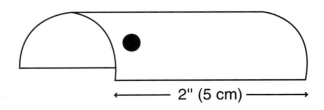

← 2" (5 cm) →

Patterns for Clothing *(cont.)*

Stencil for Sheep

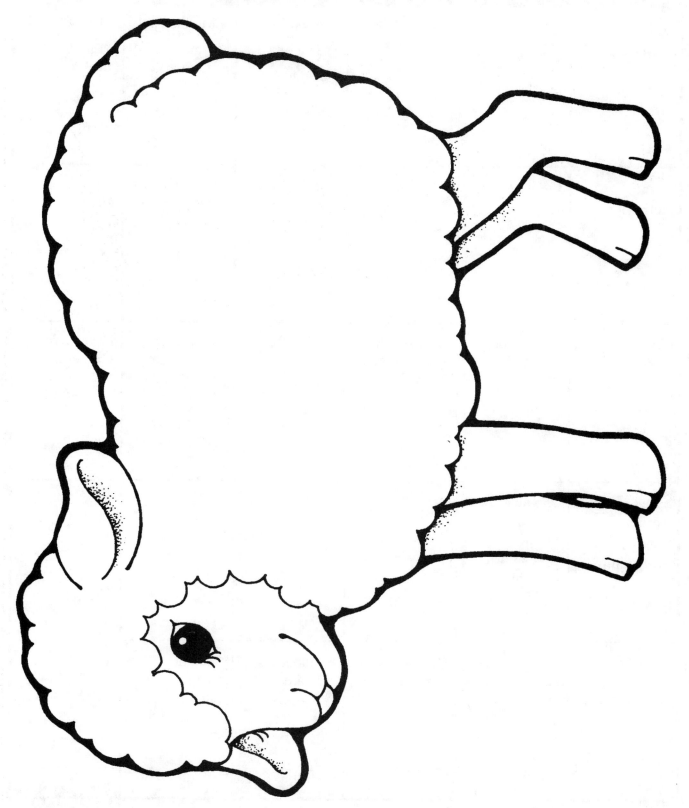

Ten Plans for Color

	Day One	**Day Two**	**Day Three**	**Day Four**	**Day Five**
Individual Activities	• Dribble Paint • Crepe Paper Dance • Separate Colored Cereal	• Tissue Paper Painting • Flower Rub • Boil Marigolds	• Marker Art • Hand Art • Scented Colored Markers	• Marble Roll • Water Surface Painting	• Feely Box • Easel Painting • Paint with Shower Puffs
Group Activities	*Color Dance*	*Planting a Rainbow*	*Purple, Green, and Yellow*	*The Mixed-Up Chameleon*	*Seven Blind Mice*
Games	Ball, Hoop, and Ribbon Activities	Ball, Hoop, and Ribbon Activities	Marker Relay	Red Light, Green Light	Pretend You Cannot See
Songs, Action Poems, Fingerplay	"Come and Get the Red Lollipop" or others on recordings all week				
Transitions	Dance to the next area.	Green leads to next area.	Purple leads to next area.	Stick out tongues and catch flies	Walk like animals.

Ten Plans for Color *(cont.)*

	Day Six	**Day Seven**	**Day Eight**	**Day Nine**	**Day Ten**
Individual Activities	• Water Paint Fence • Spatter Paint • String Paint	• Torn Paper • Loofah Prints • Puffy Paint	• Warming Tray Art • Old Crayons • Shaved Crayon Melt	• Hard-Boiled Egg Roll • Flower Print	• Old Slides • Glob Smear
Group Activities	*Oh, Were They Ever Happy!*	*Little Blue and Little Yellow*	*My Crayons Talk*	*A Color of His Own*	*Red Is Best*
Games	Paintbrush Run	There's Music in the Colors	Crayon March	Find a Favorite Color	Color Song (Hap Palmer)
Songs, Action Poems, Fingerplay	"If You're Happy and You Know It"	"There's Music in the Colors"	Same as Day Seven	Same as Day Seven	"Color Song"
Transitions	Pretend to paint on the way to next area.	Dance to "There's Music in the Colors."	Blue leads to next area.	Yellow leads to next area.	Red leads to next area.

Room Preparation for Color

Bulletin Board

A plan for the color bulletin board is on page 110. Place a rainbow over the houses which are cut from primary and secondary colors. Scatter the figures of children near the houses.

Mobile

You may wish to use paintbrushes for the crosspieces seen on page 111. Cut out cans of spilling paint, using the pattern. For each can make sure that the spilling paint is a different color.

Dress-Up Area

Make sure that there are many colored hats, mittens, and bright-colored pieces of clothing.

Extended Activity

This week communicate by clapping once if you want to say "yes" and twice if you want to say "no."

Suggested Literature for Color

Carle, Eric. *The Mixed-Up Chameleon.* Harper & Row Publishers, Inc., 1975.
Ehlert, Lois. *Planting a Rainbow.* Harcourt, Brace, Jovanovich, 1988.
Hubbard, Patricia. *My Crayons Talk.* Henry Holt & Co., 1996.
Jonas, Ann. *Color Dance.* Greenwillow Dance, 1989.
Lionni, Leo. *A Color of His Own.* Alfred A. Knopf, 1975.
Lionni, Leo. *Little Blue and Little Yellow.* Astor-Honor, 1959.
Munsch, Robert. *Purple, Green and Yellow.* Annick Press, Ltd., 1992.
Spiers, Peter. *Oh, Were They Ever Happy!* Doubleday Press, 1978.
Stinson, Kathy. *Red Is Best.* Annick Press, 1982.
Young, Ed. *Seven Blind Mice.* Philomel, 1992.

Materials

- finger-paint paper
- finger paint
- liquid starch
- meat baster
- crepe paper
- scarves or ribbons
- colored cereal
- Styrofoam egg cartons
- colored tissue paper
- manila paper
- glue
- paint brayer
- tempera paint
- marigolds or grape or onion skins
- coffee filters
- colored markers
- scented markers
- marbles
- chalk
- sandpaper
- fabric
- string
- bolts
- thread spools
- wood pieces
- seeds
- shower puffs
- pie pan
- string
- scraps of construction paper
- loofah sponge
- flour
- salt
- ketchup-type squeeze bottle
- paper plate
- warming tray
- foil
- crayons
- old muffin tin
- wax paper
- metal grater
- hard-boiled eggs
- old film slides
- bleach
- fine-line marker
- newsprint

Activities for Color

Individual Activities

Dribble Paint

Mix finger paint with liquid starch to a runny consistency. Place finger-paint paper (glossy side up) on an easel. Use a meat baster and squeeze up some of the mixture. Then slowly squeeze it out and let it dribble down the page. Use several colors and dry flat. Make sure it is dry before it is taken home.

Crepe Paper Dance *(Color Dance)*

Have the children hold lengths of crepe paper, scarves, or ribbons and pretend to dance. Notice how the colors flow behind the children.

Separate Colored Cereal

Use colored circular cereal or colored puffed cereal and separate according to color. A fiber egg-carton can be marked with markers or circles of colors and the correct cereal colors put in each section. Or, large pieces of colored paper can be placed on the table, and the cereal can be placed on each piece of paper, according to the matching color.

Tissue Paper Painting

Have colored tissue paper that bleeds, a pan of water, and manila paper. Cut the tissue paper into four-inch (10 cm) squares and crunch up so children can hold them and dip. Have the children dip the tissue paper in water and then press it on the manila paper. The tissue should color the paper. Use many colors for the children to create their own designs.

Flower Rub *(Planting a Rainbow)*

The day before this activity, dribble school glue on the pattern on page 112. Allow it to dry. The next day, have children rub a brayer over the pattern. Use tempera paint. Place a sheet of manila paper over the flower and rub with hand to get a print. Take the paper off and allow to dry.

Boil Marigolds *(Planting a Rainbow)*

In separate containers, boil marigolds, purple Concord grapes, purple onions, brown onion skins, or anything green ahead of time. Remove the marigolds, grapes, onions, and greens from the water. Retain the water. Show children the unboiled items and explain that the teacher has boiled them and that the water has a certain color. Notice how the marigolds leave a brownish yellow hue, not gold. Fold coffee filters into triangle shapes, and dip them into the dye from the plants. Hang them as an open circle to dry.

Marker Art *(Purple, Green, and Yellow)*

Draw with colored markers. Allow each child to draw something he or she really likes.

Hand Art *(Purple, Green, and Yellow)*

Draw around the hand with a pencil. Decorate the finger nails with colored markers.

Scented Colored Markers *(Purple, Green, and Yellow)*

Use scented markers. Have children smell the markers and try to identify the fragrances. Then have them draw objects that the markers smell like.

Activities for Color *(cont.)*

Individual Activities *(cont.)*

Marble Roll

Use glass marbles. Prepare pans of different tempera paint colors. Place some marbles in each pan and roll them around to get the colors on the marbles. Place a piece of manila paper in a 9" x 13" (23 cm x 33 cm) metal pan. Place one set of marbles in the pan and roll them around. Take them out and then place another color of marbles in the pan. Roll them around. Take them out. Keep on until as many colors as the child wishes to use are put in the pan.

Water Surface Painting

Place a dishpan of water on a table. Allow it to set and make sure that no one jiggles the table. Have a child gently shave chalk dust onto the surface of the water by rubbing or scraping a piece of chalk with a table knife. After several colors have been rubbed off, gently place a piece of manila paper over the surface of the water. The chalk will be picked up by the paper and can be hung up to dry. Since the surface of the water has been broken, the remaining chalk pieces will drop to the bottom of the pan. Begin again with another child to rub chalk with the table knife over the still surface of the water.

Feely Box *(Seven Blind Mice)*

Place textured items in a paper bag. Sandpaper, fabric, string, bolts, spools of thread, wood pieces, seeds, and any items of texture work well. Have children try to identify items by putting a hand in the bag and feeling. Is it easy? Can you identify by just feeling and not seeing?

Easel Painting

Place many colors of tempera paint in the easel rack. Always place colors from light to dark according to the hand preference of the child. Have children experiment with painting a stroke of one color on paper and next to it another color. How many strokes can be placed on the paper?

Paint with Shower Puffs

Puffs tied in the center with white cord and a hanging loop can be donated by parents who have extras or can be purchased from drugstores or bath shops. Place tempera paint in pie tins. Have children hold the strings tightly and dip the puffs in paint. Dab on large sheets of paper. Make sure that you have a separate puff for each color.

Water Paint Fence *(Oh, Were They Ever Happy!)*

If the weather is nice, have the children go outside and paint a fence or wall with clear water. Use a large bucket and wide paintbrushes. Have them pretend they are painting with colored paint.

Spatter Paint

Cover the table with plenty of newspaper since the paint may spread when brushed over the screen. Use a cardboard square, triangle, or circle to place on a sheet of paper. Dip an old toothbrush in colored tempera and gently rub over a piece of screening. The spatter will land on the sheet of paper and on the cardboard shape. Remove the cardboard to reveal that shape in the original color of the paper.

Activities for Color *(cont.)*

Individual Activities *(cont.)*

String Paint

Wind string randomly around a brayer. Prepare a tin with tempera paint and roll the brayer over the paint. Then roll the brayer over a piece of paper. The pattern will repeat itself as it is rolled out. Try several colors of tempera.

Torn Paper *(Little Blue and Little Yellow)*

Use leftover construction paper for this project. Have children tear large, medium, and small circles for this activity. Arrange and glue on contrasting colors of construction paper. Use with *Little Blue and Little Yellow* and show the pictures in the book.

Loofah Paints

Use loofah sponges to print with tempera on paper. Use different colors and try moist sponges versus dry sponges.

Puffy Paint

Mix equal parts of flour and salt. Add water to the desired liquid consistency so that it will squirt out of a ketchup-type squeeze bottle. Add blue tempera paint in one squeeze bottle and yellow tempera paint in another squeeze bottle. Squeeze the paint onto a paper plate. Try putting the yellow and the blue on top of each other to see if they will blend.

Warming Tray Art

Keep an electric warming tray at low temperature. It may have to be tested at different temperatures to see what is needed to melt crayons. Each manufactured electric tray is different. When it is at the correct temperature, place foil on the tray and manila paper over the foil. Have the children draw any picture they want with crayons. The wax will melt, and the colors will be more brilliant.

(Caution must be used whenever children are near heated appliances.)

Old Crayons

Remove the paper from short crayons that are no longer usable. Heat an oven to 150° F (66° C) and use a very old muffin tin. Place mixed colors of crayons in the cups of the tin and put it in the oven. Watch as the crayons melt and remove when they have blended together. (Different brands of crayons melt differently.) When the crayons have cooled, have the children color with them. The experience of handling bulk crayons plus many colors in each one causes interesting results. Compliment each finished product. The muffin tin can be cleaned with very hot water.

Shaved Crayon Melt

Shave old crayons onto wax paper, using an old metal grater. Mix up the colors. Have children pick up the shavings and mix them on a sheet of wax paper. Place another sheet of wax paper on top. Place a sheet of newspaper over that and press with an iron. The crayons will melt. Excess wax paper can be trimmed off, and the wax paper creations may be hung in the window.

Activities for Color *(cont.)*

Individual Activities *(cont.)*

Hard-Boiled Egg Roll

Hard-boil some eggs. Roll each egg in a different color of tempera paint. Place a 9" x 12" (23 cm x 30 cm) piece of manila paper in 9" x 13" (23 cm x 33 cm) metal cake pan. Place one egg on top of the manila paper and roll it around. Remove. Place another color of egg in the pan and roll it around. When the paper has the desired design, remove it from the pan.

Flower Print

Pick local flowers. Hold the stems and press flowers into tempera paint. Then press them on manila paper. Make patterns with different colors and different flowers.

Old Slides

Before this activity, dip old slides in bleach to remove pictures. Have each child draw a flower on the slide with a pencil-type or fine-line marker. Use an overhead or slide projector to see the finished products.

Glob Smear

Fold a sheet of paper in half. Open. Place a glob of any color tempera paint in the center. Refold. Press on the outside of the paper and try to spread the paint around in the middle. Open the paper and note how the pattern is the same on both sides.

Group Activities

Color Dance

Commercially made colored plastic pieces can be purchased and used to show the mixture of color by holding them up to the light. If these cannot be found, use colored cellophane or plastic wrap. Show children that if red and yellow are put on top of each other and held up to the light, they make orange. Then take out the blue and yellow and show how they blend to make green. (To get the proper blend of colors, pure color must be used and can be best achieved by using colors held to the light. If this is not possible, use water and food coloring. Make sure that an equal number of drops are used for each color.)

Read *Color Dance* to the children. If plastic or cellophane colors were used to show how colors mix, review this again with the children. Then take out the crepe paper, scarves, or ribbons and have the children dance to "Ball, Hoop, and Ribbon Activities for Young Children." The music used on the record is classical.

Continue dancing as everyone moves to the next area.

Activities for Color *(cont.)*

Group Activities *(cont.)*

Planting a Rainbow

If the weather is nice and it is planting time, take the children outside and begin planting a flower garden. Have the parents bring in seed packets for different flowers for the area. Have the children look at the pictures on the seed packets and decide where the flowers are to be planted. Remember, it is their garden! Mark the spot where the seeds are planted with a tongue depressor which has the name of the flower written on it. Then make a diagram showing where the flowers have been planted. Then take the children back inside and read *Planting a Rainbow*. (Or if the weather is nice, read the story outside.) After reading the story, look at the packets of flower seeds and show what colors will occur where. Use a marker to block out the colors of their garden on the diagram. See if they have planted a rainbow.

Everyone wearing anything green leads to the next area.

Purple, Green, and Yellow

Talk about all the drawing activities that were done before the children gathered together. Bring out the plain markers and the scented markers in separate containers. Count how many markers are in each container. Say "Let's read a book about someone who used markers, too."

Read *Purple, Green, and Yellow*. There may be some reaction about the story, so discuss it with the children. If no comments are made, put the markers on a tray and have the children identify colors. Cover the tray with a towel and put a hand under the towel, remove one marker, and hide it behind your back. Then remove the towel from the tray and ask if the children can identify which color is missing. Replace the marker, rearrange the markers, cover with a towel, and take one away again. Keep on doing this until children have had a chance to identify all the colors.

Everyone wearing anything purple leads to the next area.

The Mixed-Up Chameleon

Ask children if they ever had days where they wished they were someone else. Have them close their eyes and see if they can see something or someone else they would rather be. If they are willing, write down what they would like to be, but do not put down any child's name. Say, "Everyone sometimes would prefer to be someone or something else. Do you know what a chameleon is? It can change its colors so that it blends in with the bushes, the green of the trees, or the gray of the rocks. Sometimes it would rather be just like that something else."

Read *The Mixed-Up Chameleon*. As the teacher reads the story, make sure to point out the colors of the animals on the right side of the page and the drawings of the animals on the left side of the page. It would be valuable to read the story again. Say, "What was the special thing that the chameleon could do but the animals in the zoo could not? It would catch a fly with its tongue. Is there something special that people can do but animals in the zoo cannot?" (*Write down the children's answers.*)

As the children move to the next area, have them stick out their tongues and pretend to catch flies.

Activities for Color *(cont.)*

Group Activities *(cont.)*

Seven Blind Mice

Cut mice from red, yellow, blue, green, purple, and orange. Use the pattern on page 113. Place the mice in a paper bag. Pull them out one at a time and have children identify the colors. Then tell them the seven mice are blind. That means that they cannot see and so they have to feel things to tell what they are. This is their adventure.

Read *Seven Blind Mice*. After reading the story have different plastic animals or stuffed animals in a box. Animals cut out of sandpaper, textured wallpaper, velvet, fake fur, etc., can be used also. Have one child at a time close eyes, reach in the box, and identify the animal without looking. After each child has a turn, have them put the items back in the box and then walk to the next area as the animal each took out of the box.

Oh, Were They Ever Happy!

Fill a cardboard tube from the center of toweling with different colors of tissue paper. Pull the colors out one at a time. Ask children what colors they are. "What can colors be used for? Could they be used to paint a house?" Ask if their house or a friend's house has ever been painted. "What color was it? Who did it? What tools were used? Was a ladder ever used? Today we are going to read a book about a house that was being painted. Listen and watch the pictures and see if your parents or a friend would be happy about this paint job."

Read *Oh, Were They Ever Happy!* After reading the story, ask if the children think that their families would be happy about the paint job. "Look at the pictures and see how the paint was added. A pretend house might look good like the pictures in the book but not a real house. Maybe it is better to throw away old paint. What do you think?"

Walk, pretending to paint on the way.

Little Blue and Little Yellow

Ask children if they have a special friend. "Who is your friend? Can you give your friend a hug if he or she is in the room? Sometimes colors give each other a special hug, and then the colors really blend and become another color." Use two empty honey bear containers. In one have the color blue made with liquid tempera paint and thinned with water. In the other have liquid yellow tempera paint also thinned with water. Call one *Little Blue* and the other *Little Yellow*. Have them pretend to give each other a hug. When they do this, have a little of the yellow poured into a separate glass container and a little of the blue also poured into the container. Swirl around and stir with a spoon. Say, "What has the color become? Their hug has created another color! I wonder if other hugs from other colors can cause the same thing to happen?"

Activities for Color *(cont.)*

Group Activities *(cont.)*

Little Blue and Little Yellow (cont.)

Read *Little Blue and Little Yellow*. After reading the story, ask if other colors give hugs and if they create new colors. See whether the children can figure out what colors make up green, orange, and purple. (Younger children cannot figure out the secondary colors, but some older children can.) Use drops of food coloring in a clear glass container to show how red and yellow make orange, blue and yellow make green, and red and blue make purple. Follow up with any songs from Wally Strickland and James Earle's recording *There's Music in the Colors*.

Dance to the next area, using any song on the recording.

My Crayons Talk

Show the cover and read the title of the book to the children. Say, "I never heard of crayons that talked, have you? Do crayons have mouths or tongues? How in the world can they talk? Let's think about it a little bit. If you were a red crayon, what would you say—if you had a mouth? Red is very active. Red is the color of fire and sunburn. Ouch! I don't think that red would speak gently. What do you think red would say?" See whether children can come up with an expressive word such as ouch, wow, or roar. When children listen to the book, see whether they come up with the same words as the colors say.

Read *My Crayons Talk*. Take out a box of crayons. Show the crayons one at a time to the children. Have them really look at the crayon color. Is it dark, or is it light? Is it a happy color or a sad color? What does the color make you feel inside? Then list the colors and beside each list a word that the children think that color would say.

Children wearing anything blue lead to the next area.

A Color of His Own

Ask the children if they know what a chameleon is. (If *The Mixed-Up Chameleon* was used before, this explanation may not be necessary). Try to find a picture of a plastic replica to show the children. Say, "Chameleons can change their colors so they blend in with the things around them. For example, if they are on an orange leaf, they become orange. That way, nothing can find them." Show children the cover of the book *A Color of His Own*. Ask children what they think the chameleon's own color will be.

Read *A Color of His Own*. After reading, ask what the chameleon's favorite color was. See what answers the children give. (*It was the color of his friend, and the two would stay together and blend in with the surroundings.*) Ask the children if they have a favorite color. Write down the names of the children in the class and then write down their favorite colors. Ask each why it is his or her favorite. Children wearing anything yellow lead to the next area.

Activities for Color *(cont.)*

Group Activities *(cont.)*

Red Is Best

Ask children if they remember the story of the chameleon who had a color of his own. What did the children decide were their favorite colors? Say, "Did anyone decide on red? Today we are going to read a book about someone who thought that red was best."

Read *Red Is Best*. Ask, "What were her favorite things that were red? But what was her reason for feeling that red was really needed? (*Her red pajamas kept monsters away.*) Do you ever feel that you have monsters in your room? Would red pajamas keep them away? What are some other things that would keep them away?"

Children wearing red lead to the next area.

Games

Red Light, Green Light

Prepare a red circle and a green circle. Red means stop and green means go. Have the children in a straight line, facing the teacher. When the green circle is held up, the children walk (not run) towards the teacher. When the red circle is held up, everyone stops. Continue until everyone has made it to the teacher's line.

Marker Relay

Make two lines of children, one behind the other. Place a box of colored markers about three yards to the front of the first child. Have the first one run to the box of markers, select one, and take it back to the end of the line; the next child first in line then runs to the markers. They keep on running to the box of markers until everyone has a marker in his or her hand. Everyone then sits down and tells the others the color of his or her marker.

Pretend You Cannot See

Have each child pick a friend. One child closes his or her eyes, and the other one leaves the eyes open. Have them walk around the room hand in hand, the one with open eyes helping the other not to bump into things or people. Then exchange roles and have the child who had closed eyes keep them open and help the non-seeing friend make his or her way around the room. After everyone has had a chance to guide a friend, sit down and talk about the feelings they had when not being able to see.

Paintbrush Run

Have all children sit in a circle and close their eyes. One child hides the house paintbrush. Then have all open their eyes and try to find the brush. Take turns until everyone has had a chance to hide the paintbrush.

Activities for Color *(cont.)*

Games *(cont.)*

Crayon March

Each child picks a favorite "talking" crayon from the pile of crayons. Have the child hold it in front of himself or herself with arms extended. Chant or singsong the following words as they parade around the room.

> Yackity, clackity, yum, yum, yum.
> Sometimes my crayons say that,
> and sometimes ho-hum!

Find a Favorite Color

Each child by now has identified his or her favorite color. Have the children go around the room and each find an object that is that color. Have them return to the group and tell the others what their favorite color is and what the object is. Then have the children return each object in the room.

Songs, Action Poems, and Fingerplay

"Come and Get the Red Lollipop"

(Tune: "Here We Go Round the Mulberry Bush")

Come and get the red lollipop, red lollipop, red lollipop.

Come and get the red lollipop,

(Here sing the first and last names of a child.)

Prepare lollipops by cutting two circles at least five inches (13 cm) in diameter from construction paper. Make sure that all the primary and secondary colors are used. Tape a tongue depressor in the center of one and then glue the two pieces of construction paper together. Cover with clear stick-on plastic. Fan out the lollipops and have one child come forward as the song is sung and pick out the color.

Additional Literature

Ehlert, Lois. *Color Zoo.* Lippincott, 1990.

Hammett, Carol and Elaine Beuffel. *Ball, Hoop, and Ribbon Activities for Young Children.*

Jenkins, Ella. *I Know the Colors of the Rainbow.*

_____. *Play Your Instrument and Make a Pretty Sound.*

Strickland, Willy and James Earle. *There's Music in the Colors.* Kimbo, 1976.

Cassettes and CDs

Jenkins, Ella. *I Know the Colors of the Rainbow.* Activity Records, Inc., 1981.

Palmer, Hap. *Learning Basic Skills Through Music, Volume I.* Educational Activities, Inc., 1971.

Patterns for Color
Color Bulletin Board

Patterns for Color *(cont.)*

Color Mobile

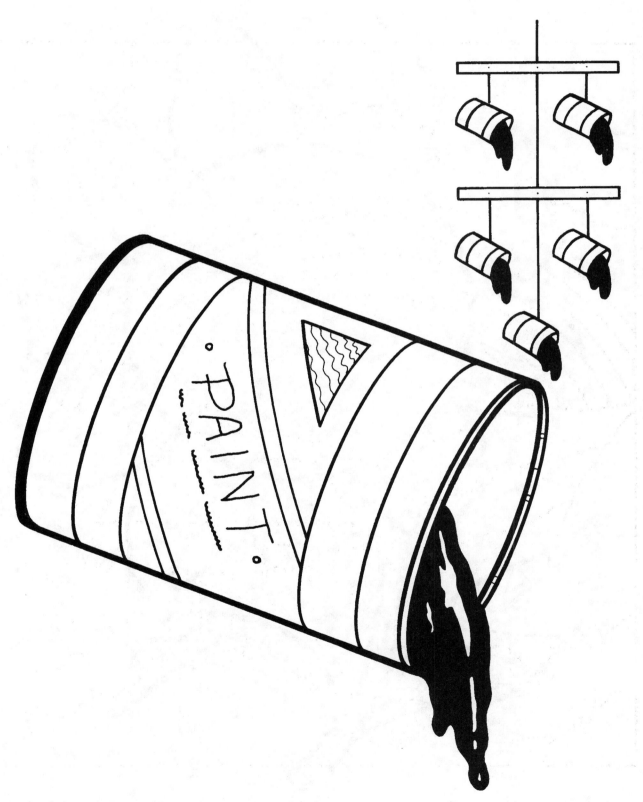

Patterns for Color (cont.)

Pattern for Flower Rubbing

Patterns for Color *(cont.)*

Pattern for Seven Blind Mice

Nine Plans for Communication

	Day One	**Day Two**	**Day Three**	**Day Four**	**Day Five**
Individual Activities	• Newspaper Hat • Newspaper Puppet • Newspaper Snowflakes • Comic Strip Match	• Mirror Image • Peep Box • Write Your Own Book	• Pretend Glasses • Fancy Glasses	• Magnifying Glass • Hole Punch	• Listen to Shells • Listen to Tape of Children's Voices
Group Activities	"Newspaper Tree"	*The Eye Book*	*Arthur's Eyes*	*Roly Goes Exploring*	*The Ear Book*
Games	Snowpaper Fight	"Put Your Hands up in the Air"	"Put Your Hands up in the Air"	"Put Your Hands up in the Air"	Dance to Music
Songs, Action Poems, Fingerplay	"Where Is Thumbkin?"	"If You're Happy and You Know It" (Use for the rest of the week.)			"Touch"
Transitions	Walk around pretending to deliver papers.	Pretend to cover eyes but peek through open fingers.	Pretend to cover eyes but peek through open fingers.	Pretend to cover eyes but peek through open fingers.	Hold ears out to hear as you walk around.

Nine Plans for Communications *(cont.)*

	Day Six	**Day Seven**	**Day Eight**	**Day Nine**
Individual Activities	• Insect Pictures • Telephone	• Hum • Magazine Ears	• Comb and Tissue Paper • Tambourines	• Identify Smells • Pop Popcorn • Finger-Paint Smells
Group Activities	*The Very Quiet Cricket*	*A Button in Her Ear*	*Ty's One-Man Band*	*Arthur's Nose*
Games		Dance to Music	• Rhythm Band • "Let's Hide the Tambourine"	
Songs, Action Poems, Fingerplay	"If You're Happy and You Know It" (Use all week.)			
Transitions	Hop like a cricket.	Hop as if dancing.	Parade to next area.	Hold nose up in air as if smelling something.

Room Preparation for Communication

Make a television screen from a flat box about 12" x 18" (30 cm x 46 cm). Cut out one 18" (46 cm) side to make a TV screen. Put dowels on each shorter side. Attach a roll of paper to each dowel and wind up to one side. Have the children draw pictures to say something to another person. Pretend it is a TV screen. Use the dowel on one side and roll the paper to make the pictures move from one side to the other.

Bulletin Board

Use the pattern on page 127 as a background and hang telephone shapes from the lines for each child. Place a name and phone number on each one.

Housekeeping

Have old phones or pretend telephones, radios, and daily newspapers from the area.

Materials

- newspapers
- masking tape
- fabric flowers
- Styrofoam pieces
- rubber bands
- scissors
- comic strips
- mirrors
- manila paper
- shoebox
- waxed paper
- tagboard
- decorations for fancy glasses
- magnifying glass
- hole punch
- shells
- audio tapes
- tin cans
- string
- old magazines
- comb
- tissue
- dinner-size paper plates
- yarn
- lima beans
- popcorn

Suggested Literature for Communication

Brown, Marc. *Arthur's Eyes.* Little, Brown & Co., 1979.

Brown, Marc. *Arthur's Nose.* Little, Brown & Co., 1976.

Carle, Eric. *The Very Quiet Cricket.* Philomel Books, 1990.

LeSieg, Theo. *The Eye Book.* Random House, 1968.

Litchfield, Ada B. *A Button in Her Ear.* Doubleday & Co., 1976.

Newth, Philip. *Roly Goes Exploring.* Philomel Books, 1977.

Perkins, Al. *The Ear Book.* Random House, 1968.

Walter, Mildred Pitts. *Ty's One-Man Band.* Four Winds Press, 1980.

Activities for Communication

Individual Activities

Newspaper Hat

Fold according to the following instructions.

1. Put four sheets of newspaper over the head.
2. Shape the newspaper to the head and use masking tape to secure the form.
3. Roll up remaining newspaper below the tape and decorate.

Newspaper Puppet

Make a puppet following the instructions in the diagram.

1. Cross two rolls of newspaper and secure with rubber bands.
2. Draw a face on the vertical roll above the arms.

Newspaper Snowflakes

Use a quarter page of a newspaper to fold into quarters. On an angle, cut away and discard the upper half of the folded sheet as shown in the diagram. Snip circles, triangles, and square shapes out of the remaining folds of paper. Unfold the remaining triangle, and it becomes a snowflake.

1. Fold in half.   2. Fold again.   3. Cut away and discard.

   Use remaining triangle to cut circles, triangles, and square shapes.

Comic Strip Match

Show children a simple comic strip that they would be interested in. Four frames is about the sequence level of young children. Read the story to them and notice how the story progresses. Cut apart simple comic strips and see if the children can reassemble the story in sequence.

Mirror Image

Have children look in a mirror at their eyes. On paper have them draw their faces with the eyes. (It will depend on their developmental level as to how they perceive their eyes.) Then have them color their eyes with crayons or markers.

Peep Box

Use a shoebox which has the middle third of the top cut out. Place a piece of waxed paper in that space. Cut a peephole on one end of the box. Inside the box on the opposite end, place stars and moon on black paper. Have the children take turns looking in the box.

Activities for Communication *(cont.)*

Individual Activities *(cont.)*

Write Your Own Book

Have children walk around and explore the room. Then have them write their own book about the room. This can be dictated to the teacher, or the children can "pretend" write. Then have the children draw any pictures that show the room.

Pretend Glasses *(Arthur's Eyes)*

Use the pattern on page 129 to make glasses for each child. In the center of each lens, place colored cellophane or plastic wrap. Have children walk around the room and notice how the color in the glasses changes the appearance of items in the room.

Fancy Glasses

Using the pattern for pretend glasses at the end of this unit, make cardboard glasses stencils for the children to trace around on paper. Have the children make them very fancy and elaborate. Glue on sequins, flat buttons, lace, etc.

Magnifying Glass

Use many sizes of magnifying glasses to explore the room. See how things get bigger if looked at under the magnifying glass. Some magnifying glasses make things smaller if flipped to the other side. See how things look when made to appear smaller.

Hole Punch

Use scrap construction paper, manila paper, or typing paper. Put out hole punches for the children to punch holes in the paper. Make patterns with the cutout dots and add color by using markers or crayons.

Listen to Shells

Use large shells and small shells from the beach. If possible obtain a large conch shell. Put it up to the children's ears and ask if they can "hear the ocean." Talk about what might cause this.

Tape of Children's Voices

As the children arrive at school, have a tape recorder placed to record their voices. Play the tape back in small groups and see if they can identify the persons speaking.

Insect Pictures *(The Very Quiet Cricket)*

Use the pictures on page 130. Tell the children that insects have voices and listen to one another "speak." Have the children look at the pictures while the teacher reads the names of each insect to them. Count how many legs each insect has.

Activities for Communication *(cont.)*

Individual Activities *(cont.)*

Telephone

Use two tin cans and make a small hole at the bottom of each. (An ice pick works well.) Make a large knot in a 4' to 6' (1.3 m to 2 m) string, feed the string through the hole (with the knot on the inside of the can) and run it through the bottom of the other can. Tie another knot and pull the string taut. Have one child hold one can to his or her ear while another child pulls the string taut and talks into the other can. The first child should be able to hear the other child speak. To make many pretend phones, use paper cups and tie them in the same manner.

Hum

Have the children hum. Have them place their fingers on their throats and feel the sound of humming. Say, "Did you ever think that you could feel sound?"

Magazine Ears

Go through old magazines and find pictures of ears. Cut them out and glue them on paper in a design or collage.

Comb and Tissue Paper

Cover a new comb with tissue paper. Have a child try to hum a tune and feel the vibrations while humming. Be sure to change the tissue paper when the next child wants to hum a tune.

Tambourines

With markers or crayons have children decorate the outside bottom of two dinner-size paper plates. Put the two plates together so that the artwork shows. Punch holes about one inch (2.5 cm) apart around the plate (for younger children, tape around the edges with masking tape). Wind yarn through the holes to keep the plates together. Prior to closing the two plates, place lima beans in the center, and then close the two so that the beans will not fall out. Shake the tambourine!

Identify Smells

Let the children walk around the room and see if they notice any smells. Write down what smells the children detect during the walk.

Finger-Paint Smells

Add spices such as cinnamon to the finger paint. See if the children can notice the difference.

Pop Popcorn

Pop popcorn and notice the smell. The finished product can be eaten for a snack or glued on paper to make a design. Do not put salt on popcorn if it is to be used for a glue-on project.

Activities for Communication *(cont.)*

Group Activities

"Newspaper Tree"

Assemble four large sheets of newspaper in the following manner.

Roll up and place a piece of string around the roll to keep it together. Sometimes a piece of tape works also. Then tell the following story.

Once upon a time there was a little pointer finger that felt very lonely. *(Have children show the teacher the pointer finger.)* He wanted a friend very much. He looked low on the ground for a friend. *(Have children move pointer low on the ground.)* He looked high up for a friend. *(Have the children move the pointer finger high up and wiggle it, as if looking for a friend.)* What was he to do? He was so lonely.

"I know," said Pointer, "I will climb a tree and look for a friend." So he walked one way, looking for a special tree. And he walked another way, looking for a special tree. *(Have the children walk their pointers on the floor as if looking for a special tree.)* All of a sudden he saw just what he was looking for! It was a very special tree. It was white and black. *(Begin tearing the top of the newspaper roll as diagramed.)*

And it was growing before his eyes! *(Pull the inside center tears up, and the tree will pull out and appear to be growing.)*

"Oh, how wonderful! I will climb it to find a friend!" So Pointer climbed and climbed and climbed to see if a friend was at the top of the tree. *(Teacher wiggles pointer finger slowly up to the top of the tree.)* Pointer looked and looked and looked, but he could not find anyone up on the top of the tree.

He slowly started to cry, but all of a sudden the wind began to blow. It blew harder and harder, and the tree started to sway from side to side. *(Have the newspaper tree sway from side to side.)* Pointer became very frightened. "Oh, my," he said. "I have come up so high to look for a friend, and now the wind is going to blow me from the tree."

All of a sudden Thumb appeared from the other side of the tree. He said, "I will help you down to the ground." So the two of them held together and slid down the trunk of the tree. *(Push the pointer finger and thumb together and slide down the tree.)* When they got to the bottom, Thumb said, "Pointer, I was here all the time. But you never looked close enough to find me. I will always be your friend."

(This story can be used for Valentine's Day. For Valentine's Day prepare a red valentine with a thumbprint on it. Have Thumb give it to Pointer, saying "Thumbody Loves You.")

Pretend you are delivering papers and throwing them on the house steps as you move to the next area.

Activities for Communication *(cont.)*

Group Activities *(cont.)*

The Eye Book

Ask children if they know what color their eyes are. Use the chart pattern on page 128. See how many brown eyes, blue eyes, and green (hazel) eyes there are. Then ask what their eyes see during the day and what do they see at night. Then read them *The Eye Book.*

After reading the book, ask if the people and animals in the book see the same things the children see every day. Conclude with everyone saying "Hooray for eyes!"

Have children walk to the next area with hands over eyes but fingers separated to see through.

Arthur's Eyes

Show pictures of Arthur on the cover of the book. Say, "Arthur had difficulty seeing, and he had to get glasses. Let's read the book *Arthur's Eyes* and see if he had trouble with his glasses."

Read *Arthur's Eyes.* Ask, "When Arthur did not have on his glasses, what happened to him? Why did he decide that it was okay to wear glasses?" (*His teacher needed them to read.*) "But what was the reason that made wearing them so special?" (*Francine wore fancy glasses with no glass in them.*) Then see how many in the class wear glasses. There probably will be very few and maybe none. Walk around the school and see if there is anyone in the school who wears glasses. Return to the room and say, "I guess it is okay to wear glasses. It makes you see better."

Roly Goes Exploring

Ask children what the word "exploring" means. Write down the answers on a piece of paper. Then explain that it means to travel around and try to find something new. Or it could mean to look closely at something. The teacher explains that he or she knows something by the name of Roly who wants to explore. "Let's see who Roly really is and what he wants to explore."

Read *Roly Goes Exploring.* As the book is read, show and count the green page shapes. Stop and figure out the problems that Roly has on each page. As the pages are turned, make sure that the white page is turned with the green page. After reading the book, point out that there is something special about the book. Say, "The white pages have dots on them. This is a special type called *Braille.* Some children cannot see—even if they use a magnifying glass. These children are called *visually impaired,* and they use their hands to feel their special type of printing. That way they can read the same thing as children who can see."

Have children come up and feel the dots. Then read the book again and point out that not only do the shapes have names like "dot" and "rectangle" that are written in Braille but there are also open spaces on the page. That way if you cannot see, you can feel the shape. Then visually impaired children can learn just the same way as children who can see everything.

Have children feel the Braille and the open shapes. Have them close their eyes, pretend they cannot see, and then touch the dots and shapes.

Activities for Communication (*cont.*)

Group Activities (*cont.*)

Roly Goes Exploring (*cont.*)

If possible, have a visually impaired person visit the classroom. Have the person show the special cane and show the colors on that special cane. Perhaps that person also has a dog that he or she would be willing to show the children. It is important for young children to understand all "challenged" individuals.

The Ear Book

Play the tape of the children arriving at school. See if the class can identify each person speaking. Then take out a clock and see what sound the clock makes. Try other sounds such as a bell ringing, a drum drumming, and water dripping. Ears help us tell what the sounds are. Read *The Ear Book*.

After reading the book, have the children close their eyes. Ask them to see if they know the sounds you are going to make. Then the teacher performs the following sound-making actions:

- tears paper
- pours water
- jingles keys
- rings bells
- bounces ball
- knocks on wood

- claps hands
- scratches paper
- coughs
- cuts with scissors
- staples
- tears tape

Have the children walk to the next area with their hands holding their ears out to hear everything said.

The Very Quiet Cricket

Again play recorded voices of children as they come into the room. See if they can identify the persons talking. Then show the picture of the cricket on the cover of *The Very Quiet Cricket*. Say, "Sometimes people keep lucky metal crickets on their fireplaces." These can be purchased at garden stores. If you can find one, show that to the children also. Then ask what sound a cricket makes. "Are they ever quiet? Let's find out."

Read *The Very Quiet Cricket*. At the end, have the children listen to the sound made by the book. Ask children if they think that the cricket will be quiet again. "What do you think he will say the next day?" (*Write down what the children think he will say.*)

With hands rubbing together, have the children try to imitate the cricket sound. Then let them go around the room, hopping like crickets.

Activities for Communication *(cont.)*

Group Activities *(cont.)*

A Button in Her Ear

Information: This book is meant to show the children that some children need help hearing just like the ones who need help seeing. For younger children, it would be better to tell the story and show the pictures. For older children, the teacher may be able to read the whole story.

Ask children if they remember the stories of Arthur who needed glasses and Roly and the use of Braille. Review the stories. Show the book with the Braille in it again. Explain that sometimes people need help hearing, too. They are called "hearing impaired." This is a story about Angela and how she got help hearing.

Read *A Button in Her Ear.* Explain that sometimes Angela could not hear the words correctly, and so her answers were wrong. Examples: *Paul/ball, this/kiss, burn/learn, bed/red, gown/Sue Brown.* It was important for her to hear so that she could learn in school. Ask the children if they know of someone who has a hearing aid. Discuss how they feel about the person.

Ty's One-Man Band

Information: This book is very good for older children. For younger children, use the video tape of *Ty's One-Man Band* from Reading Rainbow, distributed by GPN/WNED-TV.

Ask the children if they have ever heard a band playing. Have they ever heard just one person play all the instruments? Say, "One time a man came to a small town and said he was a one-man band. This is his story." Either play the tape or read *Ty's One-Man Band.*

After reading the story, have the children play their homemade tambourines to rhythm-band music. Next have the rhythm-band instruments out and have the children play them to the Ella Jenkins record at the end of the unit.

Depending on the age of the children, this is a good book to introduce children to the fact that the man has a physical disability. One of his legs is partially made of wood. But it does not stop him from doing what he wants, and no one in the town notices that there is something different about him. There are commercially made dolls which have disabilities, and they will make a good addition to the room at this time. (*Note:* Different areas use different terms. "Disability, impaired, and challenged" are used. "Handicapped" usually is frowned on. Check with the special education people in your area to see which term may be preferred. There may be another term they would like used.)

Activities for Communication *(cont.)*

Group Activities *(cont.)*

Arthur's Nose

Ask the children what book was their favorite story in the unit on communication. Talk about the books that were their favorites. Then explain that people who cannot see or hear use other senses to help themselves. They use taste and touch and even smell. Say, "We use smelling to help us, even though we can see and hear. Let's go for a walk around the building and see if we notice any special smells. When some special smells are found, let's stop, close our eyes, and see if we can identify them."

When you return to the room, read *Arthur's Nose*. Say, "Arthur did not know how important his nose was. He wanted to change it to look like someone else's nose. Our noses are very important. If you could not see or hear, you would need to smell to help you know what is nearby. But all people need their noses to smell bad things and good things. If we smell bad things, it means 'watch out!' If we smell good things, it makes us very happy." (*This would be a good time to talk about fire safety and to have a firefighter visit the school.*)

Have children hold their noses up in the air as if smelling something as they walk to the next area.

Activities for Communication *(cont.)*

Games

Snowpaper Fight

Make two fortresses facing each other, about two or three yards (two or three meters) apart. Use a wider space if students are older. Hollow blocks work well for this, or you may tip a table on its side and have the children gather behind it. Wad up a ball from a single sheet of newspaper. Have the children make a stack of them for their snowpaper fight. Divide the class in two and have one group behind one fortress and the other group behind the other fortress. Let them proceed to throw paper balls at one another.

March

Use rhythm-band instruments and march to John Phillip Sousa's marches.

Dance to Music

Use dance music and have the children pretend they are dancing in the wind. Use crepe paper streamers or scarves to swirl behind them.

Rhythm Band

Use Ella Jenkins' *Play Your Instrument and Make a Pretty Sound* to introduce children to the rhythm band.

Records, Cassettes, and CD Music Sources

Palmer, Hap. *Getting to Know Myself*
"Touch"

Palmer, Hap. *Learning Basic Skills Through Music, Volume I*

"Put Your Hands Up in the Air"

Palmer, Hap. *Learning Basic Skills Through Music, Volume II*
"Let's Hide the Tambourine"

Activities for Communication (cont.)

Songs, Action Poems, and Fingerplay

"Where Is Thumbkin?"

(Traditional)

Where is Thumbkin? Where is Thumbkin?

Here I am, here I am.

How are you today, sir?

Very well, I thank you.

Run away, run away.

(Have both hands behind back. As finger is named,

pull it out and nod to other fingers.)

(Return one finger at a time to your back.)

Where is Pointer? Where is Pointer?

Here I am, here I am.

How are you today, sir?

Very well, I thank you.

Run away, run away.

(Repeat with Middle Man, Ring Man, and Pinky.)

"If You're Happy and You Know It"

(Traditional)

If you're happy and you know it, clap your hands.

If you're happy and you know it, clap your hands.

If you're happy and you know it,

Then your face will surely show it.

If you're happy and you know it, clap your hands.

If you're happy and you know it, tap your toes.

If you're happy and you know it, tap your toes.

If you're happy and you know it,

Then your face will surely show it.

If you're happy and you know it, tap your toes.

(Continue with "stomp your feet," "shake your hands," "wave your arms," "wink

your eye," "wiggle your nose," and "nod your head.")

Records, Cassettes, and CD's

Palmer, Hap. *Getting to Know Myself.* Educational Activities, Inc., 1972.

Palmer, Hap. *Learning Basic Skills Through Music, Volume I.* Educational Activities, Inc., 1969.

Palmer, Hap. *Learning Basic Skills Through Music, Volume II.* Educational Activities, Inc., 1971.

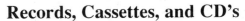

Patterns for Communication

Communication Bulletin Board

Patterns for Communication *(cont.)*

Eye Graph

blue	brown	green or hazel

Patterns for Communication *(cont.)*

Pattern for Glasses

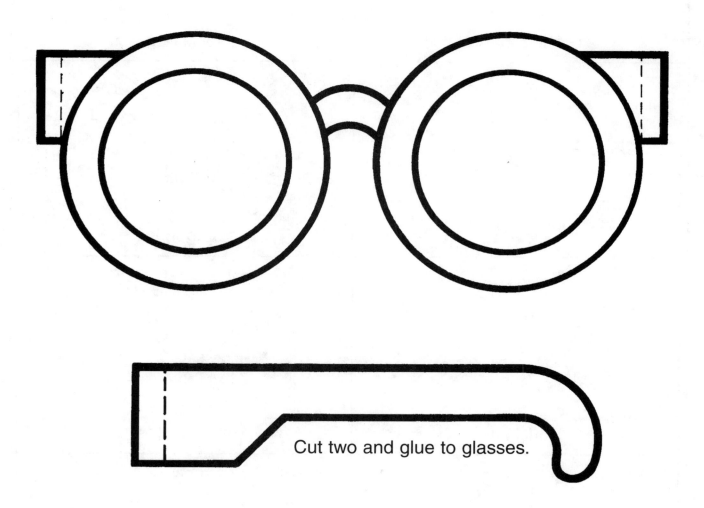

Cut two and glue to glasses.

Patterns for Communication (cont.)

Insect Pictures

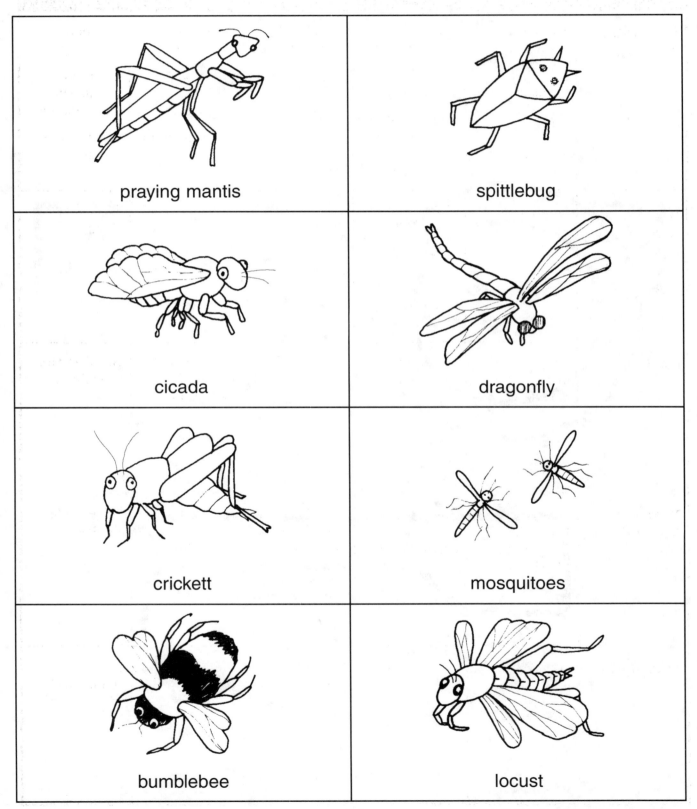

praying mantis

spittlebug

cicada

dragonfly

crickett

mosquitoes

bumblebee

locust

Five Plans for Cookies

	Day One	Day Two	Day Three	Day Four	Day Five
Individual Activities	• Stamp with Cookie Cutters • Match Cookie Shapes • Paint at Easel	• Draw Around the Child • Sort Buttons • Decorate Gingerbread with Frosting	• Make Play Dough Cookies • Draw Around Cookie Cutters • Block House	• Cookie Factory • Sandpaper Gingerbread Cookie • Block House	• Cookie Factory • Cooked Spaghetti Decoration • Pretend to Bake
Group Activities	Gingerbread Story	Own Cookie Story	Cookie Jar Story	*If You Give a Mouse a Cookie*	*The Doorbell Rang*
Games	Gingerbread, Where's Your Cookie?	Hot Cookie	Hot Cookie	Who Stole the Cookie from the Cookie Jar?	Beanbag Hot Oven Toss
Songs, Action Poems, Fingerplay	"Do You Know the Gingerbread Man?"	"Do You Know the Gingerbread Man?"	"Do You Know the Gingerbread Man?"	"Do You Know the Gingerbread Man?"	"Five Little Cookies"
Transitions	Gingerbread runs and walks.	Gingerbread hops and jumps.	Walk to wall to hang story.	Pretend to be mice.	Follow "Grandma."

Room Preparation for Cookies

Bulletin Board

Use the pattern of the cardboard-box oven described on page 135 and make from construction paper, oaktag, or butcher paper. Cookie patterns on page 145 can contain the names of children in the class or can be decorated with markers or rickrack and buttons.

Mobile

Use the pattern on page 142. Use corrugated cardboard or glue two pieces of poster board together. Or cut out many shapes of gingerbread people and hang them from the ceiling.

Name Tags

See the pattern on page 23 in Introduction to School.

Puppet Stage

Decorate the outside of a puppet stage with rickrack to look like frosting.

Make stick puppets using the pattern on page 143. Glue craft sticks or tongue depressors on the back. Felt finger puppets can be made using the pattern on page 144. Glue or sew two parts of felt together with a slot in the middle of one to put fingers in for the feet. Decorate with plastic eyes, red-hots, buttons, and rickrack. All can be hot-glued with a glue gun.

Suggested Literature for Cookies

Egielski, Richard. *The Gingerbread Boy.* Laura Geringer Books, 1997. (modern version)

Hutchins, Pat. *The Doorbell Rang.* Greenwillow Books, 1986.

Numeroff, Laura Joffe. *If You Give a Mouse a Cookie.* HarperCollins, 1985.

Schmidt, Karen. *The Gingerbread Man.* Scholastic Inc., 1967.

Materials

- manila paper
- butcher paper
- tie pin
- sample wallpaper book
- buttons
- lunch bags
- food coloring
- colored construction paper
- sandpaper
- cookie cutters
- brown tempera markers
- salt
- yarn
- newsprint for easel
- sheet of thin sponge
- kitchen utensils
- crayons
- flour
- spaghetti

Extended Activity

If a mailing is sent out just before the summer, ask the parents to send postcards from their vacation spots. Have parents sign the card or letter with a gingerbread cookie outline. Read to the children all the spots to which the gingerbread person has traveled. Use a map to show where children live and compare it to locations where the postcards are from. Which is the farthest away, and which is closest? Place the cards on the bulletin board low enough for the children to see.

Activities for Cookies

Individual Activities

Stamp with Cookie Cutters

Place a sheet of thin sponge in a shallow pan or pie tin. Place tempera paint on the sponge. Stamp the cookie cutter on the sponge and then on the paper. Other materials such as potato mashers, pastry brushes, measuring spoons, small sieves, and measuring spoons may be used to print also.

Match Cookie Shapes

Use the patterns on page 145 to cut shapes from sample wallpaper or construction paper. Cut two from each color or design. Let the children match the shapes and place them on a paper plate.

Paint at Easel

For younger children, use brown tempera to paint a gingerbread man. For older children, put out yellow, red, and blue. Start with the yellow and add other colors over it to see if the children can discover that all three colors can blend to brown.

Draw Around the Child—Life-Size Gingerbread Person

Place a roll of brown paper or white butcher paper on the floor. Have each child lie on the paper and draw around the child for a silhouette. Then have each child draw himself or herself as a gingerbread person. Use markers or crayons to make eyes, nose, mouth, and buttons down the front. Jiggly lines around the figure give a frosting effect. You may also decorate with real fabric, buttons, or rickrack.

Sort Buttons

Use any buttons but call them "gingerbread cookie buttons." Use egg cartons and have the students place the buttons in separate spaces according to color, size, or shape.

Decorate a Cardboard Gingerbread

Pre-cut gingerbread shapes from cardboard, using the pattern on page 146. Mix equal parts of salt and flour. Add water until you reach frosting consistency. Place the mixture in a ketchup squeeze bottle. Squeeze thin lines to form frosting trim and squeeze dots for eyes and buttons.

Make Play Dough Cookies

Mix two parts flour to one part salt. Add a scant one part water gradually until it resembles dough. Have the children roll out the dough and use cookie cutters to form the cookies. Children can pretend they are baking the clay on a Styrofoam tray in a housekeeping oven. After school, put the clay cookies on a metal tray and leave them in the 150° F (65.5° C) oven overnight. The next morning take them out of the oven. Then let the children play with them in the housekeeping area.

Draw Around Cookie Cutters

Have children draw around cookie cutters on paper. Then have the children decorate the drawings with crayons or markers.

Activities for Cookies *(cont.)*

Individual Activities *(cont.)*

Block House

Use hollow blocks to make a house for gingerbread cookies. Use kindergarten blocks to decorate.

Cookie Factory

Cut circles for cookies. Set up a store with a cash register and shopping cart. One child is the grocer, another is the bagger, and the others are customers. Cookies can be sold in lunch bags. Prepare stickers with pictures of cookies and the price. Some are to be sold for five cents and others for ten cents. Explain that the ten-cent bag has twice as many cookies as the five-cent bag. Have them bag the cookies and see if they understand the concept of "twice as many."

Sandpaper Gingerbread Cookie

Cut gingerbread from sandpaper, using the pattern on page 146. *Optional:* Hot-glue a sandpaper shape to heavy cardboard. Use colorful yarn to decorate gingerbread. The yarn will stick to the sandpaper like Velcro. Then it can be taken apart and rearranged.

Cooked Spaghetti Decoration

Cook spaghetti and drain but do not rinse. The starch in the spaghetti will cause it to "glue" to cardboard. Cut cardboard circles to form cookies. Have children take one strand of spaghetti at a time and place it on a cookie. Let them make it swirl or leave it straight around the edges. For decorative effect, the spaghetti may be tinted by mixing in a few drops of food coloring.

Housekeeping and Cooking

In the housekeeping area pretend to bake cookies for the cookie factory. Pretend to roll out cookies using a rolling pin and pretend dough. Arrange "cookies" on a cookie sheet and place in the oven. Set a timer and wait until the cookies are "baked." Take them out and pretend to eat.

Gingerbread Cookie

Introduce the story by putting different herbs (ginger, thyme, rosemary, bay leaf, oregano, lavender, rose petals, nutmeg, etc.) in small plastic bags. Have children smell the different spices and herbs. Ask them which one they liked best. Which one reminded them of pizza or spaghetti? Which one reminded them of cookies? of flowers? Then tell the children that some cookies are made with a spice called *ginger.* Have children smell the ginger. Say, "There was once a story written about something made from ginger. What do you think that the name of the story is?"

Read one of the many versions of *The Gingerbread Man* story. After reading the story, prepare a tray with different baking items on it—different cookie cutters, measuring spoons, small measuring cups, and hand mixers. Cover with a towel. Have all close their eyes—and don't peek! Put your hand under the towel, remove an item, and hide it behind you. Now remove the towel and have the children guess what is missing. When the children guess what is missing, replace the items, rearrange, cover, and repeat.

Activities for Cookies *(cont.)*

Individuals Activities *(cont.)*

Gingerbread Cookie *(cont.)*

To move to the next activity, point out that the gingerbread man ran away. Ask, "Is there another way we can move inside the building besides running (walk slowly, walk backwards, hop, walk on tiptoes)?" Move to the next area of activity.

Group Activities

Review the Story of the Gingerbread Cookie

Bring out a large cardboard box or use the oven from the housekeeping area. If the box is used, it can be plain or it can be decorated to look like an oven. Tell the children that the box is a magic oven. Ask the children to guess what is inside. Open the oven and pull out a green gingerbread cookie which has been precut, using the pattern on page 145. Ask the children what color it is. Then pull other cookies of different colors from inside the oven. Discuss the colors. Can cookies really be those colors? (They can if they have frosting!)

Talk about the story of the Gingerbread Cookie. Did he have frosting? What did it taste like? Then have children dictate their own story of what happened to that Gingerbread Cookie. Write down on a large sheet of paper what they dictate. If they get to a point where they don't know what to say, read what has been dictated. Point to each word as you read. That way they will know that you read from top to the bottom of the page and from left to right, and they will think of ways to continue the story.

For a variation, you may want to start with questions such as these:

- *Suppose the fox had not eaten the gingerbread cookie? Where would the cookie have gone?*
- *Whom would the cookie meet? Suppose that the cookie had never run away? What would have happened?*

Find a place in the room to hang the story. Have the children help you hang it, and then read their wonderful story again. When parents arrive, show them the story their children helped to write.

Cookie Jar, Cookie Jar, What Do You See?

Cookies are not just in the shapes of people like the gingerbread person. They can have other shapes and even colors plus taste, too. Have them taste red apples, lemons, blueberries, oranges, green grapes, and purple grapes. Could cookies be made of these fruits? Perhaps some could, but others could be used to make frosting for the cookies. The color of the fruit can be used to make the color of the frosting. Food coloring can be added to make the color of purple or green grapes. Make up the following story (page 136) in book form, using the shape pattern of a cookie jar on page 141 or merely read the story to children.

Activities for Cookies *(cont.)*

Group Activities *(cont.)*

Cookie Jar, Cookie Jar, What Do You See?

(Based on *Brown Bear, Brown Bear, What Do You See?* by Bill Martin, Jr.)

Cookie jar, cookie jar, what do you see?

I see a red cookie looking at me.

Red cookie made of red apples, what do you see?

I see a yellow cookie looking at me.

Yellow cookie made of lemons, what do you see?

I see a blue cookie looking at me.

Blue cookie made of blueberries, what do you see?

I see a green cookie looking at me.

Green cookie colored like green grapes, what do you see?

I see an orange cookie looking at me.

Orange cookie made of oranges, what do you see?

I see a purple cookie looking at me.

Purple cookie colored like purple grapes, what do you see?

I don't see, but I feel children's hands pulling at me!

Children, Children, what do you pull out?

Cookies that are red, yellow, blue

And green, orange and purple too.

After reading the story, have children taste the fruit again. What are their favorite fruits? Have a large sheet of paper. Print each child's name on the sheet and the child's favorite fruit after the name. Place on the bulletin board or on the wall so the parents can read when they come to pick up the child.

If You Give a Mouse a Cookie

Ask children if they ever had a mouse in the house. What kind of food did it get into? Did it ever get into cookies? Show different types of real cookies and ask which one a mouse would really like to eat. Then show the picture on the cover of the book and read the title. Say, "Let's find out what happens if you give a mouse a cookie."

Read *If You Give a Mouse a Cookie*. After reading the book ask the children what happens if you give a mouse a cookie? Ask, "What was your favorite thing that the mouse did? Mine was that he colored a picture with crayons." Take out a container that has several boxes of mixed-up crayons. Take out one color and ask children to name the color and then to find more crayons of the same colors in the container. Continue with all the crayons.

After the crayons are all put back, have the children pretend they are mice that like to drink milk and then crawl over to another area.

Additional ideas can be obtained by using *Mouse Cookies—10 Easy-to-Make Cookie Recipes* by Laura Numeroff and Felicia Bond, HarperCollins, 1995.

Activities for Cookies *(cont.)*

Group Activities *(cont.)*

The Doorbell Rang

Have children bring pictures of Grandma or some special friend. Ask them to tell about Grandma or the friend and whether they cooked and baked something special. Say, "We are going to read a book about a grandma who makes special cookies."

Read *The Doorbell Rang*. As you read the first few pages, note that there are two lines that repeat themselves. "Nobody makes cookies like Grandma," said Ma as the doorbell rang. Have the children say these lines with you as they occur in the book. You may want to read it a second time so that those who have not caught on can have the chance to say the lines with you. They may even want you to read it a third time.

Cut twelve circles out of construction paper. After you have read the book, ask the children how many cookies were on the first plate. If there were six for Sam and six for Victoria, how many would that make? Count out six circles for Sam and six circles for Victoria. Place Sam's in one pile and Victoria's in another pile. Go through the book page by page. Have the children pretend to be the other characters in the story. Take the cookies from the first two piles and divide them up as the story progresses. Before Grandma enters, count how many children there are in the story and look at the number of cookies. Ask, "How many cookies did each one have until Grandma came with a new plate? Grandma brought in another plate. I wonder how many were on that one?"

Then bring out a plate of cookies and have the children follow "Grandma" (the teacher) to the snack area.

Games

Gingerbread Man, Gingerbread Man, Where Is Your Cookie?

Have one child seated on a chair with his or her eyes closed. This child has his or her back to the rest of the class. Under the chair, place the cookie to be stolen. The rest of the class sits in a line at least three yards (three meters) away. One child tries to sneak up and remove the cookie without the child hearing the theft. If he or she does hear, the child cries, "I caught you," and the caught child then sits on the seat. If that child, however, is able to steal the cookie, he or she returns to the spot he or she occupied and places hands behind the back. In order to confuse the child on the chair, all children place their hands behind their backs. The child in the chair then has three tries to catch the culprit. The child who stole the cookie then sits on the chair to detect the next thief.

Activities for Cookies *(cont.)*

Games *(cont.)*

Hot Cookie

Play this game like Hot Potato. Have the children sit in a circle, play music, and pass around a pretend cookie, pretending it is very hot. When the music stops, shout "Hip, hip, hooray!" to the child holding the cookie. This approach will make the child feel good about himself or herself. Then start the music again and when the music stops, shout "Hip, hip, hooray!" again. Play as long as the children are interested.

Beanbag Hot Oven Toss

Use the oven from the housekeeping area as the target for the toss. Open the door of the oven and leave it wide open. Have each child try to toss three bean bags into the oven. Gauge the distance the children stand away from the oven according to the ages of the children playing the game.

Who Stole the Cookie from the Cookie Jar?

(Traditional)

Have the children sitting in a circle. Have them say the first line of words together.

Children: *Who stole the cookie from the cookie jar?*

Teacher: *Mary stole the cookie from the cookie jar.*

Mary: *Who, me?*

Children: *Yes, you.*

Mary: *Couldn't be!*

Teacher: *Then who stole the cookie from the cookie jar?*

Mary: *John stole the cookie from the cookie jar.*

John: *Who, me?*

Children: *Yes, you.*

John: *Couldn't be!*

Children: *Then who stole the cookie from the cookie jar?*

(Continue until all the children have a turn being the accused thief.)

Activities for Cookies *(cont.)*

Songs, Actions Poems, and Fingerplay

"Do You Know the Gingerbread Man?"

(Tune of "Do You Know the Muffin Man?")

Do you know the gingerbread man, the gingerbread man, the gingerbread man?

Do you know the gingerbread man

Who lives up on the hill?

He popped out of the oven one day, oven one day, oven one day,

He popped out of the oven one day

And ran far, far away.

He came upon a woman that day, woman that day, woman that day,

He came upon a woman that day

And ran far, far away.

He came upon a man that day, a man that day, a man that day,

He came upon a man that day

And ran far, far away.

(Continue with a cow and any other animals he saw in your particular story. Each version has different animals in it. *The Gingerbread Boy* by Richard Egielski has a rat, construction workers, musicians, policeman, and a fox.)

Final verse:

He came upon a fox that day, fox that day, fox that day,

He came upon a fox that day

Say, "And neither has been seen since they swam the river that day."

(Hold up hands, shrug shoulders, and shake head in bewilderment.)

Activities for Cookies (cont.)

Songs, Action Poems, and Fingerplay (cont.)

"Five Little Cookies"

Five little cookies sitting on a plate.
(Hold up all five fingers on one hand.)

The first one left because it was late.
(Put down one finger.)

The second one left because he rolled off.
(Put down two fingers.)

The third one left in an angry huff.
(Put down three fingers.)

The fourth one left all covered with jelly.
(Put down four fingers.)

The fifth one left because he was lonely.
(Make a fist.)

The little plate said, "Oh, my, it's getting cold."
"I guess I'll just stay here until I'm . . .
(pause)

"Full of Grandma's warm, warm cookies."

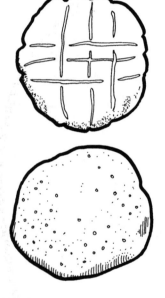

Holiday Follow-Up

A December holiday follow-up to this theme is to make tree decorations for a present to the children. Teachers cut a gingerbread cookie out of a sheet of cork available in a hardware or craft store. Use the pattern on page 146. To give the frosting effect, use commercially made puffy paint or fine bathtub putty. Jiggly eyes, red-hots for the nose, a thin ribbon bow at the neck, puffy paint for the mouth and buttons complete the figure. Put a thin gold thread at the top to hang the cookie from the holiday tree. On the back place the teacher's name, school, and year.

Additional Literature

Alesworth, Jim. *The Gingerbread Man.* Scholastic, 1998.

Scieszka, Jon and Lane Smith. *Stinky Cheese Man and Other Fairly Stupid Tales.* Viking, 1992.

Patterns for Cookies

Bulletin Board Pattern for Cookies

Place names of children in class on gingerbread cookies. Place cookies around the cookie jar.

Cookie
Jar

Patterns for Cookies *(cont.)*

Mobile Pattern for Cookies

Cut from brown poster board. Either glue two pieces together or use corrugated cardboard. Use tub caulking to give a frosting effect.

Patterns for Cookies *(cont.)*

Stick Puppet Pattern for Cookie Puppet Stage

Patterns for Cookies *(cont.)*

Pattern for Gingerbread Finger Puppet of Felt

Cut two out of felt. On one glue on jiggly eyes, embroider red dots for nose and several for mouth. Sew on heart buttons. Cut the other felt piece in half (horizontally) below arms. Sew all pieces together while sewing on small rickrack to represent frosting trim.

From the back put fingers in leg part and have gingerbread walk.

144

Patterns for Cookies *(cont.)*

Patterns for Cookies (cont.)

Pattern for Cardboard Gingerbread to Frost and Sandpaper Gingerbread

Five Plans for Dogs

	Day One	Day Two	Day Three	Day Four	Day Five
Individual Activities	• Mail Carrier • Police Officer • Teacher-Supplies Collage	• Dress Up for School • Bone Prints • Yellow Tempera Paint	• Blue Tempera Paint • Water Table • Bubbles in Margarine Tubs	• Make Pretzels • Dog Rubbings • Zigzag Fold	• Magnets • Biscuits • Make Peanut Butter
Group Activities	*The Ugliest Dog in the World*	*Spot Goes to School*	*Wake Up, Mr. B*	*Pretzel*	*That Magnetic Dog*
Games	Hanky Drop	Stuffed Dog Toss	Dog Feeding Dish Relay	Doggie, Doggie, Where's Your Bone?	Hot Bone
Songs, Action Poems, Fingerplay	All week use "B-I-N-G-O" and "Puppy Dogs" with work-glove puppet.				
Transitions	Pick up mail.	Walk around, looking for Spot things.	Walk like a pet.	Stretch and walk.	Hug a magnet friend.

Room Preparation for Dogs

Bulletin Board

Use pictures of various breeds of dogs from magazines or famous paintings of dogs from a library or museum. Or use dog patterns on pages 157 and 159 and print names of children on them.

Name Tags

See the pattern for a dog name tag on page 24 in Introduction to School.

Puppet Area

Use the pattern for dogs made from plastic film containers on page 156. Cover the sides of the container with paper. Draw on the dog's face. Use pattern for the top of the head and attached ears and cut this from felt. Glue to the top of the container.

Five Puppies from Work Gloves

Use a white cotton work glove and fill the ends of each finger with cotton. Tie string around each fingertip where the cotton stuffing ends and make a bow in front. Glue on jiggle eyes and draw faces with a permanent marker. Place the wrist cuff of the glove over a wide-top plastic container. Push puppies into the container and have them looking out the top. See sample patterns on page 215.

Suggested Music for the Week

Grand Canyon Suite by Ferde Grofé

Suggested Literature for Dogs

Dale, Penny. *Wake Up, Mr. B.* Candlewick Press, 1994.
Hill, Eric. *Spot Goes to School.* Putnam, 1984.
Rey, Margaret. *Pretzel.* Harper & Row, 1944.
Whatley, Bruce. *That Magnetic Dog.* Henry Holt, 1996.
Whatley, Bruce. *The Ugliest Dog in the World.* Henry Holt, 1995.

Materials

- several shades of blue construction paper
- newsprint for easel
- old stamps
- hole punches
- rubber stamps and stamp pads
- yellow and blue tempera paint
- water
- margarine containers
- lima bean seeds
- toweling
- cinnamon sugar
- cooking oil
- manila paper
- envelopes
- staplers
- tape
- bone cookie cutters
- blue finger paint
- dish soap
- ingredients for pretzels
- zip-lock bag
- tubes of biscuits
- unsalted peanuts

Activities for Dogs

Individual Activities

Mail Carrier *(The Ugliest Dog in the World)*

The post office needs lots of help handling all the mail. Give the children envelopes and old stamps. The stamps can be collected by saving Christmas seals and stamps sent out from various organizations. Have the children pretend they are writing letters. Some children may want to send a letter to a friend or parent. Each child should dictate the letter to the teacher. Place it in an envelope and show them where the stamps are to be placed. Make a mail box out of a shoebox. Cut a slot in the top for the children to mail the letters. Letters to be actually mailed should later be taken to the post office.

Police Officer *(The Ugliest Dog in the World)*

Police officers wear blue uniforms. Give the children many shades of blue construction paper size 9" x 6" (23 cm x 16 cm). Show them how to hold one part of the paper with one hand. Then starting at the top, begin tearing with the other hand. Have them tear the paper in different sizes and paste it on a sheet of contrasting color. The result will be a collage of blues that make up the blue of the uniform.

Teacher-Supplies Collage *(The Ugliest Dog in the World)*

Teachers have to use all kinds of things to help them do a good job. They need staplers, hole punches, tape, ribbons, stamps, and stamp pads. Place all these items out for students, plus manila paper. Have the children experiment and see what the resulting collage is.

Dress Up for School *(Spot Goes to School)*

Have the clothes in the dress-up area resemble clothes used for going to school. Or have doll clothes ready for dress-up. Have children pretend that they are getting ready for the first day at school. What kinds of clothes should they wear? Where will they walk, and what will they say?

Bone Prints *(Spot Goes to School)*

Purchase bone cookie cutters at a bakery supply store. Have a pan of tempera paint with a layer of thin sponge over it. Have children place the bone cookie cutters in the paint and then stamp on a piece of manila paper. For more than one color, use separate pans for each color. Count how many bones are on each picture. Would there be enough for the little dog? What about a big dog?

Yellow Tempera Paint *(Spot Goes to School)*

Set up an easel with newsprint or place newsprint on a table. Have children paint a dog or cover the paper with yellow tempera paint. Then try to put a dab of brown over it with a sponge to form Spot's spot. If children do not want to touch the sponge with their hands, snap a clamp clothespin onto the sponge. The child can then hold the clothespin and not get his or her hands smeared.

Blue Tempera Paint *(Wake Up, Mr. B)*

Cover a 9" x 12" (23 cm x 30 cm) sheet of manila paper with blue tempera paint. The teacher and the child sprinkle Epsom salt on the paper, and the paint is allowed to dry. When completely dry, it will appear like shimmering stars.

Activities for Dogs *(cont.)*

Individual Activities *(cont.)*

Water Table *(Wake Up, Mr. B)*

Fill a water table with water and place sailboats in it. A small plastic tub filled with water and boats is just as much fun.

Bubbles in Margarine Tubs *(Wake Up, Mr. B)*

Punch a hole in the middle of one side of a soft plastic container. Then put a little dishwashing liquid and a little water in the container. Mix. Cut the lid in half and place on the container. Place a straw in the hole and have children blow so that the bubbles come out of the open space on the lid. It is better to have the child sit at a table while doing this. Also, do not do this activity with little children since they may suck in rather than blow out.

Finger Paint with Blue *(Wake Up, Mr. B)*

Cover a table with newspaper. Place the shiny surface of finger-paint paper on newspaper. Use a wide paintbrush to cover the paper with a thin coat of water. Place two tablespoons of finger paint on paper and have children move their hands, fingers, sides of hands, and fists to the mood music from the *Grand Canyon Suite*.

Make Pretzels *(Pretzel)*

Make pretzels with children, using the rebus recipe on page 158. If made at beginning of the class, the pretzels will be ready to eat in about an hour.

Dog Rubbings

Use the pattern of a dog on page 157. The day before, drizzle craft glue on the outline. Allow this to dry for 24 hours. Have children place typing paper on top of the outline. Rub over it with pencil to make an outline of the dog.

Zigzag Fold *(Pretzel)*

Cut paper strips about three inches (8 cm) wide and nine inches (23 cm) long. Show children how to fold the strips back and forth like a fan. Talk about how things such as people and animals grow. Then show how the paper pulls out or expands. Younger children may have a difficult time with folding paper back and forth and may need assistance.

Stuffed Dog

Place a stuffed dog in the housekeeping area. Have the children try to place the doll clothes on the stuffed dog. Where would he or she go all dressed up?

Magnets *(That Magnetic Dog)*

With whatever types of magnets the teacher can accumulate, have the children experiment. Colored pliable magnetic shapes can also be purchased from educational surplus stores. Any of the magnets can be attached to a cookie sheet made from steel. This gives a nice surface to experiment on.

Activities for Dogs *(cont.)*

Individual Activities *(cont.)*

Biscuits *(That Magnetic Dog)*

Explain that biscuits are made from wheat seeds which are ground into flour. Purchase tubes of premixed biscuits and take them out of the package. Direct children's attention to how the biscuits "explode" when they are taken out of the package. Have children place the biscuits on a pan with enough space between each. Bake for snacks. Dip in cinnamon sugar when they come out of the oven.

Make Peanut Butter *(That Magnetic Dog)*

Purchase unsalted peanuts. With the children watching, use a blender to grind the peanuts. Add about a teaspoon of oil or more to make the peanut butter creamier. Point out that peanuts are really seeds, and we have used a blender to grind them up and make them smooth. Say "Our teeth could grind them up too, but that would not make peanut butter!"

Group Activities

The Ugliest Dog in the World

Show the children a dictionary and explain what kind of book it is. Tell them to pretend that they are dictionaries and that they know what all the words used mean. Write down words on a sheet of paper. (Have a large sheet of paper ready so that all the children can see what you write.) Try words like "candy, house, paper," etc., and then go to abstract words such as "happy, sad," etc. Conclude with the word "ugly." Write down their definition of ugly on a large sheet of paper in front of the class. Then say, "Let's read a story about an ugly dog."

Read *The Ugliest Dog in the World* up to the second to last page. At that point, take the class around the building and ask the secretary, the building engineer, and other teachers what they would do if they had the ugliest dog in the world. Make sure all adults are notified of your coming and the time. (You may want to suggest answers to the question the children will ask.) Return to the room and conclude by reading the last page in the book. Then talk about the answers that the people in the building have given. Ask if they think these were good answers. Ask how the "ugly dog" would feel if he heard the answers.

Pretend to be a mail carrier who has dropped the mail. Pick up envelopes as you go to the next area.

Spot Goes to School

Show the children a picture of Spot from the cover of the book. Tell the children that Spot is starting school just as they are. Ask, "How did you feel the first day of school?" Have the children express themselves. Say, "Let's see if Spot felt the same way you did."

Read *Spot Goes to School.* On every page there is a flip picture. Have children guess on each page what is under the flip section. After reading the story, walk around the classroom and then the playground to see if you have the same things that Spot did. What things were the same? What things were different?

Activities for Dogs *(cont.)*

Group Activities *(cont.)*

Wake Up, Mr. B

Show the cover of the book and read the title to children. Ask, "Who do you think Mr. B is?" Write their answers on a large sheet of paper on an easel. Say, "We will find out who has answered correctly after we read the book."

Read *Wake Up, Mr. B* and have the children narrate the pictures. Then read the list that the children dictated at the beginning. Review who everyone thought that Mr. B was. Who guessed correctly? Ask, "Was Mr. B a good pet? Why?" Then walk like a dog on all fours to the next area.

Pretzel

Cut out the pattern of the dachshund (page 159) and then cut it in half in the center of the body. Then glue accordion pleats at the center, connecting the two parts of the body. Show the dog to children with the pleats held together. Dachshunds are very long dogs, but some dogs are even longer. Pull out the pleats to lengthen the dog. If you do not have time to make the pull-out Pretzel, show the picture on the front of the book and then turn to the back of the book to show how long Pretzel really was. Say, "I wonder how such a long dog spends his time! Let's find out by reading the book."

Read *Pretzel*. After reading the book, ask children why the dog was called Pretzel. Show the picture of Pretzel shaped like a pretzel. Talk about making pretzels during interest time or make them following the story. Then have the children stretch to the ceiling and to the floor. Have them pretend to be Pretzel by stretching as they walk to the next area.

That Magnetic Dog

Show the magnets that were used during activity time. Explain that magnets can pick up certain things. Have out paper items along with metal items that can be picked up with the magnets. Have children try to pick up all the items. Make a pile of those things that a magnet will pick up and a pile of those things that a magnet will not pick up. Sometimes we talk about people or dogs that are like magnets. They have certain things that pull toward them like magnets. We are going to read a story about a magnetic dog.

Read *That Magnetic Dog*. After reading the story, ask children what they can do with magnets (*pick things up*). What was the final thing that the magnetic dog picked up? (*a can of dog food*) Have some empty metal cans for the children to try the magnets on. Can a magnet pick up a metal can? If so, then I guess that Skitty must have been a magnetic dog!

Magnets pull towards each other if they are a match. Can children find one friend that they could be a magnet to? Hug that friend and be a magnet!

Activities for Dogs *(cont.)*

Games

Hanky Drop

Have the children sit in a circle. Have one child with a handkerchief in his or her hand walk around the outer portion of the circle. The child walking around the circle then drops the handkerchief behind another child. That child picks up the handkerchief and chases the first child around the circle until they reach the spot vacated by the second child. If the first child is tagged, or if he or she reaches the spot last, that child becomes the next to walk around the circle. That child has two turns to drop the handkerchief! No one is winner or loser. Always make sure that everyone has a chance to walk around the circle and drop the handkerchief.

Stuffed Dog Toss

Use a large sheet or blanket and have a child hold each end. Place stuffed dogs in the center and have the children toss them to see whether they go high or low. Roll the dogs around in the blanket. Alternate children so that all have a turn tossing the stuffed dogs.

Dog Feeding Dish Relay

Form two lines of children, one behind the other. Place a dog feeding dish about three yards in front of each line. Give each child in the line a paper cutout of a bone (or you can use dog food bones). Call "Start!" and have the first child in each line run up to the bowl and place a bone in it. Then the child is to run back to the next person in the line and tag that person, who then runs up to the bowl and places a bone in it. Keep repeating this until all the bones are in the dishes and then yell, "Hooray, the dogs will all have food!"

Doggie, Doggie, Where's Your Bone?

(See instructions in Introduction to School on page 18.)

Hot Bone

(This is based on the Hot Potato game in Introduction to School on page 18.)

Activities for Dogs *(cont.)*

Songs, Action Poems, and Fingerplay

BINGO (B-I-N-G-O)

(Traditional)
There was a farmer had a dog,
And Bingo was his name.
B-I-N-G-O
B-I-N-G-O
B-I-N-G-O
Bingo was his name-o.

(Sing a second time, omitting the letter "B." Clap instead. Sing the verse again and keep dropping a letter for each verse, clapping for each dropped letter until the entire name is simply clapped.)

"Puppy Dogs"

Five little puppy dogs
(Hold up five fingers and bend each down as verse progresses.)

At a dog house door,
One didn't like the crowd,
Then there were four.
Four little puppy dogs
Running 'round the tree.
Mother calls one puppy home,
Then there were three.
Three little puppy dogs
Playing with a shoe.
Bingo ran to chase a cat,
Then there were two.
Two little puppy dogs
Having so much fun.
Rover went to find a bone,
then there was one.
One little puppy dog
Sitting in the sun.
He went running home,
And then there was none.

Additional Literature

Day, Alexander. *Good Dog, Carl.* Simon & Schuster, 1985.
Eastman, P. D. *Go, Dog, Go.* Random House, 1961.
Graham, Amanda. *Who Wants Arthur?* G. Stevens Publishers, 1987.
Keats, Ezra Jack. *Whistle for Willie.* Viking Press, 1964.
Nodset, Joan L. *Go Away, Dog.* HarperCollins, 1997.

Patterns for Dogs

Bulletin Board for Dogs

Put doghouse in center and dogs from name tag pattern around it. Place names of children on the dogs.

Patterns for Dogs *(cont.)*

Plastic Film Container Dog

1. Cut above piece from typing paper or draw on dog color construction paper.
2. Use hot-glue gun to attach at seam in back. Make sure one dot of glue attaches the drawing to the plastic container.

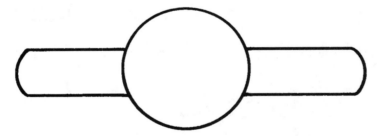

3. Cut from felt and glue onto the top of the container.

4. Put two fingers in the bottom to move the puppet.

Patterns for Dogs *(cont.)*

Dog Glue Rubbing

Patterns for Dogs *(cont.)*

Pretzel Recipe

1  flour

2 tablespoon sugar

1 teaspoon salt

1 dry yeast

1½ warm water

1 egg

Combine and warm water.

Beat and add to and . Add 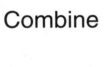 ,

 , and . Knead  . Pinch off

pieces and make a snake shape.

Shape into a pretzel . Place on greased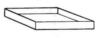

cookie sheet.

Brush with water and coarse . Bake at

425° for 10–15 minutes. Makes about 26 .

Patterns for Dogs *(cont.)*

Pattern for Pretzel with Accordion Pleats

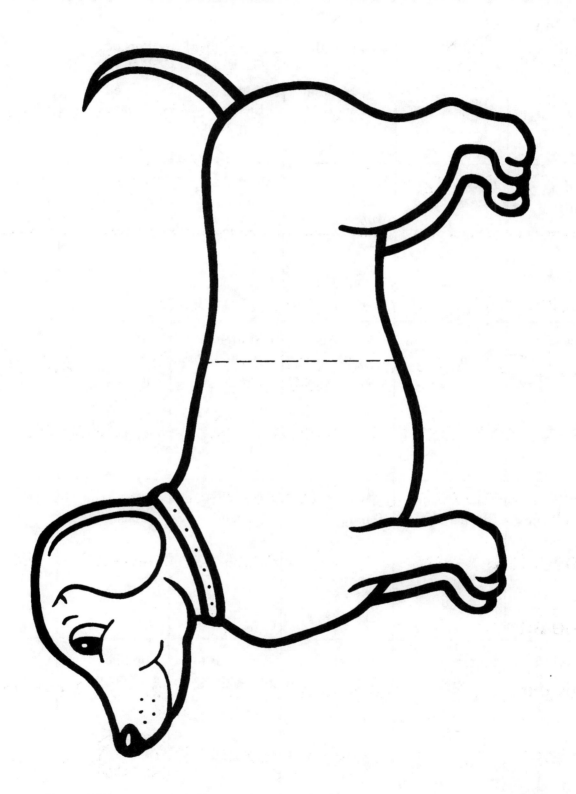

Five Plans for Elephants

	Day One	Day Two	Day Three	Day Four	Day Five
Individual Activities	• Leaf Rubbings • Elephant Trunk in a Plate • Leaf Stencil	• Sock Nose • Paint with Gray • Elephant in a Circus Cage	• Crayon Melt • File Folder Game • Edible Elephant Play Dough	• Bubbles • Popcorn Pictures • Stuffed Animals	• Paper Snips Collage • Scissors, Stapler, Hole Punch, and Tape
Group Activities	*The Elephant Tree*	*When the Elephant Walks*	*Elmer*	*Ten Out of Bed*	*Babar's Busy Year*
Games	"A Tree Fell Down"	• Song About Colors • Rope Walk	• Stuffed Animal Toss • Hot Peanut	• Stuffed Animal Toss • Elephant, Elephant, Where's Your Peanut?	Elephant Parade
Songs, Action Poems, Fingerplay	"The Elephant"	"There Were Ten in a Bed"	"The Elephant"	"The Elephant"	"The Elephant"
Transitions	Pretend to pick up the leaves.	Walk like the animals on the tray.	Red leads to the next area.	Hop like jumping on a bed.	

Room Preparation for Elephants

Bulletin Board

The pattern for the bulletin board is on page 167. The background is a circus scene. In the foreground is a line of elephants. The teacher can put the names of the children in the class on the elephants.

Name Tag

The pattern for the elephant name tag is on page 25.

Puppet Stage

The patterns for stick puppets of an elephant and a mouse are on page 168.

Extended Activity for the Week

Place peanuts in the shell in the room. Every day use a different container for the children to count them into. Every time they put a peanut in the container, make sure they say only one numeral.

Suggested Literature for Elephants

Dale, Penny. *The Elephant Tree.* Putnam, 1991.

Dale, Penny. *Ten Out of Bed.* Candlewick Press, 1994.

De Brunhoff, Laurent. *Babar's Busy Year.* Random House, 1990.

Kasza, Keiko. *When the Elephant Walks.* Putnam, 1990.

McKee, David. *Elmer.* Lothrup, Lee, Shepard, 1991.

Materials

- light and dark green construction paper
- newsprint for easel
- gray tempera paint
- scissors
- sock
- file folder
- bubble mixture
- popcorn
- hole punch
- typing paper
- manila paper
- crayons or markers
- nine-inch paper plate
- electric warming tray
- ingredients for elephant play dough
- bubble wands
- stapler
- transparent tape

Activities for Elephants

Individual Activities

Leaf Rubbings *(The Elephant Tree)*

Place paper over a leaf taped on the table. Rub over paper with a heavy crayon or chalk.

Elephant Trunk in a Plate *(The Elephant Tree)*

Tear small pieces of light green, dark green, and brown construction paper for leaves. Use a dinner-size paper plate and precut hole in center for the elephant trunk. Cover the plate with torn pieces of construction paper and glue on. Use old socks to put on children's hands and thrust through the hole for the elephant's trunk.

Leaf Stencil *(The Elephant Tree)*

Using the pattern on page 169, make a stencil of cardboard for various leaf shapes. Place the stencil on manila paper. Use chalk to stroke outward from the stencil so that the chalk flows onto the paper. Remove the stencil, and the open area represents the leaf.

Paint with Gray

Use tempera paint and set up the easel so children can paint anything they want with the gray paint. Have them think of elephants or have a picture of an elephant near the easel.

Elephant in a Circus Cage (difficult for young children)

Have child draw an elephant on a 9" x 12" (23 cm x 30 cm) sheet of manila or white paper. Then fold in half a sheet of the same size construction paper, and mark the paper as illustrated. Cut out the black sections and open. Place the construction paper over the drawing of the elephant. Glue circles to the bottom to make wheels for the circus wagon.

Edible Elephant Play Dough

1 cup peanut butter	1 cup powdered milk
1 cup oatmeal	1 cup honey

Mix ingredients the day before and place in the room to experience the smell that elephants love.

File Folder Elephant Game

The pattern for the game is on pages 170 and 171. Use dice or a numbered spinner for moves.

Crayon Melt

Using an electric warming plate or tray, place manila paper (construction paper is too thick) on the surface. Have the children draw on paper and watch the crayons melt. If the child wears mittens, it will prevent the hands from getting warm.

Activities for Elephants (cont.)

Individual Activities (cont.)

Bubbles

Use prepared bubble mixture and a small bubble wand. Wave in the air and have bubbles float around the room. (Use only if you have carpeted floors or if you are doing all activities outside.)

Popcorn Pictures

Pre-pop popcorn. Do not use butter or salt. Tell children that it is a favorite circus snack, but they are going to use it to make a design. Children can then glue popcorn onto colored construction paper to make their own designs. Crayons or markers can also be used.

Stuffed Animals

Put out a variety of stuffed animals and blankets in the housekeeping area. Have the children pretend they are having a slumber party and cuddle with the stuffed animals.

Scissors, Stapler, Hole Punch, and Transparent Tape

Have the children experiment with these on a sheet of paper.

Collage

Put out small snips of leftover construction paper. On a table, place sheets of 9" x 12" (23 cm x 30 cm) light colored paper and nontoxic school glue or glue stick. Have them create their own pictures by gluing small pieces on the large sheet of paper.

Group Activities

The Elephant Tree

Show leaves from different types of trees, such as elm, maple, and willow. Explain that each tree is different, especially the willow whose branches bend down and move as if they are dancing when the wind blows. Then ask, "But have you ever seen an elephant tree?"

Read *The Elephant Tree*. Read up to the part where it says, "But we still couldn't find the elephant tree. Never mind, Elephant. Wait and see." Stop here and say, "I think we should ask the maintenance man if he has seen an elephant tree. Maybe the principal has seen one, too." Make sure you have contacted the people and indicated the time and the question that will be asked. Walk around the building and ask various people if they have seen the elephant tree.

Return to the room and continue reading. If you have had the children make the paper plate with the sock trunk coming out of the leaves, you could have them pretend the ending of the story.

Make a classroom tree. Start with a branch. Walk around outside and have children pick up leaves, sticks, acorns, pine cones, and/or litter. Return to the room and tie these items on a branch. The branch can either be hung from the ceiling as a mobile or placed in a coffee can with plaster of Paris.

Activities for Elephants (cont.)

Group Activities (cont.)

When the Elephant Walks

Make a paper plate with a sock pushed through the middle for an elephant's trunk. Add eyes and ears, using the pattern on page 172. Put a hand in the sock and talk to the children. "Hi, boys and girls. Do you know what I am? What is this sticking out of my face?" Have everyone clasp hands and pretend they have trunks also. Have them swing their trunks from side to side and then up in the air. Say, "Let's find out what happens when an elephant walks."

Read *When the Elephant Walks*. After reading the story, display various plastic animals on a large Styrofoam or cafeteria tray. Talk about the animals and whether they are found in zoos or circuses. Cover the tray with a cloth and reach under and remove one animal. Hide this animal behind your back. Remove the cloth and see if the children know which one is missing. Continue until the children have had a chance to identify each missing animal. Keep moving the animals on the tray to make it just a little harder.

Then have them walk to next area like the animals on the tray.

Elmer

Make lollipops of different circles of construction paper. Make two of each color. Place a craft stick or tongue depressor between the two circles and cover with clear plastic stick-on paper. Hold them in your hand like a fan. Singsong the following:

"Come and Get the Red Lollipop"
(to the tune of "Mulberry Bush")

Come and get the *(color)* lollipop, *(color)* lollipop, *(color)* lollipop,

Come and get the *(color)* lollipop, *(child's name)*.

Talk about the different colors. Then show a picture of Elmer on the cover of the book. Say, "Let's listen to this story."

Read *Elmer*. After reading the story, have the children identify colors in their clothing. Find what color is predominant. Then explain that we are going to sing a song and it is going to ask what color they have on. Think about only one color you have on and stand up when the recording says that color.

"Who Is Wearing Red Right Now?"

Who is wearing red right now, red right now, red right now?

Who is wearing red right now?

Stand up, WOW!

Children dressed in red lead to the next area.

Activities for Elephants *(cont.)*

Group Activities *(cont.)*

Ten Out of Bed

Say, "When you go to bed at night, do you sleep with a very special animal? It is so nice to cuddle with the animal. Do you have more than one favorite toy or animal that you take to bed?" Have each child name the animal or toy that he or she takes to bed.

"Sometimes we just take a blanket to bed. We are going to read a story about a little boy who had 10 things in bed with him. How many is 10?" Have the children hold up all their fingers. "They all were not really tired and decided to play something before falling to sleep. I wonder what they decided to play."

Read *Ten Out of Bed.* Ask, "Of all the animals that were in the bed, which one was the biggest? (*elephant*) Which one was the littlest? (*mouse*)" Show the pictures of the animals again and discuss which one each of them would like to have in bed.

Then talk about all the things that the animals did before falling asleep. They pretended to be at the beach, acted, played pirates, danced, played ghost, went camping, and pretended to be monsters. All of these activities made them sleepy. Have the children act out the different activities and then pretend to go to sleep.

Babar's Busy Year

Say, "Babar had children, and they liked to play different things at different times of the year. Do you do different things at different times of the year? What do you do in fall, winter, spring, summer? Let's find out what Babar's family did."

Read *Babar's Busy Year.* Say, "Everyone wanted summer to last forever except Isabelle. Why did she want summer to end?" (*School would start.*) "What are some things you would like to do in school? Why?"

Games

"A Tree Fell Down"

Have children form a circle. Use a handle of a broom and hold either high to go under or low to go over.

Palmer, Hap. *Easy Does It.*

"The Elephant"

Palmer, Hap. *Learning Basic Skills Through Music, Volume I.*

Stuffed Animal Toss

Place many animals in a blanket. Have one child on each end of the blanket hold onto the edges. Have the children toss the blanket up and down. Then place animals in the blanket and toss them in the air. See which one goes the highest.

Activities for Elephants *(cont.)*

Games *(cont.)*

Rope Walk

Use a long rope and tie knots about 12" to 18" (30 cm x 46 cm) apart. Make enough knots for half of the number in the class. Then go for a walk and have two children hang onto each knot with one child on each side of the rope.

"Elephant, Elephant, Where's Your Peanut?"

Follow "Doggie, Doggie, Where's Your Bone?" in Introduction to School on page 18.

Hot Peanut

Play as Hot Potato. Instructions are in Introduction to School on page 18.

Elephant Parade

Have children put their two hands together and extend arms down to represent an elephant's trunk. Line up one behind the other to form an elephant parade. March around the room using music or have each child take a turn leading the parade.

Songs, Action Poems, and Fingerplays

"The Elephant"

(Traditional)

Right foot, left foot, see me go,

(Put weight on first one foot, then the other, swaying from side to side.)

I have big ears and I walk slow.

I come plodding down the street

With my trunk and big four feet.

(Extend arms together in front and swing like a trunk.)

"There Were Ten in a Bed"

(Traditional)

There were ten in a bed and the little one said,
"Roll over, roll over."

So they all rolled over, and one fell out.

There were nine in a bed . . . *(Continue with one less number each time the verse is said.)*

There were none in the bed, and the little one said,
"EVERYONE COME BACK!"

Additional Literature

Jackson, K. *Saggy Baggy Elephant.* Golden Press, 1973.

Riddell, Chris. *The Trouble with Elephants.* Lippincott, 1988.

Sheppard, Jeff. *The Right Number of Elephants.* Harper and Row, 1990.

Young, Ed. *Seven Blind Mice.* Philomel Books, 1992.

Records, Cassettes, and CD's

Palmer, Hap. *Learning Basic Skills Through Music, Volume I.* Educational Activities, Inc., 1971.

Palmer, Hap. *Easy Does It.* Educational Activities, Inc., 1977.

Patterns for Elephants

Bulletin Board

Use circus tent in background and put elephant parade in foreground. Children's names should be put on elephants.

Patterns for Elephants *(cont.)*

Puppets for Puppet Stage

Color and glue on craft sticks.

Patterns for Elephants *(cont.)*

Leaf Stencil

Leaf shapes for maple, elm, locust, and other shapes need to be cut out.

Patterns for Elephants *(cont.)*

File Folder Game for Elephants

See two mice and hide in trees—lose a turn.

See three mice and hide in water—lose 2 turns.

Find an elephant friend—go ahead 1 space.

Patterns for Elephants *(cont.)*

File Folder Game for Elephants *(cont.)*

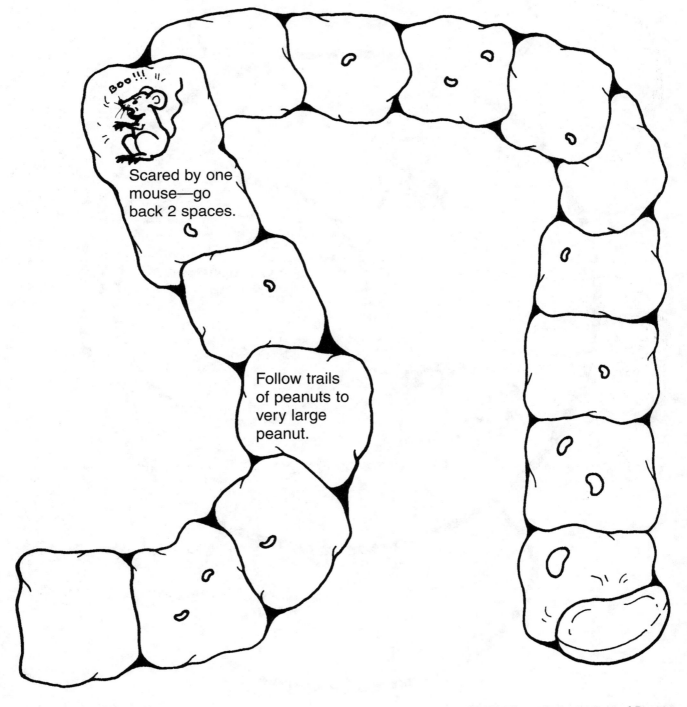

Patterns for Elephants (cont.)

When the Elephant Walks Pattern

Cut open for
sock on
hand.

Ten Plans for Families

	Day One	Day Two	Day Three	Day Four	Day Five
Individual Activities	• Doll House • Animals and Their Babies • Draw a Place to Sleep • Stencils of Stars	• Bird Feeder Bagel • Owl Puppets • Paint with Feathers	• Dye Eggs • Torn-Paper Pictures	• Dolls • Baby Bottles • Easel Paint	• Empty Baby Bottles • Tasty Baby Food
Group Activities	*Time for Bed*	*Owl Babies*	"Bird Story"	*Carl's Afternoon in the Park*	*More, More, More, Said the Baby*
Games	Mother Bird and Babies	Baby Rattle Band	Mother Bird and Babies	Doll Rock	Doll Rock
Songs, Action Poems, Fingerplay	"Two Lil' Blackbirds"	"Little Bird"	"Patty-Cake"	"Mother's Knives and Forks"	"There Was an Old Woman"
Transitions	Pretend to carry a doll.	Swoop like Mama Owl.	Flutter like Baby Bird.	Crawl like Carl.	Pretend to be big.

Ten Plans for Families *(cont.)*

	Day Six	Day Seven	Day Eight	Day Nine	Day Ten
Individual Activities	• Grandma's Face • Maze to Grandma's House • Favorite Adult Card	• Measure Children • Measure Objects • Make Footprints	• Workbench • Wood Sculpture • Chairs of Different Sizes	• Wash Windows • Vacuum Floor • Wash Clothes	• Mice Rubbings • Big Bro Find Little Bro Maze
Group Activities	*When I Was Little*	*Higher on the Door*	*Peter's Chair*	*Once Upon a Time*	*Watch Out! Big Bro's Coming!*
Games	Little and Tall Relays	Jump Up and Down	Musical Chairs	Musical Chairs	The Little House
Songs, Action Poems, Fingerplay	"Grandma's Spectacles"	"This Is The Way Dad Goes to Work"	"Mother's Knives and Forks"	"This Is the Way We Wash the Clothes"	"Two Lil' Blackbirds"
Transitions	Take grandparent's hand.	Reach high.	Paint with imaginary paintbrushes.	Vacuum way to next area.	Follow Big Bro to next area.

Room Preparation for Families

Bulletin Board

If possible, use famous paintings of families. If they are not available, use the patterns on page 187. These can be enlarged, and the finished products can be colored with markers.

Dramatic Play and Housekeeping

Have dolls, doll clothes, blankets, wigs, glasses, adult dress-ups, and aprons ready for the children.

Large Box for House

Packing boxes from stoves and refrigerators make very good pretend houses. Cut out the door and windows. Have the children decorate the house with markers, crayons, and tempera paint.

Teacher Preparation

If owl pellets are to be used for "Owl Babies," contact a science supplier or Pellets, Inc., P.O. Box 5484, Bellington, Washington 98227, for information. Dissect the pellets to see the small bones and hair not digested by the owl. Try to reconstruct the bones to put together a small mouse or animal. These pellets are sanitized, but you may wish to wear surgical gloves.

Suggested Literature for Families

Alborough, Jez. *Watch Out! Big Bro's Coming!* Candlewick Press, 1997.

Day, Alexander. *Carl's Afternoon in the Park.* Farrar, Straus & Giroux, Inc., 1991.

Fox, Mem. *Time for Bed.* Harcourt & Brace, 1963.

Keats, Ezra Jack. *Peter's Chair.* Harper & Row, 1967.

Prater, John. *Once Upon a Time.* Candlewick Press, 1993.

Stevenson, James. *Higher on the Door.* Greenwillow Books, 1987.

Waddell, Martin. *Owl Babies.* Candlewick Press, 1992.

Williams, Marcia. *When I Was Little.* Walker Books Ltd., 1989.

Williams, Vera B. *More, More, More, Said the Baby.* Scholastic, 1990.

Famous Paintings

- Mary Cassett. *Young Mother Sewing, Maternal Caress, Children Playing on the Beach*
- Edgar Degas. *Woman Ironing*
- Thomas Eakin. *Baby at Play*
- Claude Monet. *The Cradle*
- Pierre-Auguste Renoir. *The Artist's Family*

Materials

- manila paper
- fabric
- plastic animals and their babies
- glue
- pencils
- dried bagels
- peanut butter
- bird seed
- film canister
- feathers
- plastic lids
- white crayons
- cooked eggs
- 12-inch squares of fabric
- blue, brown, green construction paper
- string
- rice
- bay leaves
- milk
- baby food
- light blue and pink tempera
- hammer
- nails
- large Styrofoam meat trays
- sandpaper
- safety glasses
- wood
- Styrofoam squares
- toothpicks
- red and brown onion skins
- cardboard

Activities for Families

Individual Activities

Doll House

Have dolls and a doll house available for the children to play with. Emphasize the bedroom and cut pieces of fabric to make the bed and to wrap the baby dolls in.

Animals and Their Babies

Have many plastic animals with their babies for the children to play with. Have the Lincoln Logs out, plus barns and fences to make homes for the animals.

Draw a Place to Sleep

Put out manila paper for the children to draw their sleeping places and the surroundings. Also put out fabric for them to make the rug and the curtains. Glue these onto the picture.

Stencils of Stars

Use the patterns on page 188 to cut different sizes of stars from plastic lids. Have the children draw around them with white crayon on dark blue paper. Encourage them to use different sizes and make patterns.

Bird Feeder Bagel

Obtain a dried bagel and have the children coat it with peanut butter. Then roll it in bird seed. Put string through the center and hang it from a tree. Make sure that the bagel hangs near a branch the birds can sit on and eat their seeds.

Owl Puppets

Make owl puppets using the pattern on page 189 for the film canister babies and the pattern on page 190 for the mother.

Paint with Feathers

Set up the easel or the table and have the children paint with feathers. These can be found in some areas but are best purchased at craft stores. Long feathers with strong centers work best.

Dye Eggs

Bring hard-boiled eggs. Have squares of white cotton fabric about 12" x 12" (30 cm x 30 cm) on which to place each egg. Place onion skins from brown and red onions around the egg. Also scatter some rice and bay leaves on the fabric so that it is close to the egg. Pull up the fabric around the egg and tie it with string as tightly as possible. The teacher places the eggs in boiling water for about 10 minutes. Take them out and allow them to cool. Unwrap the eggs and notice that there is no color in the places where the rice and bay leaves were. Where the onion leaves touched the egg, shades of brown occur.

Activities for Families *(cont.)*

Individual Activities *(cont.)*

Torn-Paper Pictures

Tear strips of brown shades of construction paper so that they can be made to look like a bird's nest. Glue these onto a sheet of contrasting colored backing paper. Either draw the branch that the nest is on or glue more torn paper onto the backing paper to represent the branch. Tear green construction paper leaves for the branch and for flowers on the ground. Glue these onto the backing paper.

Dolls

Put out dolls and doll clothes plus blankets for the children to use in dramatic play or housekeeping. Have the children wash the dolls, using soapy water, towels, wash cloths, and brushes.

Baby Bottles

Use plastic baby bottles or baby jars. Fill each one with a different amount of milk. Have the children line them up, starting with the least amount of milk and progressing to the most amount of milk. Have other children check to see if the order is correct. Mix up the the bottles and start again.

Easel Paint

Use light blue and pink tempera paint. Paint something that a baby would like.

Empty Baby Bottles

Use the empty baby bottles and have the children pretend to feed the dolls. Make sure that the dolls are wrapped in blankets so they feel secure while eating.

Tasty Baby Food

Have samples of baby food for the children to taste. Applesauce, pudding, and cereals are likely to be the most appealing to the young children.

Grandma's Face

Use a Styrofoam meat tray and draw Grandma's face with pencil. This will make a line in the Styrofoam. Use a paintbrush or brayer to coat the tray with tempera paint. Place a piece of manila paper on the tray and have the children rub over it with their hands. Take the paper off the tray, and the face outline should be the color of the paper while the rest is the color of the paint.

Maze to Grandma's House

Use the pattern on page 191 to find the way to Grandma's house.

Activities for Families *(cont.)*

Individual Activities *(cont.)*

Grandparent or Favorite Adult Day

Have a grandparent or a favorite adult visit for the day. Have the children and the adults each make a special card to give to each other. Use construction paper, lace, ribbon, and stickers for the card.

Measure Children

Place a strip of paper on the frame of the door. Have the children line up one by one and see how tall they are on the door frame. Place each child's name next to his or her mark.

Measure Objects in the Room

Use fabric or metal measures to measure items in the room. Children can dress as construction workers to complete this task. Also give them each a pad of paper so that they can draw what they have measured and what the numeral was on the tape.

Make Footprints

Show a baby footprint. Then have children take their shoes off and compare the sizes. Draw around the child's foot. Measure how big it is. Write the numeral on the foot. Also draw around the shoe. Write the numeral on the shoe print. Compare the sizes. Ask, "Which is larger? Why?"

Workbench *(Peter's Chair)*

Have hammer, nails, sandpaper, safety glasses, and wood at the workbench. Have children make whatever they want. Make sure there are only a few at the bench at one time, however.

Wood Sculpture *(Peter's Chair)*

Have scraps of wood available. Sometimes building sites will collect scraps for a school. Some school supply companies have scraps of many shapes for purchase. Use a flat piece to serve as the base. Use white glue on other pieces to make a creation. Styrofoam pieces, thread spools, toothpicks, and other items can be added. The creation can be painted the next day and sent home when dry.

Chairs of Different Sizes

Find chairs in the building that are of sizes different from the classroom chairs. Place them around the room and have the children try them out. The teacher can write down any unusual comments.

Wash Windows

Have spray bottles available for the children to spray the windows and then clean with toweling.

Vacuum Floor

Have children pretend to clean the house. Use a dusting cloth, broom, and a toy vacuum cleaner. Put aprons on both the boys and the girls and have them pretend to clean the house.

Activities for Families *(cont.)*

Individual Activies *(cont.)*

Wash Clothes

Have children wash small doll clothes in a pan of soapy water. Rinse in another pan. Wring the clothes and hang them outside to dry or hang them on a line in the room to dry.

Mice Rubbings *(Watch Out! Big Bro's Coming!)*

Reproduce the patterns on page 192. Glue paper to cardboard. Use school glue to drizzle lines over the patterns of mice. Allow to dry overnight. Have the children place newsprint over the mice and rub with pencils or chalk. Or use a brayer to coat the pattern with tempera paint. Place manila paper over the pattern and rub gently. The paper will pick up the raised portion, and the other part will stay the paper color.

Big Bro Find Little Bro Maze

Use the pattern on page 193 to have Big Bro look for his brother.

Group Activities

Time for Bed

Ask the children what kinds of places they sleep in. "Is it a bed, cot, bunk bed, sofa?" Show pictures of animals in the book *Time for Bed*. Ask, "What kind of bed do you think they had? Let's read the book and find out."

Read *Time for Bed*. Ask, "If it was time for bed, do you think it was the morning or the nighttime? Were there stars in the sky, or was the sun shining?" Prepare the peep box described on page 117 and have the children look inside to see the stars. Have a box of purchased stars about one-inch (2.54 cm) in size. Place about 10 in a jar. Have the children guess how many are in the jar. Write down all the numerals that they say. Then take the stars out and count them. Ask children if they think that is as many stars as there are in the sky. Explain that they are to look at the sky and see if they can count the stars.

Owl Babies

Explain that owls live in trunks of trees and like to be awake at night. Show pictures of the three baby owls in the book *Owl Babies*. They are white when they are babies. Place the three owl-baby puppets on fingers. Have them wiggle and say "Hi" to the children. Say, "Let's listen to their story."

Read *Owl Babies*. Each time Bill says, "I want my mommy," have the children say it with him. As "And she came" is read, have another adult swoop in with the mother-owl puppet on the hand. This story can be read the first time, and then have the puppets act it out the second time.

Activities for Families *(cont.)*

Group Activities *(cont.)*

Owl Babies (cont.)

Follow this up with older children by talking about what the owls eat. They really like to eat mice. Sometimes they cannot digest all the animal parts, so they cough up some. This coughed-up part is called an owl pellet. Explain that we have some owl pellets that were ordered from a company that makes them sanitary and okay to touch. The teacher can open a pellet and take apart the bones as the children watch. Say, "Let's try to put the bones together and see if the owl ate a mouse or something else."

"Bird Story"

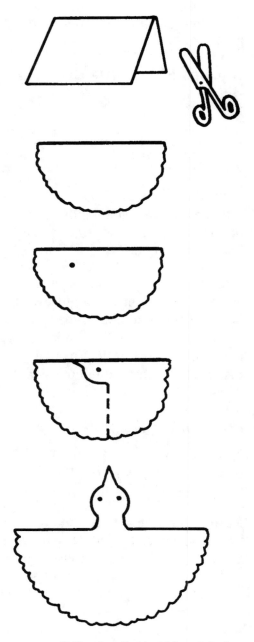

Talk about the *Owl Babies* story. What was the children's favorite part of the story? Say, "Your teacher knows another story about a bird." (*Fold a piece of typing paper in half horizontally.*)

"Once upon a time, Mama Bird and Papa Bird went flying over the land to see if they could find a good place to build a nest. Mama saw a locust tree that looked very good, and Papa saw an evergreen tree that he thought would protect them from the wind. They just could not decide where a good space would be. Then they spotted a tall maple tree. That is just the spot, they agreed. So they landed in the tree and began to build their nest." (*Tear the nest shape from the paper.*)

"Then Mama laid her egg. She sat on the egg to keep it warm and waited for it to hatch. Papa went off to find food every day. But Mama got very bored just sitting on the egg, and she wished she could talk to somebody. Then one day a little bug landed on the branch and said 'Hi!'" (*Put a dot on nest according to the pattern.*)

"They talked all day, but at the end of the day the little bug had to go back to her home. The next day, Mama Bird was lonesome again. But another bug landed on the branch." (*Put a dot across from the other dot on the opposite side of the folded paper.*)

"They chatted all day, but this bug had to go home when the sun began to set. Mama was very lonesome waiting for Papa to come home with the food. Then all of a sudden, she heard, 'Peep, peep, peep.'" (*Tear a baby bird from the paper. Then refold in the opposite direction.*) 'My goodness, it is Baby Bird!' Then she and Papa Bird were very happy because they were a family."

Activities for Families *(cont.)*

Group Activities *(cont.)*

Carl's Afternoon in the Park

Bring a baby doll to the area. Wrap it in blankets and sing "Rock-a-Bye Baby." Ask, "Do any of you children have a baby at home? How about a baby cousin or a friend's baby? Who takes care of the baby? What is done to take care of the baby? Sometimes babies grow up a little bit, and then they start to walk. Do any of you have a brother or sister who has just started to walk? Who takes care of the child?"

"Do you think a dog could take care of a baby or a small child?"

Read *Carl's Afternoon in the Park*. After reading the story, ask if Carl was a good babysitter. Since it is a picture book with very little writing during most of the book, show the pictures and have the children narrate what is happening.

More, More, More, Said the Baby

Ask children, "What are some of the favorite things that your mommy, daddy, or favorite person does to you? Does anyone remember having that person count your toes and say,

> *This little piggy went to market.*
> *This little piggy stayed home.*
> *This little piggy had roast beef.*
> *This little piggy had none.*
> *This little piggy cried, "Waa-waa," all the way home.*

(Point to big toe and continue with the next toe until all the toes are pointed to.)

"Some little children love to have this done to them. They say, 'More, more, more' to the person who does it. Today we are going to read about three children who had favorite things done to them. See if any of the things are the favorite things that you like."

Read *More, More, More Said the Baby*. After reading the story, ask the children if any of the actions in the story were things they liked to have done to them. What were they? Then have all the children take off their shoes and point to the big toe and say, "This little piggy went to market." Follow with the rest of the rhyme. Then let's see who is really big now and can put their shoes back on again. Then have them pretend to be big and walk to the next area.

When I Was Little

Let the teacher recount some of the things that he or she remembers when Granny came to visit. "Granny would say things like 'It is bad luck to step on cracks in the sidewalk,' and 'I had to walk a mile to school in the snow!'" Since this could be "Grandparents Day," have the grandparents tell what they remember from when they were young. (It would be a good idea to have the children sitting in a circle with the grandparents behind them or have the children sitting in the grandparents' laps.) Make sure that all the grandparents have a chance to share!

Activities for Families *(cont.)*

Group Activities *(cont.)*

When I Was Little *(cont.)*

Then read *When I Was Little*. Ask the grandparents if they say some of the same things to their grandchildren. What things in particular? Have the children do "Grandma's Spectacles" and then take the grandparent's hand and walk to the next area.

Higher on the Door

Let the teacher take down the door frame tape measure and point out who is the tallest in the class. Then go down the tape and show where each child's name is. Say, "It isn't important how tall you are because we know that everyone will grow." Ask how many children are measured on the door frame by their parents or another important person. "When was the last time you were measured? On a birthday? Fourth of July? Let's read a book about being measured on the door frame."

Read *Higher on the Door*. Then ask the children what they would do if they grew as high as the top of the door frame. Write down their answers and keep them in their journals.

Walk to the next area, pretending to reach to the top of the door frame.

Peter's Chair

Place different-sized chairs in front of the group of children. Point out to the children that there are different-sized chairs in the room today. Ask, "Did everyone try sitting in them? Which did you like the best?" Then see which chair was the favorite of most of the children. "Why do you think everyone liked a certain one? There was a little boy named Peter, and he had a favorite chair. He wasn't sure that he wanted to share it with anyone. You listen to the story and find out why."

Read *Peter's Chair*. After reading the story, ask the children why Peter did not want to share his chair with Sue. (He already had shared his highchair, cradle, and crib.) Say, "He was so upset, what did he decide to do?" *(Run away.)* "What did he discover about his chair? *(He was too big to sit in it.)* "So he and his dad did what with the chair?" Ask the children if they ever had problems with big or little brothers and sisters. What were they? How did they solve the problems?

Have the children pretend to have paintbrushes in hand and paint their way to the next area.

Activities for Families *(cont.)*

Group Activities *(cont.)*

Once Upon a Time

Ask children if they have ever heard "Once upon a time." Hopefully, they will say that it is the beginning of a fairy tale. Say, "We have a book and the title is *Once Upon a Time*. Let's see what happens in the story."

Read *Once Upon a Time*. After reading the story, sing the following songs to the tune of "Mulberry Bush." Point to the activities in the book that match the activities in the song.

> *This is the way Dad goes to work, goes to work, goes to work.*
> *This is the way Dad goes to work, early in the morning.*
> Verse Two: *Mom washes clothes.*
> Verse Three: *Mom washes windows.*
> Verse Four: *Mom vacuums the floor.*
> Verse Five: *Mom plants the garden.*
> Verse Six: *Mom drinks her coffee.*
> Verse Seven: *We find the people.*

Say, "What did we sing in verse seven? Find the people! Let's look at the pictures again." Have the children look carefully at each page and find the "once-upon-a-time" characters hidden in the picture. What story do they tell about?

Then have the children move to the next area, pretending to vacuum the floors.

Watch Out! Big Bro's Coming!

Ask children how many of them have a bigger brother. Ask, "What do you do with your brother?" Then ask if anyone has a big sister. (This will include more children.) "What special things do you do with her? We are going to read a book about a big brother."

Read *Watch Out! Big Bro's Coming!* After reading the story, ask what kind of animal Big Bro is. He really is a mouse. Go through the book again and this time point out what each animal thought "big" really was. To a mouse, it was a few inches tall. Show how big a few inches is on a ruler. The bigger the animal, the taller that animal thought Big Bro really was. The teacher should stretch out hands and arms for each animal. For the frog, it was a few more inches then the mouse, but for the parrot, the wing span was quite wide. The chimpanzee has long arms, and when he stretches out his arms they seem even longer. The elephant was the biggest animal, so he thought that Big Bro was even bigger than he was. When Big Bro came, all the animals thought he was tiny, but the mouse still thought he was big. Only Big Bro's voice made him rough and tough.

Have the children line up to see who is the tallest and who is the smallest. Have the smallest child be the leader "Big Bro" or "Big Sis" and have all the children follow him or her to the next area.

Activities for Families *(cont.)*

Games

Mother Bird and Babies

Have one child be the mother or father bird. That child covers his or her eyes. All the other children hide. Mother or Father uncovers eyes while all the other children gently chirp. Mother or Father finds the children by the sounds of their voices. The first or last one found becomes the next parent.

Baby Rattle Band

Have children bring their baby rattles (if saved). Teacher may want to round up some rattles to complete the band. Have children shake the rattles to any recording. March around the room shaking the rattles. If there are not enough rattles, use maracas or any rattle type of instrument.

Little and Tall Relays

Have children line up against the wall according to height. Have the tallest first, ranging down to the smallest. Make two lines for a relay with alternating heights. There should be a tall followed by a short. Pass a ball over the head. Then have the first in line run to the back and pass the ball again over the head. Keep on until all have changed positions once. The relay can be repeated by passing the ball between the legs.

Doll Rock

Spread a sheet out on the floor. Place one child at each end of the sheet and have them hold the sheet. Place a doll in the center and pretend to rock the baby while singing "Rock-a-Bye Baby."

Musical Chairs

Have one line of chairs with alternating chairs facing the opposite direction. Make sure that there is one less chair than children. Have children make a circle around the chairs. When the music starts, have the children walk around the chairs until the music stops. Everyone finds a chair and sits down. One child will not have a chair. Say, "Hip, Hip, Hooray for _____!" Have that child again join the group and march around the chairs.

Records, Cassettes, and CDs

Palmer, Hap. *Easy Does It*. "Birds in a Circle."

Palmer, Hap. *Learning Basic Skills Through Music, Volume I*. "The Birds."

Palmer, Hap. *Walter the Waltzing Worm*. "All the Ways of Jumping Up and Down.

Raffi. *Everything Grows*. "The Little House."

Activities for Families *(cont.)*

Songs, Action Poems, and Fingerplay

"Two Lil' Blackbirds"

(Nursery Rhyme)

Two lil' blackbirds sitting on a hill,
(Put two hands behind back.)
One named Jack,
(Pull out one thumb and wiggle for Jack.)
And the other named Jill.
(Pull out the other thumb and wiggle for Jill.)
Fly away Jack,
(Put one hand behind back.)
Fly away Jill.
(Put other hand behind back.)
Come back Jack,
(Pull out one hand and wiggle thumb.)
Come back Jill.
(Pull out the other hand and wiggle thumb.)

Continue by saying that the birds sat on other things and have other names. The names should be the opposite of each other with the last one rhyming with the item sat on.

Suggestions:

Two lil' blackbirds sitting on ice,
One was mean and the other was nice.

Two lil' blackbirds sitting on a stump,
One was smooth and the other was a lump.

Two lil' blackbirds sitting on a chair,
One was bald and the other had hair.

"Little Bird"

(Nursery Rhyme)

Once I saw a little bird come hop, hop, hop;
So I cried "Little bird, will you stop, stop, stop?"
I was going to the window to say "How do you do?"
But he shook his little tail, and away he flew.

"Rock-a-Bye Baby"

(Nursery Rhyme)

Rock-a-bye baby on the tree top.
When the wind blows, the cradle will rock.
When the bough breaks, the cradle will fall;
Down will come baby, cradle and all.

"Grandma's Spectacles"

(Traditional)

These are Grandma' spectacles.
(Bring index finger and thumb together and place against face as if wearing glasses.)
This is Grandma's hat.
(Bring finger-tips together in a peak over head.)
This is the way she folds her hands,
(Clasp hands together.)
And lays them in her lap.
(Lay hands in lap.)

Activities for Families *(cont.)*

Songs, Action Poems, and Fingerplay *(cont.)*

"Patty-Cake"
(Nursery Rhyme)

Patty-cake, patty-cake, baker's man,

Bake me a cake as fast as you can.

Pat it and prick it and mark it with "B."

Put it in the oven for Baby and me.

"Mother's Knives and Forks"
(Traditional)

Here are Mother's knives and forks.
(Interlock fingers, palms up.)

This is Father's table.
*(Keep fingers interlocked and
turn palms down.)*

This is Sister's looking glass,
(Make peak of two forefingers.)

And this is Baby's cradle.
(Add peak of little fingers.)

"There Was an Old Woman"
(Nursery Rhyme Changed)

There was an old woman who lived in a shoe.

She had so many children, she didn't know what to do.

She gave them some soup and a big slice of bread,

And hugged them so tightly and sent them to bed.

"This Is the Way Dad (Mom) Goes to Work"
(Tune: Mulberry Bush)

*Form a circle. Perform actions. Then hold hands and go
around in a circle on "early in the morning."*

This is the way Dad goes to work, goes to work, goes to
work.

(Stand in place and pretend to run or drive a car.)

This is the way Dad goes to work, early in the morning.

(Put hand above eyes, look for the sun, and blink eyes.)

This is the way Mom washes clothes, washes clothes,
washes clothes.

(Pretend to scrub clothes on a washboard.)

. . . Mom washes windows . . .

(Pretend to swirl cloth in front of imaginary windows.)

. . . Mom vacuums floors . . .

(Pretend to push vacuum in front of you.)

. . . Mom plants a garden . . .

(Stoop down and pretend to dig in ground and plant seeds.)

. . . Mom drinks her coffee . . .

(Hold pretend cup in hand and put up to mouth.)

Records, Cassettes and CD's

Hap Palmer. *Easy Does It.* Educational Activities, Inc., 1977.

Hap Palmer. *Learning Basic Skills Through Music, Volume 1.* Educational Activities, Inc., 1971.

Hap Palmer. *Walter the Waltzing Worm.* Educational Activities, Inc., 1982.

Raffi. *Everything Grows.* Homeland Publishing. (Troubadour Records), 1987.

Videos

Peter's Chair. Children's Circle. Weston Woods, 1983.

Tight Times. Reading Rainbow. Distributed by GPN/WNED-TV.

Patterns for Families

Bulletin Board for Families

Patterns for Families *(cont.)*

Star Stencil

188

Patterns for Families *(cont.)*

Owl Babies

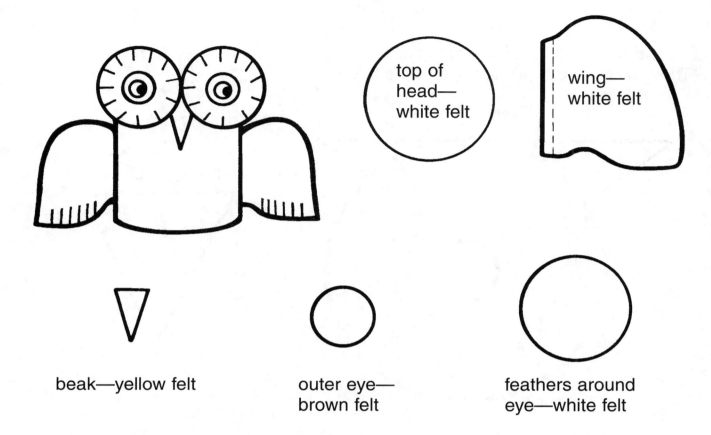

beak—yellow felt

outer eye—
brown felt

feathers around
eye—white felt

Cover empty plastic film canister with coating of glue.

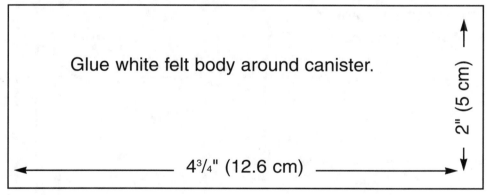

Glue white felt body around canister.

2" (5 cm)

4³/₄" (12.6 cm)

Directions

1. Glue top of head to container.
2. Glue on wings and feathers around eyes.
3. Then put brown circles in center of each eye.
4. Glue jiggly eyes in the center of each brown circle.
5. Glue beak between eyes.

Patterns for Families *(cont.)*

Owl Mother

Cut two from brown construction paper.
(They will extend over the edge of the bag.)

fringe around eye

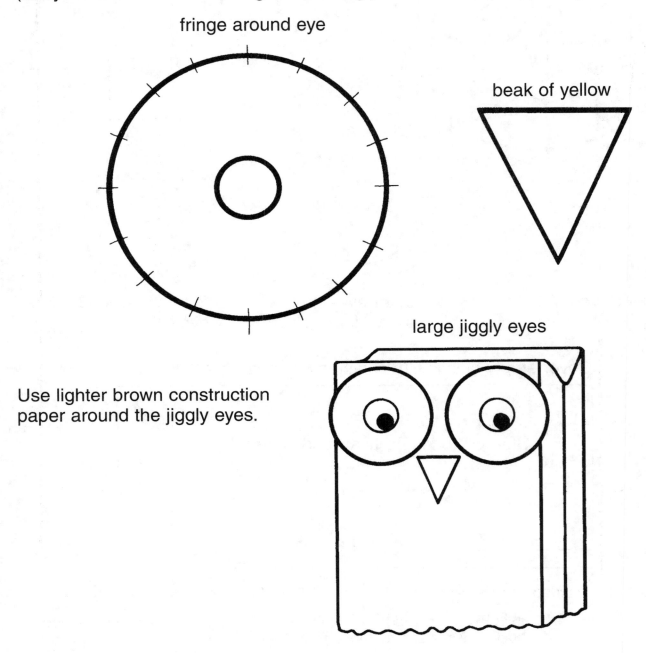

beak of yellow

large jiggly eyes

Use lighter brown construction
paper around the jiggly eyes.

Use the bottom of a lunch bag for the puppet face.

Patterns for Families *(cont.)*

Maze to Grandma's House

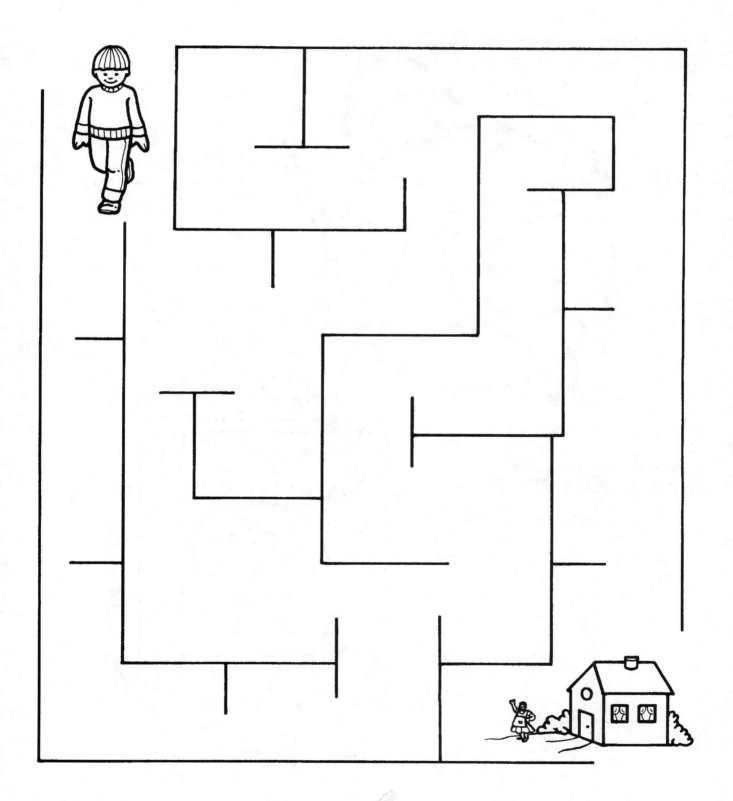

Patterns for Families *(cont.)*

Rubbing Pattern for Big Bro

Patterns for Families *(cont.)*

Big Bro Find Little Bro Maze

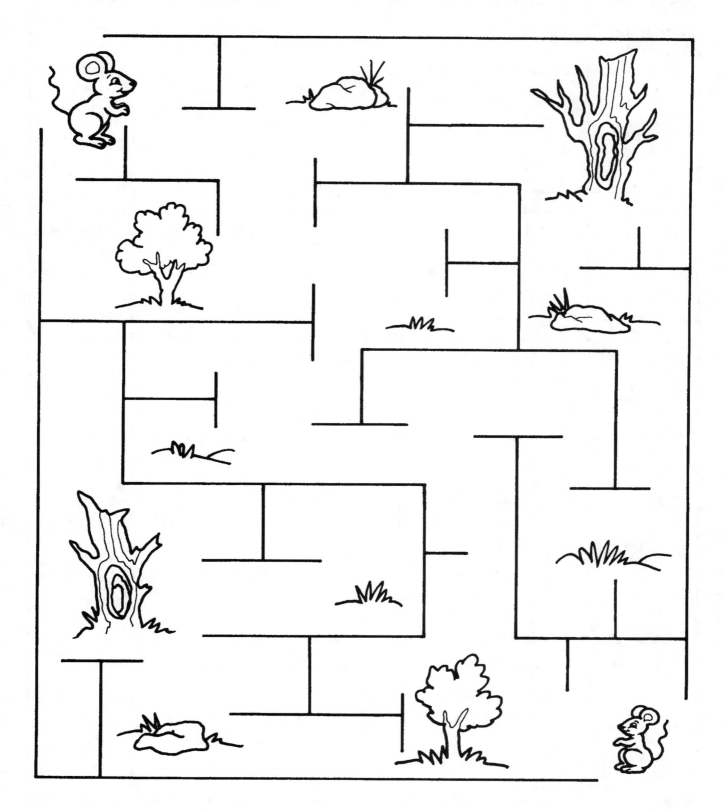

Ten Plans for Food

	Day One	Day Two	Day Three	Day Four	Day Five
Individual Activities	• Scented Dry Glue • Lunch Bag Puppets • Prepare Lunch Bags	• Mice Prints • Print with Apples • Paint Puffs	• Make Vegetable Soup	• Housekeeping • Vegetable Concentration • Seed Catalogue Collage	• Spaghetti Art • String Tinted Macaroni • Classify Tinted Macaroni
Group Activities	"Lunch Bag, Lunch Bag"	*Lunch*	*Stone Soup*	*Growing Vegetable Soup*	*Strega Nona: An Old Tale Retold*
Games	Lunch Bag Dump Relay	Lunch Bag Throw	Soup Pot Toss	Soup Pot Toss	Follow the String
Songs, Action Poems, Fingerplay	"We All Made Lunch Today"	"We All Made Lunch Today"	"We All Made Lunch Today"	"We All Made Lunch Today"	"We All Made Pasta Today"
Transitions	Rub tummy as if just eating lunch.			Rub tummies and say "yum, yum!"	Pretend you have a fat tummy like Anthony.

Ten Plans for Food *(cont.)*

	Day Six	Day Seven	Day Eight	Day Nine	Day Ten
Individual Activities	• Paint Toast • Paint with Pastry Brush • Pretend Bread	• Paint with Kitchen Utensils • Muffin Liner Art (a & b)	• Pancake with Holes • Housekeeping Pancakes	• House-keeping Cereal • Soup Pot Art • Sizes of Animals	• Cardboard Boxes • Tin Cans • Good Food
Group Activities	*The Little Red Hen*	*If You Give a Moose a Muffin*	*Pancakes, Pancakes*	*The Fat Cat*	*Gregory, the Terrible Eater*
Games	Lazy Day	Muffin Liner Colors Game	Pancake Flip	Soup Pot Toss	Kick the Can
Songs, Action Poems, Fingerplay	"We All Made Bread Today"	"We All Made Muffins Today"	"We All Made Pancakes Today"	"To Market, to Market"	"Peanut Sitting on a Railroad Track"
Transitions	Pretend to sweep the floor.		Walk, pretending to be chewing a pancake.		Pretend to kick a can.

Room Preparation for Food

Bulletin Board

Plans for bulletin board are on page 207. The pattern includes food groups. If the pattern is not large enough to cover the bulletin board, cut the marks for the puzzle pieces. Spread out on the bulletin board with space between pieces.

Mobile

A mobile can be created by hanging a large mixing spoon from the ceiling. From the mixing spoon, hang kitchen items such as measuring spoons, pastry brush, cheese cutter, cherry stone remover, etc. Another mobile can be created by using frosting tips in sequence and keeping a knot between them.

Housekeeping

Tables, tablecloths, kitchen utensils, and menus are needed.

Special Idea for the Teacher

Burn scented candles in the classroom, making sure that they cannot be reached by the children.

Famous Paintings

Display a print of Pablo Picasso's *Le Gourmet*.

Suggested Literature for Food

Brown, Marcia. *Stone Soup*. Scribner, 1975.
Carl, Eric. *Pancakes, Pancakes*. Simon & Schuster, 1990.
dePaola, Tomie. *Strega Nona: An Old Tale Retold*. Prentice-Hall, Inc., 1975.
Ehlert, Lois. *Growing Vegetable Soup*. Harcourt Brace & Co., 1987.
Fleming, Denise. *Lunch*. Henry Holt and Company, 1992.
Galdone, Paul. *Little Red Hen*. Dutton Children's Books, 1991.
Kent, Jack. *The Fat Cat*. Parent's Magazine Press, 1971.
Numeroff, Laura Joffe. *If You Give a Moose a Muffin*. Laura Geringer Books, 1991.
Sharmatt, Mitchell. *Gregory, the Terrible Eater*. Simon & Schuster, 1980.

Materials

- lunch bags
- glue
- shower puffs
- seed catalogues
- food coloring
- milk
- dry cereal
- plastic animals
- foil
- iron
- string
- cans and sponge covers for cans

- construction paper
- scents
- tempera paint
- spaghetti
- rubbing alcohol
- white play dough
- leftover construction paper
- cardboard boxes
- magazine pictures of good food
- beanbags
- muffin liners

- manila paper
- apples
- beef stock
- macaroni
- white bread
- food pictures from magazines
- wheat paste
- tin cans
- wax paper
- soup pot
- paper plates

Activities for Food

Individual Activities

Scented Dry Glue

Squeeze small amounts of glue on different spots on the paper. While the glue is still moist, add drops of peppermint, lemon, almond, etc., extracts on the glue. Allow to dry overnight. The next day have the children smell and see if they can identify the odors.

Lunch Bag Puppets

Have the children create a face on a lunch bag. Let them glue on buttons for eyes and draw the nose and mouth with markers. Hair can be created with yarn or cotton.

Prepare Lunch Bags

Have lunch bags in the dramatic play area. Have pretend food from housekeeping and pretend to make a sandwich and pack a lunch.

Mice Prints *(Lunch)*

Press a finger on a black stamp pad. Then press the finger onto a piece of typing paper. Add two eye dots to one side of the print and a tail to the other end. Now you have a mouse. Make more than one mouse, adding a mouse house or hole in the wall. Use markers to add a cat.

Print with Apples *(Lunch)*

Cut an apple in half horizontally. Use a pie tin with a thin sponge resting in red tempera paint. Press the flat part of the apple onto the sponge. Then press the apple onto a sheet of paper and notice that the print has a star shape in the middle. Show children that the star is from the pattern of seeds within the apple.

Paint Puffs *(Lunch)*

Use shower puffs to paint. Place different colors of tempera in pie tins. Put puffs in one color and press onto manila paper. Then try other colors. During group activity compare their paintings with the way the mouse looked after eating all the food for lunch.

Make Vegetable Soup

Have pots and pans, hot pads, dishes, and pretend food in the housekeeping area. Have the children pretend they are cooking soup. Put vegetables in pots, place them on the stove, and then remove them, using hot pads. Serve pretend soup to friends sitting at the table.

Vegetable Concentration

Use patterns on pages 211 and 212 to make vegetable concentration cards. Reproduce and cut up. Mix up the cards and place them facedown on the floor. Have about three children play the game at once. Each takes a turn lifting one card and seeing if he or she can find the matching one. If the cards do not match, place both facedown and the next child takes a turn. Keep on until all the cards are matched.

Activities for Food *(cont.)*

Individual Activities *(cont.)*

Seed Catalogue Collage

Use old seed catalogues and let children cut out favorite vegetables and plants and paste on sheets of manila paper. Arrange in whatever way they want. It is their collage!

Spaghetti Art

Boil spaghetti until cooked. Do not rinse. Allow to cool and add food coloring. Supply sheets of shirt cardboard or heavier paper. Have the children make designs by using one strand of spaghetti arranged on the cardboard. Younger children will have to be supervised since they like to put globs of spaghetti on the cardboard, and it does not dry.

As a variation, wind cooked spaghetti randomly around toilet paper tubes. Roll them in a pan of tempera paint and then on a sheet of manila paper. Make several different rolls so that several colors can be put on the same sheet of paper.

String Tinted Macaroni

Have macaroni that is straight and can be threaded. About a day before class, place uncooked macaroni in a glass jar with about $1/3$ cup of rubbing alcohol and about 10 drops of food coloring. Add about one cup of uncooked macaroni to the mixture and toss around until the macaroni is tinted. Remove and place on newspaper to dry overnight. Do this with several colors and then mix the dried colors up. This should not be done while the children are in the room. The next day, have the children string the macaroni by using yarn needles with double string and a tied macaroni at the end. Make a necklace.

Classify Tinted Macaroni

Use the tinted macaroni and have the children classify according to color. Empty egg cartons work well as containers to divide up the colors.

Paint Toast

Mix food coloring with milk. Use a pastry brush to spread on white bread. Toast and use for snack time.

Paint with Pastry Brush

Place newspaper on a table and use manila paper to paint on. Use tempera paint and pastry brushes of different types and have the children experiment painting with them.

Pretend Bread

In the housekeeping area, place white play dough and small loaf tins. Have the children pretend to knead the dough, form into loaves, and place into loaf tins. Place the tins in the pretend oven and wait until they are done baking. All who have helped make the bread can pretend to eat it. Anyone who did not help cannot help eat it!

198

Activities for Food *(cont.)*

Individual Activities *(cont.)*

Paint with Kitchen Utensils

Spread newspaper on the table. Put out paper to print on and potato mashers of different types, spatulas, cookie cutters, slatted spoons, forks, doughnut cutters, and any other kitchen utensils available. Prepare a pie tin with tempera paint under a thin sponge. Have the children press down on the sponge with the kitchen utensils and then stamp them on the paper. Pie tins and sponges holding different colors can be used to make a more interesting picture.

Muffin Liner Art *(If You Give a Moose a Muffin)*

a. Have children flatten muffin liners of different colors and glue about two on a sheet of 9" x 12" (23 cm x 30 cm) manila paper. Use markers or crayons to add stems and leaves.

b. Press a finger on a stamp pad or in tempera paint and print on the muffin liners. Make many colors of fingerprints on the muffin liners.

Pancake with Holes *(Pancakes, Pancakes)*

Use the pattern on page 213 to resemble a pancake. Cut holes in various spots on the pancake according to the pattern. Cut pictures of food from a magazine and place them under the pancake with holes. Have children guess what the magazine food picture is by looking through the holes in the pancake.

Housekeeping Pancakes *(Pancakes, Pancakes)*

Use pretend pancakes in the housekeeping area and have the children pretend to flip them with a spatula.

Housekeeping Cereal *(The Fat Cat)*

Place dry cereal in the housekeeping area. Have children pretend to stir and make cooked cereal. Prepare other areas with dry cereal for the children to taste.

Soup Pot Art *(The Fat Cat)*

Have a large soup pot filled about $1/4$ with water. Have the children drop in pieces of leftover construction paper which has been torn into small pieces. These can be all the same color or different colors. Let the paper absorb the water, and then take the paper out and squeeze the water out of it. Add some wheat paste to the paper and mix and knead. Have the children create whatever shapes they want and allow them to dry.

Sizes of Animals *(The Fat Cat)*

Pile up as many of the soft plastic animals as you can in the room. Have the children sort them according to size (small, medium, and large).

Cardboard Boxes *(Gregory, the Terrible Eater)*

Try to get as many types of boxes as are available. Try shoeboxes, cartons, and empty refrigerator boxes. Have the children stack, decorate them with markers, and play to their hearts' content!

Activities for Food *(cont.)*

Individual Activities *(cont.)*

Tin Cans *(Gregory, the Terrible Eater)*

Wash empty cans about the size of soup cans. Have the children cover them with wrinkled foil. Let them take these home to use as containers for pencils.

Good Food *(Gregory, the Terrible Eater)*

Have the children go through magazines and look for good food to eat. Teacher may have to work with the children on this. Sometimes a picture of the food groups helps. After the children have found the pictures, place wax paper on top and underneath. The teacher irons them together by using newspaper on top of wax paper and underneath wax paper.

Group Activities

"Lunch Bag, Lunch Bag"

Make a lunch bag book ahead of time, using the patterns on pages 208 and 209. Put pictures on each side of a lunch bag and join the book together with yarn or string through holes punched a few inches from the top and bottom.

Lunch Bag, Lunch Bag, What Do You See?

Lunch Bag, Lunch Bag, what do you see?
I see white bread looking at me.
White Bread, White Bread, what do you see?
I see a green lettuce leaf looking at me.
Green Lettuce Leaf, Green Lettuce Leaf, what do you see?
I see a red tomato looking at me.
Red Tomato, Red Tomato, what do you see?
I see yellow cheese looking at me.
Yellow Cheese, Yellow Cheese, what do you see?
I see brown mustard looking at me.
Brown Mustard, Brown Mustard, what do you see?
I again see white bread looking at me.
White Bread, White Bread, what do you see?
I see a lunch-making mother looking at me.
Lunch-Making Mother, Lunch-Making Mother, what do you see?
I see Alex looking at me.
Alex, Alex, what do you see?
I see my school friends eating lunch with me.

If they were packing a lunch, what would they put it in? Show a lunch bag to the children. What is their favorite lunch bag food? On a sheet of paper, write down the names of all the foods suggested. After each food, list the names of the children who like that food. Determine which is the most popular lunch food. Ask, "Did you ever wonder what a lunch bag thinks about all the food put inside it?"

Activities for Food *(cont.)*

Group Activities *(cont.)*

"Lunch Bag, Lunch Bag" *(cont.)*

Then take out the story of *Lunch Bag, Lunch Bag* and read it. After reading the story, take out lunch bags which have buttons, cookies, apples, etc., in them. Twist them shut at the top. See if the children can figure out what is in the bags by shaking, smelling, and touching the bags. Have them walk to the next area while rubbing their tummies.

Lunch

Review the popular lunch items written down the day before. Did any of the children change their minds? Ask, "What if you were a mouse and had favorite lunch items. What do you think a mouse would like?" (*Write down the children's answers.*) " Let's read a book about a mouse's lunch."

Read *Lunch*. As the story is read, notice that one page says "He ate a crisp white—," but the item eaten is not told until the following page. As the teacher reads, he or she should stop at the "—" and have the children guess what the "crisp white —" really is. Continue with each item and have the children guess what the food item is. Read again and have children notice the colors on the mouse after eating lunch and compare them with their puff paintings done earlier.

Stone Soup

Send a note home, using the pattern on page 210. Request that the children bring in a vegetable for the soup the next day because stone soup will be made. Use this story at the beginning of the day so that the soup can cook and be eaten that day.

Say together the poem of "Old Mother Hubbard."

> Old Mother Hubbard
>
> Went to the cupboard
>
> To get her poor dog a bone.
>
> When she came there,
>
> The cupboard was bare,
>
> And so the poor dog had none.

This poem can be recited while slapping thighs and clapping hands. Ask the children, "What would you do if you could not find your dog some food? Where would you get some? There is a story about some men who lived long ago, and as they walked to the village, they knew they would not be able to convince the people to give them food. So they had a plan. See if you can figure out their plan."

Read the story of *Stone Soup.* Younger children may have to be told the story rather than reading it. After reading the story, have the children wash a stone and place it in a soup kettle. Wash the vegetables. Have the children cut up the vegetables to be placed in the kettle. The children can easily do this if a cutting board and plastic serrated knives are used. Add cans of beef bouillon to the vegetables and allow to cook until the vegetables are fairly soft.

Activities for Food *(cont.)*

Group Activities *(cont.)*

Growing Vegetable Soup

Have ready a package of green bean seeds and a pot plus potting soil to plant the seed. Ask the children if they know what to do with seeds. Go through the process of how to plant seed in a pot. Say, "What comes next? Water. If the seeds grow, what do we do with the beans?" (*Write down the answers.*) "We are going to read a story, and you try to remember what is done with the vegetables."

Read *Growing Vegetable Soup.* After reading the story, ask the children what was done with all the vegetables grown in the garden. Using a large soup pot, have the children place in the pot all the plastic vegetables from the housekeeping area. Let them use a large spoon to stir. Then have all of them pretend they are eating the soup. Pretend it is good. Rub tummies and say "Yummm, Yummm."

Walk to the next area while rubbing tummies and saying "Yummm, yummm."

Strega Nona: An Old Tale Retold

Bring out a soup pot. Show children how big it is inside. Then show a smaller pot. How much water from the smaller pot will go into the bigger soup pot? If there is water nearby, measure the number of times the smaller pot is filled with water and put in the larger pot. Ask, "Which one do you think would be better to cook the spaghetti or macaroni that we worked with today?"

Tell children that both macaroni and spaghetti have a common name—*pasta.* Say, "A long, long, time ago there was a lady named Strega Nona who lived in a town far away. She was very good at cooking pasta. Which kind of pasta do you think she would use? Let us listen to her story." (Younger children may have to be told the story since it is rather long, although very good.)

After reading the story, ask if they would feel sorry for Big Anthony. Ask, "How much pasta did he have to eat? Look at how big his tummy is on the final page." Walk to the next area while pretending to have a fat tummy.

The Little Red Hen

Use the film canister red hen puppet pattern on page 214 to tell the story. The lazy dog and mouse can be made with a worker's glove. See the patterns on page 215.

The teacher pretends to be asleep as children gather around. "Oh, my goodness, I have so many things to do that I really cannot sleep!" Ask children if they have ever fallen asleep when they knew they should be doing something. Have the children tell their stories. Say, "We are going to read a book about a red hen who worked very hard." (*Show the puppet of the red hen.*) "But some other animals in the house wanted to sleep all day." (*Show the worker's glove puppet and put animals in a plastic container. Place a wristband on the glove around the outside.*)

Read *The Little Red Hen.* Have the children repeat "Not I" when said by the cat, dog, and mouse. After reading the book, have the children retell the story using the puppets. Keep the puppets in the dramatic play area so that children can keep on retelling the story at a later time. Look at the last page as the lazy animals sweep the floors and do the dusting. Have the children walk around the room, pretending to sweep the floor.

202

Activities for Food *(cont.)*

Group Activities *(cont.)*

If You Give a Moose a Muffin

Sing together:

Do you know the muffin man, the muffin man, the muffin man?

Do you know the muffin man who lives in Drury Lane?

Yes, I know the muffin man, the muffin man, the muffin man.

Yes, I know the muffin man who lives in Drury Lane.

Ask children if they know what a muffin is. Show a muffin tin and the paper used to line the tin. Ask, "What do you think would happen if you give a moose a muffin?" Read the book *If You Give a Moose a Muffin*. After reading the book, give each child a muffin liner. See if the children know the colors. Have each one exchange the liner with someone else. Have the children identify the colors of the new liners. Play Hap Palmer's record *Learning Basic Skills Through Music, Volume I*, "Colors." Have children stand if they have a muffin liner of the color called.

Pancakes, Pancakes

Ask children what they had for breakfast. Bring out the activity using the pancakes with holes to identify food items. Ask how many children like pancakes. Say "Do you know how they are made? Let's read a book and see how pancakes are made." (Older children will be able to listen to the whole book, but younger children can be shown and told about the pictures at the beginning. At the point that Jack goes to the cellar to get the strawberry jam, begin reading on the next page.) After reading the book, review how a pancake is made. Then pretend that everyone is eating the pancake. Walk to the next area and pretend to be chewing the pancake.

The Fat Cat

Make the characters of the story, using the patterns on pages 216–222 prior to reading to the class.

Ask, "How many children have a cat at home? What does your cat eat?" The teacher says that he or she knows a cat, and it likes to eat very special food. Mention that it likes canned cat food, mice, and sometimes something very strange. Sometimes the cat is called a "fat cat." Ask, "Why do you think that the cat is called that? (*Write down the answers.*) Then tell the children that we are going to read a book titled *The Fat Cat*.

Read *The Fat Cat* to the children. Then have the children act out the story. The teacher is the cat with a large sheet around himself or herself. Pin at the neck in back. Have the children act as each character in the story, using the 6-inch (15 cm) paper plates with patterns on pages 216–222. Glue or tape a tongue depressor on each plate so that the child can hold it. As the teacher tells the story, each character crawls under the sheet so that it gets fatter and fatter. After the woodcutter opens the cat and all the children can get out from under the sheet, place a Band-Aid on the tummy of the sheet. This story can be repeated often on different days.

Activities for Food *(cont.)*

Group Activities *(cont.)*

Gregory, the Terrible Eater

Ask children if they have ever gone to a petting zoo and seen a goat. Say, "Goats will eat anything. If you ever have flowers on your purse, do not go near the goats. They will eat the flowers! But not all goats eat that way. One goat named Gregory ate the types of food we eat. And what do you think his parents thought of him? Let's read the book and find out."

Read *Gregory, the Terrible Eater.* After reading, talk about the difference between Gregory's food and his parents' food. Ask, "What was finally done so that everyone was happy with Gregory's food? Are there ever any foods that your family likes but you don't? What are they?" (*Write the children's answers down on paper.*) "What do you think you could do to make the family happy and you happy too?" (Try to have the children learn to work out eating problems.) Walk to the next area pretending to kick one of Gregory's empty cans.

Games

Lunch Bag Dump Relay

Put a beanbag in an open lunch bag. Divide the class into two groups. Have children line up one behind the other. Place the open lunch bag about three yards (3 meters) in front of each line. The first child runs to the bag, dumps out the beanbag, leaves it there, and runs back. The second child runs to the bag, puts the beanbag in the bag, and runs back. Continue in this pattern until all children have a turn.

Lunch Bag Throw

Place a beanbag in a lunch bag and twist the bag closed at the top. Stand near a taped line on the floor and try to toss the bag beyond the line. Younger children need to be near the line, but older children can be a distance away from the line.

Soup Pot Toss

Use a heavy soup pot and toss beanbags into the pot. If a lighter weight pot is used, toss plastic soup vegetables into it. If used as a class activity, have the children line up behind each other and take turns.

Follow the String

Have a piece of string placed over and under furniture. Have the children line up one behind the other. Follow the leader and follow the string. For older children, make the obstacle course more difficult.

Lazy Day

Have the class make a circle. They are to pretend it is a lazy day. First they yawn. Then they flop to the floor. They roll around as if in bed. Then they get up on hands and knees and pretend to sock the pretend pillow. Then they lie on their backs and look at the ceiling. The teacher then says "Time for breakfast!" Everyone gets up quickly and decides it is not a lazy day after all.

Activities for Food *(cont.)*

Games *(cont.)*

Muffin Liner Colors Game

Flatten paper muffin (cupcake) liners. Pass them out to the children. Make sure that all the colors are identified since there are pink and other lighter colors in the package.

Say, "If you give a moose a muffin,

He may want pink."

Have everyone with a muffin liner that is pink stand up. Continue saying the phrase and the different colors until everyone has a turn. Exchange liners and see if the children know the other colors.

Pancake Flip

Have a wide-open area for this activity. In order for the children to be pretend pancakes, have them line up one behind the other. Have them take turns, one at a time going from one side of the room to the other. Have them roll, crawl, somersault, slide on tummy, etc. Use a tumbling mat if it is available.

Kick the Can

This has been a popular activity in open fields, alleys, and streets. Now it can be adapted to the classroom by placing sponge cup covers over the cans. Have children kick the can to an open area in the classroom. Kick calmly indoors but vigorously outdoors. Just make sure that the area being kicked to is wide open!

Songs, Action Poems, and Fingerplay

"We All Made Soup Today"
(Tune: "This Is the Way We Wash Our Clothes")

We all made soup today, soup today,

Soup today, soup today.

We all made soup today, soup today.

Mmmmm, it was good!

Replace "soup" with *lunch, pasta, bread, muffins,* and *pancakes* or anything you pretended to make for the day. Make sure that you emphasize that in some cases, items of food were not made but were pretended to be made.

Activities for Food (cont.)

Songs, Action Poems, and Fingerplay (cont.)

"To Market, to Market"

(Mother Goose)

To market, to market, to buy a fat pig,

Home again, home again, jiggity jig.

To market, to market, to buy a fat hog,

Home again, home again, jiggety jog.

To market, to market, to buy a plum bun,

Home again, home again, market is done.

"Peanut Sitting on a Railroad Track"

(Traditional)

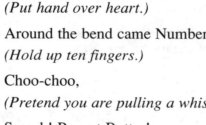

A peanut sat on a railroad track

His heart was all aflutter.

(Put hand over heart.)

Around the bend came Number Ten,

(Hold up ten fingers.)

Choo-choo,

(Pretend you are pulling a whistle.)

Smack! Peanut Butter!

(Clap hands together.)

Records, Cassettes, and CDs

Mr. Al and Stephen Fete. *Back to School.* Melody House, 1992.

Strickland, Willie and James Earle. *There's Music in Color.* Kimbo, 1976.

Patterns for Food

Bulletin Board for Food

Food Groups

1. Grain (bread, cereal, rice, pasta)
2. Vegetable
3. Fruit
4. Milk (milk, yogurt, cheese)
5. Meat and Bean (meat, poultry, fish, dry beans, eggs, and nuts)

Patterns for Food *(cont.)*

"Lunch Bag, Lunch Bag"

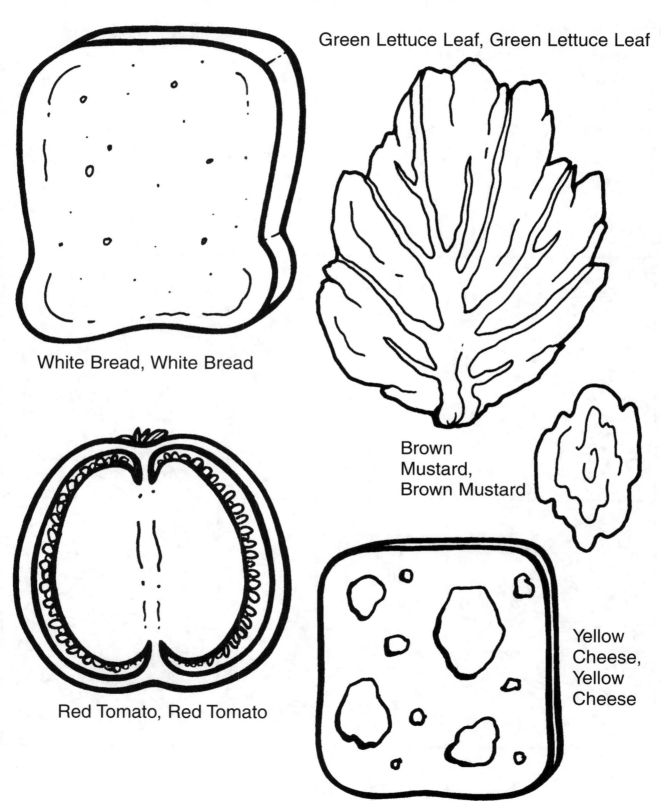

Green Lettuce Leaf, Green Lettuce Leaf

White Bread, White Bread

Brown
Mustard,
Brown Mustard

Red Tomato, Red Tomato

Yellow
Cheese,
Yellow
Cheese

Patterns for Food *(cont.)*

"Lunch Bag, Lunch Bag" *(cont.)*

Lunch-Making Mother

Alex, Alex

School Friends

Patterns for Food *(cont.)*

Note for Stone Soup

(Attach with safety pin or clip to child's top.)

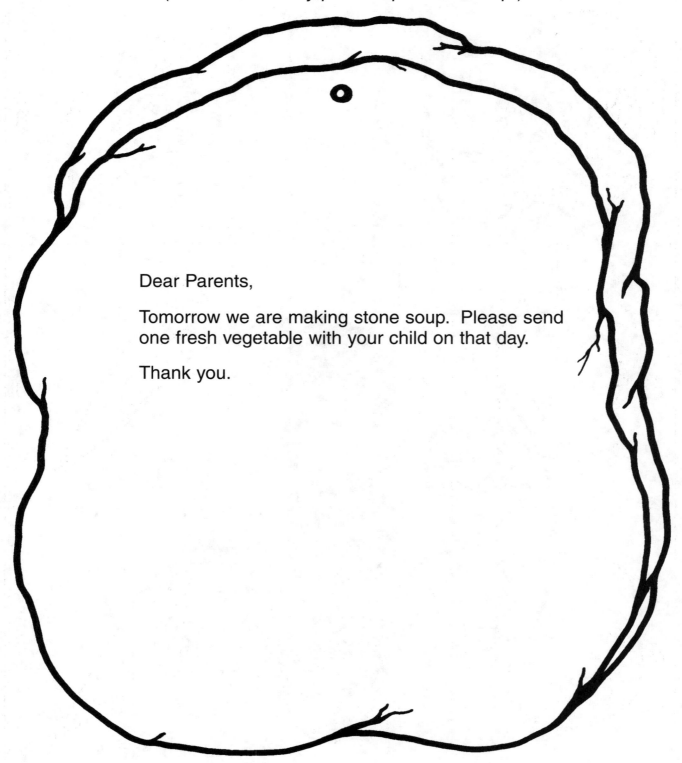

Dear Parents,

Tomorrow we are making stone soup. Please send one fresh vegetable with your child on that day.

Thank you.

Patterns for Food *(cont.)*

Vegetable Concentration Cards

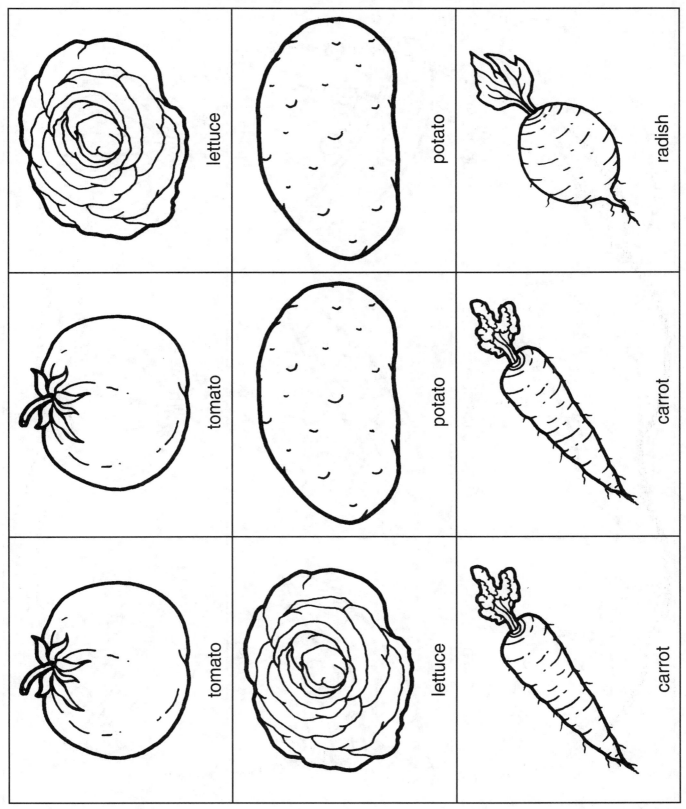

lettuce

potato

radish

tomato

potato

carrot

tomato

lettuce

carrot

Patterns for Food *(cont.)*

Vegetable Concentration Cards *(cont.)*

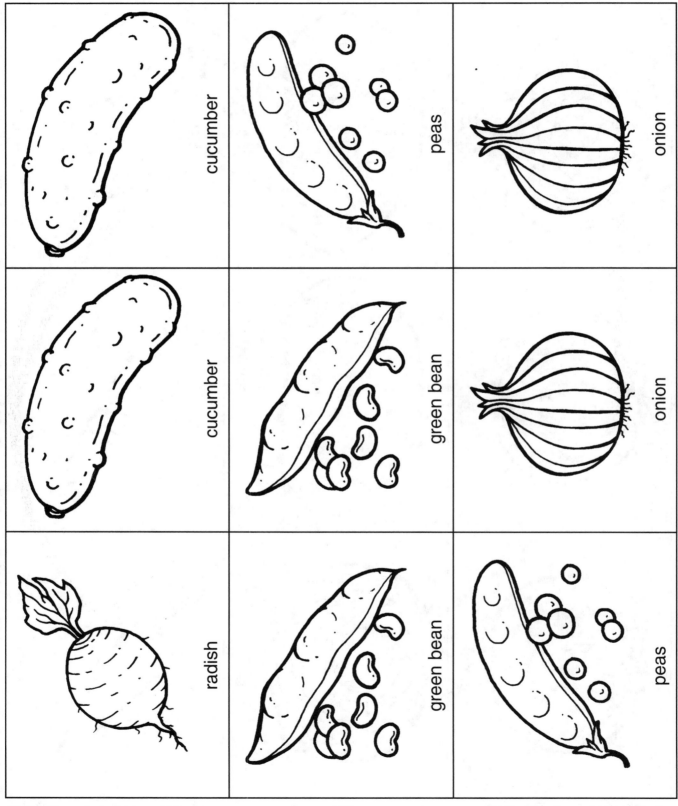

Patterns for Food *(cont.)*

Picture Identification with Pancakes

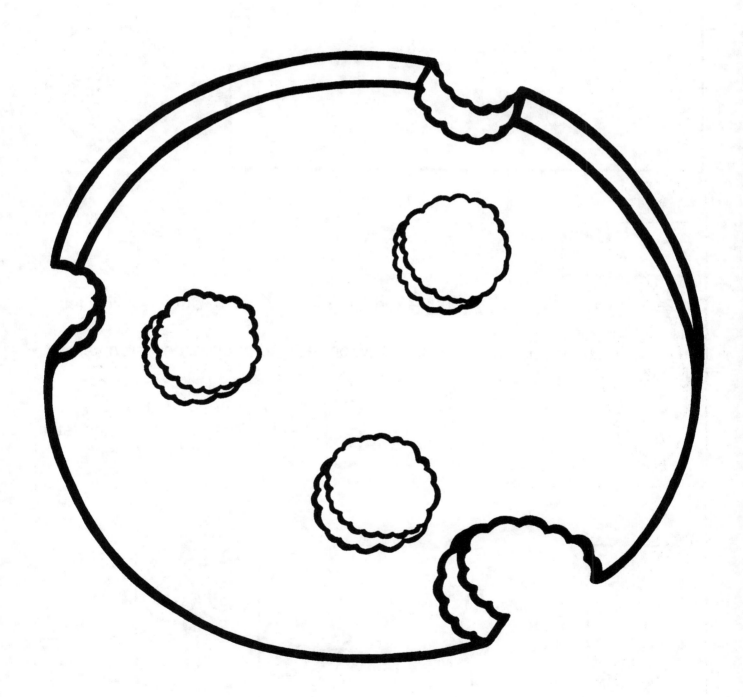

Patterns for Food *(cont.)*

Film Canister Puppet for Red Hen

body of red felt

top of head—red felt

Cut 2—red felt.

Glue together at top. Flare bottom apart and glue to top of hen.

Cut 2—red felt.

Cut 2—yellow felt.

Glue yellow on red and put jiggly eyes on yellow.

Cut from red and glue under beak. Glue at top only and let it hang loose under the beak.

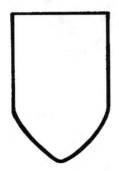

Cut 2—red felt.

Cut 1—Yellow felt.
Fold and glue at fold.

Patterns for Food *(cont.)*

Glove Puppet for Cat, Dog, and Mouse

jiggle eyes

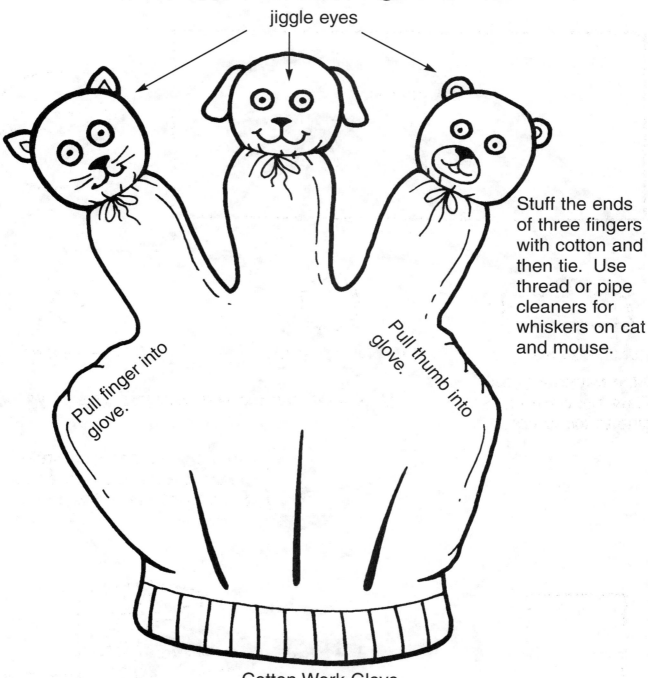

Stuff the ends of three fingers with cotton and then tie. Use thread or pipe cleaners for whiskers on cat and mouse.

Pull finger into glove.

Pull thumb into glove.

Cotton Work Glove

Cut animals' ears from felt to match the glove.

Patterns for Food *(cont.)*

Fat Cat Old Woman

Patterns for Food (cont.)

Fat Cat Skohottentot

Patterns for Food *(cont.)*

Fat Cat Skolinkenlot

218

Patterns for Food *(cont.)*

Fat Cat Five Birds

Patterns for Food *(cont.)*

Fat Cat Seven Girls Dancing

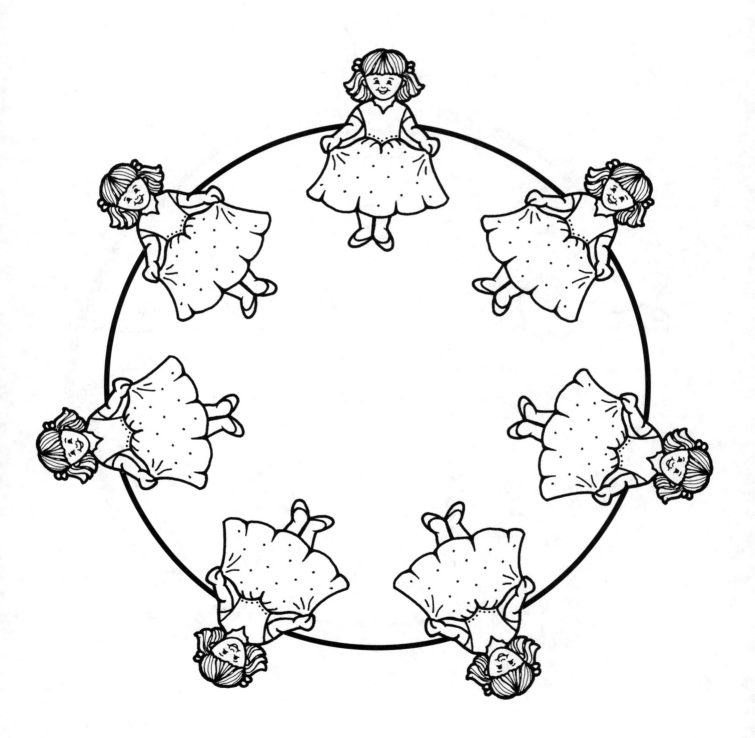

Patterns for Food *(cont.)*

Fat Cat Lady with Parasol

Patterns for Food *(cont.)*

Fat Cat Parson

Five Plans for Monkeys

	Day One	Day Two	Day Three	Day Four	Day Five
Individual Activities	• Nylon Hanger Faces • Bubble Wrap Rubbing • Stamp Print	• Make Binoculars • Kaleidoscope • Magnifying Glass	• Shaving Cream • Soap Bubbles • Dress-Up	• Body Silhouette • Mirror • Face on a Paper Plate	• Touch Box • Draw Around Fingers and Hand
Group Activities	*"Morgan Monkey"*	*Chimps Don't Wear Glasses*	*Curious George Goes to the Laundromat*	*Five Little Monkeys Jumping on the Bed*	*Hand, Hand, Finger, Thumb*
Games	Birds in a Circle	Nylon Hanger Toss	What Have You Got On?	Monkey, Monkey, Where's Your Banana?	Hot Banana
Songs, Action Poems, Fingerplay	• "Monkey Song" all week • "What Have You Got On?"	"Monkey Song" "The Elephant"	"Monkey Song"	"Monkey Song"	"Monkey Song"
Transitions	Hold head high and say "I'm proud to be me."	Wake up from a dream, walk slowly, and rub eyes.	Open and close clamp clothespin.	Jump up and down.	Parade with instruments.

Room Preparation for Monkeys

Bulletin Board

Use the patterns for the monkey and bananas in Introduction to School, pages 26 and 27. Cut out banana shapes from construction paper and put the names of children in your class on each banana. Put bananas around the monkey in the center of the bulletin board.

Puppet Stage

Cut finger monkey puppets from cardboard, using the patterns on page 231. The stage can be embellished with construction paper trees and flowers.

Doll Area

Sock and pattern for a sock monkey can be purchased at toy stores, educational supplies, and some commercial stores. Or you may also find stuffed monkeys at toy stores.

Dress-Up Area

Make sure that there are many hats in the area. Washable hats can be obtained from resale shops.

Suggested Literature for Monkeys

Christelow, Eileen. *Five Little Monkeys Jumping on the Bed.* Clarion Books, 1989.

Numeroff, Laura Joffe. *Chimps Don't Wear Glasses.* Simon & Schuster, 1995.

Perkins, Al. *Hand, Hand, Finger, Thumb.* Random House, 1969.

Rey, Margaret and H. A. *Curious George Goes to the Laundromat.* Houghton Mifflin, 1987.

Materials

- nylons
- scissors
- brayers
- toilet paper tubes
- shaving cream
- bubble hoop
- butcher paper
- paper plates
- wire hangers
- school glue
- small block of wood
- kaleidoscope
- colored construction paper
- touch box with scraps of textures
- mirror
- heavy cotton thread or yarn
- scrap construction paper
- bubble wrap
- meat trays
- magnifying glass
- liquid dish soap
- paper dolls
- manila paper
- tempera paint

Activities for Monkeys

Individual Activities

Nylon Hanger Faces *(Morgan Monkey)*

Pull wire hangers so they form an oval shape. Curl the handle to make a circle. Stretch old nylons over the thin hanger and secure with a rubber band. Have scrap construction paper out with scissors and school glue. Have the children glue on eyes, noses, and mouths to form faces.

Bubble Wrap Rubbing *(Morgan Monkey)*

Pretend that all the puffs on the bubble wrap are cheeks. Have children touch their cheeks. Say, "We just wouldn't want to pop them!" Roll a brayer in tempera paint which is in a flat pan and then roll it over the puffy packing. Place a piece of plain paper over the bubble wrap and then rub with hands. Be careful not to pop the bubble wrap! Pull off the print and let dry.

Stamp Print *(Morgan Monkey)*

Use a block of wood 4" by 4" (10 cm x 10 cm). Using Styrofoam meat trays, cut out outlines of animals or people, using the patterns on pages 232–234. Glue the Styrofoam patterns onto the bottom of the four-inch square blocks. Show the children how to stamp in the stamp pad and then on paper. They may want to draw more on the paper around the stamp print.

Make Binoculars *(Chimps Don't Wear Glasses)*

Glue or tape two toilet paper tubes together next to each other. Make a boat with hollow blocks and use the binoculars to "sight items on land."

Kaleidoscope *(Chimps Don't Wear Glasses)*

Look through a kaleidoscope. Tell friends what you see.

Magnifying Glass *(Chimps Don't Wear Glasses)*

Go around the room and look at things up close. If possible, have a teacher nearby who can write down the comments. Read the comments back to the class and keep them in a journal for the class.

Shaving Cream *(Curious George Goes to the Laundromat)*

If you can find the old type of Ivory Snow laundry soap powder, whip up some with a little water. The new soap powder will not whip, so you may have to pretend that you are using a laundry soap powder by substituting shaving cream. Place the shaving cream on a cafeteria tray or large Styrofoam meat tray and have the children finger-paint with it. Use sides of hands, palms of hands, fingers, elbows, fingernails, etc. After the design is made, place a piece of blue construction paper over the picture. Rub with hands to pick up the imprint. Let it dry before sending it home.

Activities for Monkeys *(cont.)*

Individual Activities *(cont.)*

Liquid Soap Bubbles *(Curious George Goes to the Laundromat)*

Mix a little water with liquid soap. Dip a bubble hoop in the mixture, blow, and watch the bubbles.

Dress-Up *(Curious George Goes to the Laundromat)*

Make sure there are plenty of dress-up clothes in the housekeeping area.

Body Silhouette *(Five Little Monkeys)*

Place butcher paper on the floor. Have one child lie down on the paper. Have another draw around the first person. Then have child name the arms, legs, etc., and finally draw clothes on the silhouette.

Mirror *(Five Little Monkeys)*

Have two children look in a mirror and point to parts of their faces. Then each should draw the other's face on a sheet of manila paper.

Face on a Paper Plate *(Five Little Monkeys)*

Use a paper plate to draw a face. Use cotton or yarn to glue on for hair.

Touch Box *(Hand, Hand, Finger, Thumb)*

Use a cardboard box with two holes cut out so that the hands can reach inside to touch objects. Place a piece of cardboard between the two sides to keep the hands apart. Place items with different types of textures in the box, such as sandpaper, wallpaper, fabric types, buttons, etc. Have the same items in both sides. The child reaches in and tries to find matching items from both sides.

Draw Around Fingers and Hand *(Hand, Hand, Finger, Thumb)*

Place the non-writing hand on a piece of manila paper. Draw around it with the writing hand. Draw on rings and bracelets. Then add scenes around the hand.

Group Activities

"Morgan Monkey"

Prior to telling the story, have an overhead projector set up and transparencies made, using patterns on pages 235–239. Each one is designed to overlap the other. However, they are put on one by one and not joined together until the end of the story.

Have a puppet or doll monkey for the children to look at. Say, "What kind of face does he have? What is his nose like, and what about his ears? Listen to a special story about Morgan Monkey."

Activities for Monkeys *(cont.)*

Group Activities *(cont.)*

"Morgan Monkey" *(cont.)*

Morgan Monkey lived in a warm forest and loved to swing from branch to branch. He had many friends and would swing around every day to visit them. One day some strangers went riding through the forest on Danny Donkey's back. Danny Donkey was Morgan's friend, but Morgan hid so they wouldn't find him.

The next day he swung from tree to tree to see his friends when he spotted something in the grass. He picked it up and said, "My, this animal's face is made of two circles!" *(Put up the transparency of two circles on the overhead projector. Then take it off.)*

So he swung to his friend Arnold Alligator, who lived in the water, and said, "Look what I found in the forest grass." His friend looked at it and said "My, this animal has a big smile!" *(Put up the transparency of a smile and take it off the projector.)*

"What kind of thing did I find?" said Morgan Monkey to himself. So he want to his friend Danny Donkey, who carried the people on his back as they traveled through the forest. He said, "Look what I found in the forest grass." His friend looked and said, "My, this animal has lovely big ears!" *(Put up the transparency of ears and take it off the projector.)*

Morgan Monkey said to himself, "What kind of thing did I find?" So he went to his favorite big animal friend named Leo Lion and said, "Look what I found in the forest grass." His friend looked at it and said, "My, this animal has a big, beautiful mane!" *(Put up the transparency of a mane on a lion and take it off the projector.)*

Morgan Monkey said to himself, "What kind of thing did I find?" Then he walked to an opening in the forest and went to his friend Carla Cow, who gave milk to her children. He said, "Look what I found in the forest grass." His friend looked and said, "My, but she has beautiful eyes!" *(Put up the transparency of eyes and then remove it from the projector.)*

Morgan Monkey said, "My, what kind of thing did I find?" So that day as the sun set, he gathered all his friends together. Again he said, "Look what I found in the forest grass." All his friends looked at once, and this is what they saw. *(Put all the transparencies on top of each other on the overhead projector.)* "ECCCCCHHHHH," they all said. And they all ran home. So Morgan Monkey buried the thing, and no one ever talked about it again.

Ask the children if they can figure out what Morgan Monkey found in the forest. It was a mirror! Take out a mirror and have each child look in the mirror and say what each likes about his or her face. The teacher may want to write down the positive things that the children say about their faces. If children are hesitant, say, "Your eyes are so blue!" or "Your teeth are so white!"

Move to the next area, holding heads up high and saying, "I'm proud to be me!"

Activities for Monkeys (cont.)

Group Activities (cont.)

Chimps Don't Wear Glasses

Show a pair of glasses. Put them on and ask the children if they know anyone who wears glasses. Do animals wear glasses? Why or why not?

Read *Chimps Don't Wear Glasses*. Read as far as "And you won't see a puppet show put on by pugs."

Say the following rhyme:

> "Now just close your eyes and draw with your mind.
> You might be surprised at what you will find."

Have all children close their eyes and dream up their own characters doing strange things. While their eyes are closed, write down on a large sheet of paper what they say they are imagining. Then have them open their eyes and read what has been written. Point to the words so that the children understand that reading goes from left to right and top to bottom. Then continue reading to the end of the story. Go back to what the children imagined. See if anyone thought up the same thing as the book. After class, write the children's ideas into story form and keep with the class journal.

Then have all children lie down on the floor and look up to the ceiling. Pretend there are things on the ceiling. Ask what each child sees. Some children hesitate to use their imaginations but can be stimulated by peers.

To move to the next area, have the children pretend they are waking up from a dream, rub their eyes, and slowly walk to the next area.

Curious George Goes to the Laundromat

Have a bowl of soap suds and start washing a piece of doll clothes. Say, "This is a lot of work. What could I do to make it easier?" If someone tells you to use a washing machine, ask that person, "Where can we find one?" If no one mentions a laundromat, explain that sometimes the washing machine at home breaks down or sometimes we live in an apartment where there are no washing machines, and then we have to go to a laundromat. Curious George went to the laundromat, and this is his story.

Read *Curious George Goes to the Laundromat*. After the story, explain that Mrs. Goodman was so happy that George had hung the baseball uniforms on the tree. Say, "We need lots of help to hang up the doll clothes on the line." Give each child a piece of wet doll clothes, blanket, etc. If the paint-drying rack is free of paint, have children hang up the clothes on it. Otherwise, use a low line stretched between two stationary objects. Use clamp clothespins to strengthen the children's pincer muscles in their hands.

Give each child a clamp clothespin. Walk to the next areas, using the pincer muscles to open and close the clothespin.

Activities for Monkeys *(cont.)*

Group Activities *(cont.)*

Five Little Monkeys Jumping on the Bed

Do fingerplay of five little monkeys using words from the book. Then show pictures that go with it.

Read *Five Little Monkeys Jumping on the Bed* and show pictures. When finished reading the book, ask, "What was the surprise ending? How would you like the story to end?"

Hand, Hand, Finger, Thumb

The teacher pretends to sneeze and then runs for a tissue. Talk about how important our hands are to use tissue and prevent germs from spreading. Talk about the pictures that children drew around their hands. Say "But there are other things we can do with our hands and fingers. Listen as this story is read and see if you can get some ideas."

Read *Hand, Hand, Finger, Thumb.* After reading the story, ask the children what the monkeys did with their hands. If they say "Play drums," explain that we are going to play the drums. Add, "However, we have to practice before using drums." Have the children slap their thighs as you slap your thighs. Then clap your hands and have the children clap their hands. Then have them do both slap and clap alternately. This is called "patterning" and is a good foundation for math. Then sing simple songs and pattern to the rhythm. Then give the children drums and instruments and parade around the room. Use this to transition to the next area.

Games

Birds in a Circle (*Easy Does It* by Hap Palmer)

"What Have You Got On?"
(Sing to the tune of Brother John/Frere Jacques.")
What have you go on, what have you got on?
Tennis shoes, tennis shoes?
All with tennis shoes on, all with tennis shoes on,
Please stand up, please stand up.

Continue with *fancy dress, little boy's shirt, colored socks, knitted sweater,* etc.

Nylon Hanger Toss

Pull a thin wire hanger into a long shape. Pull a nylon stocking over it and attach with a rubber band. Bend the hanger hook to make a handle. Use it to toss a yarn ball, Ping-Pong ball, or whiffle ball.

Monkey, Monkey, Where's Your Banana?

Same as "Doggie, Doggie, Where's Your Bone" in Introduction to School on page 18.

Hot Banana

Same as "Hot Potato" in Introduction to School on page 18.

Activities for Monkeys (cont.)

Songs, Action Poems, Fingerplay

"The Elephant"

See *Learning Basic Skills Through Music, Volume I* by Hap Palmer.

"Monkey Song"

(Traditional)

Little monkey likes to do,

Just the same as you and you.

(Suit actions to words.)

When you sit up very tall,

Monkey sits up very tall.

When you try to touch your toes,

Monkey tries to touch his toes.

When you try to reach up high,

Monkey tries to reach up high.

When you try to wiggle your nose,

Monkey tries to wiggle his nose.

When you jump up in the air,

Monkey jumps up in the air.

When you sit down in a chair.

Monkey sits down in a chair.

(Add your own variations.)

Records, Cassettes, and CDs

Palmer, Hap. *Easy Does It.* Educational Activities, Inc., 1977.

Palmer, Hap. *Learning Through Music, Volume I.* Educational Activities, Inc., 1971.

Patterns for Monkeys

Puppet for Puppet Stage

Cut out.

Cut out.

Insert fingers in holes to make legs.

Patterns for Monkeys *(cont.)*

Patterns for Stamp Print

(to be cut from Styrofoam meat trays for 4" [10 cm] squares of wood)

Monkey

Donkey

Patterns for Monkeys *(cont.)*

Patterns for Stamp Print *(cont.)*

(to be cut from Styrofoam meat trays for 4" [10 cm] squares of wood)

Lion

Cow

Patterns for Monkeys *(cont.)*

Patterns for Stamp Print *(cont.)*

(to be cut from Styrofoam meat trays for 4" [10 cm] squares of wood)

Alligator

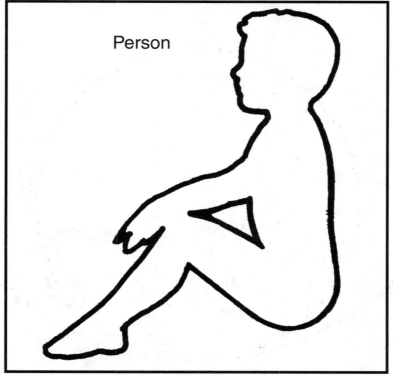

Person

Patterns for Monkeys *(cont.)*

Two-Circle Pattern for Morgan Monkey

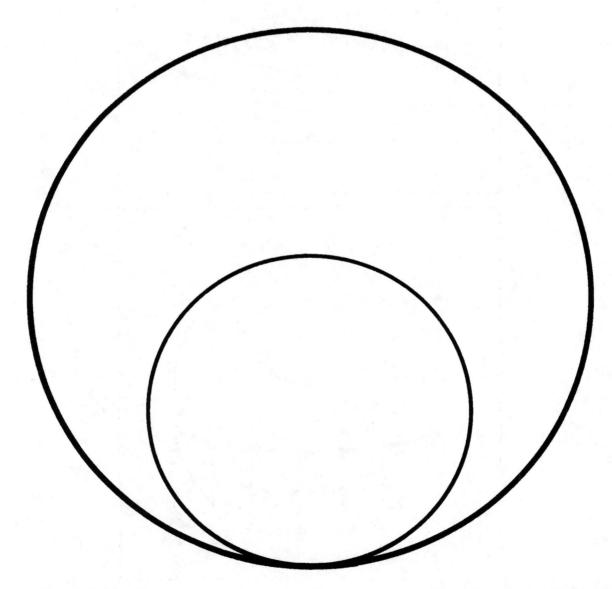

Patterns for Monkeys *(cont.)*

Smile Pattern for Arnold Alligator

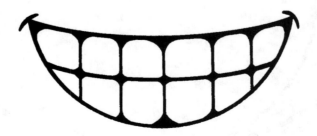

Patterns for Monkeys *(cont.)*

Ear Pattern for Danny Donkey

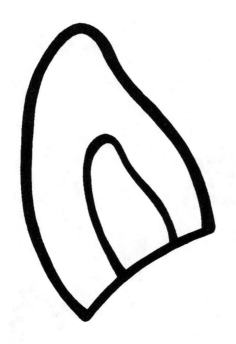 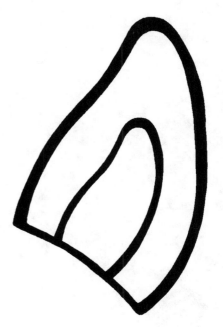

Patterns for Monkeys *(cont.)*

Mane Pattern for Leo Lion

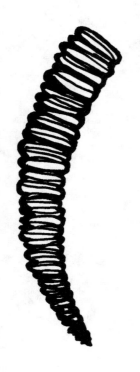

Patterns for Monkeys *(cont.)*

Eye Pattern for Carla Cow

Six Plans for Plants

	Day One	Day Two	Day Three	Day Four	Day Five	Day Six
Individual Activities	• Eggshell Grass • Grow Seeds • Clean Mud • Adopt a Tree	• Paint with Pine Branch • Paint with Flowers	• Plant Potato in Water • Potato Prints • Forsythia	• Seed Collage • Carrot Tops • Celery Tops • Scrub Vegetables	• Many-Colored Leaf • Leaf Press • A Tree Is Nice	• Muffin Liner Flowers • Flower Rubbing • Tissue Paper Tint
Group Activities	Rock and Sock Walk	Growing Things Hunt	*The Tiny Seed*	*The Carrot Seed*	*The Giving Tree*	*The Gunnywolf*
Games	Lid Toss	Pretend to Be a Seed	Pretend to Be a Flower	Pretend to Be Wheat	Falling Acorns	Basketball Hoop
Songs, Action Poems, Fingerplay	(Select one and use all week.)					
Transitions			Pretend to be a growing seed.	Pretend to dig in a garden.	Pretend to be a falling apple.	Sing "ABC Song."

Room Preparation for Plants

Bulletin Board

The pattern for the bulletin board background is on page 250. Use an overhead projector to enlarge the cloud, sun, and wind. Use the flower-rubbing pattern on page 112 in the color unit for the names of children in the class.

Mobile

Hang a stick from the ceiling so that it is horizontal with the floor. Hang leaves, pine cones, small pine branches, and other found items from the branch.

Puppet Stage

Make the puppet stage into a fruit and vegetable stand. Use vinyl or plastic fruits and vegetables, cash register, coins, bags, and shopping cart.

Housekeeping Area

Have garden gloves, sprinkling cans, shovels, shade hats, and boots.

Science

Put out plants, bulbs, seeds, and a magnifying glass. Start an amaryllis bulb. When it starts to grow, place a paper ruler behind it. Measure the growth daily by placing the date and a mark showing its height on that particular day.

Famous Paintings

- Vincent Van Gogh
  Flower Picture
  Irises (Place near an indoor iris plant.)
  Cypresses
- Edouard Manet
  The Manet Family in Their Garden

- Claude Monet
  Water Lillies
  Antibes
- Thomas Anshutz
  The Way They Live

Suggested Literature for Plants

Carle, Eric. *The Tiny Seed*. Simon & Schuster, 1987.
Delaney, A. *The Gunnywolf*. Harper & Row, Publishers, 1988.
Krauss, Ruth. *The Carrot Seed*. Harper & Row, 1945.
Silverstein, Shel. *The Giving Tree*. Harper & Row, Publishers, 1964.

Materials

- egg shells
- empty egg carton
- lima bean seeds
- tempera paint
- manila paper
- carrots
- muffin liners

- grass seed
- plastic bags
- pine branches
- newsprint
- potatoes
- celery
- toweling

- play dough
- jar
- dirt
- sharp knife
- butcher paper
- toothpicks

- vegetable scrub brushes
- yellow crepe paper
- heads of flowers
- many types of beans
- sheets of cardboard
- food coloring

Activities for Plants

Individual Activities

Clean Mud (must be mixed three days before intended use)

This activity will require 12 rolls of white toilet paper, lots of water, four small bars or three large bars of Ivory soap (grated), and three cups borax powder. Unroll the toilet paper in a large water tub and cover with water. Let it set for several days and then squeeze out the water. Add grated Ivory soap and borax. Keep kneading the borax and the soap into the toilet paper. The more the children play with the mixture, the more everything gets blended. Cover each night and the clean mud will last for weeks! It is debatable whether the children or the teachers enjoy this more.

Adopt a Tree

Adopt a special tree for the class. If there are enough trees nearby, have each child adopt a tree. Identify the tree, watch it grow, and give it hugs. Observe the changes and keep a journal of the changes. If it is a maple tree, have the children split the seed pods in the spring so each person can put one on the nose. You now have a "polly nose"!

Eggshell Grass

Save clean eggshell halves. Have the children fill the eggshells with dirt. Place grass seed on the top and sprinkle more dirt on top. Place in an empty egg carton and then place the carton in a sunny area and watch the seeds grow. When the seeds have grown to about one-half inch (1.75 cm), have the children draw faces on the eggshells so that each one looks like a person with green hair.

Grow Seeds

Explain that most plants come from seeds. Have each child place a seed in a small zip-lock bag. Moisten a paper towel that has been folded into a square. Put that in the bag. Then place a seed on top of the wet toweling. Make sure that each child has his or her name on the bag. Put in a dark space. For the next few days, have each child get his or her seed from the dark space and place it in a pocket. The body warmth will cause the bean to sprout more quickly. When the child goes home, put the seeds back in the dark spot. If lima bean seeds are used, they should sprout in about three or four days. If seeds show signs of sprouting, keep them in the dark place. Carrying them in a pocket may cause the sprouts to break off. When the seed has sprouted, show the children where the plant will grow and where the roots will grow. Have them take these home to show the family.

Paint with Pine Branch

Use a small pine branch in place of a brush when painting at the easel or table.

Paint with Flowers

Use the head of a flower for the brush and the stem for the handle. Dip in paint and brush along the paper or stamp the shape onto the paper.

Activities for Plants *(cont.)*

Individual Activities *(cont.)*

Plant Potato in Water

Place toothpicks in the side of a potato. Set in a jar so that the toothpicks rest on the side of the jar edge and the bottom of the potato rests in the water. Make sure that some eyes of the potato are in water and some are above it. Also, make sure the potato is natural, not treated with preservatives.

Potato Prints

Cut a potato in half horizontally. In the now-revealed inner potato, mark off a design with a sharp knife. Cut away the outer edge from the design. Simple shapes (triangles, squares, etc.) work well for a beginner's design. Place a thin layer of sponge in a pie tin with tempera paint. Have the children stamp on the sponge with the potato and then press the potato on a piece of paper to transfer the design.

Forsythia

Have the children draw several lines on their paper to form the branches of the forsythia bush. Cut 1" x 1.5" (2.5 cm x 3.8 cm) pieces of yellow crepe paper ahead of time. Have the children twist the long side of the paper strips in the middle. Then glue them onto the drawn branch.

Seed Collage

On a heavy sheet of paper, glue many colors, sizes, and types of beans and seeds to form a pattern.

Carrot Tops

Cut a carrot about one-half inch (1.25 cm) below the greens. Place in a shallow bowl of water and watch for growth.

Celery Tops

Cut about one-half inch (1.25 cm) away from the bottom of celery stalks. Place the stalks in different glass jars. Add red, blue, and orange food coloring to separate jars. Watch the celery stalks drink the colored water and turn the leaves that color. It may take more than an hour to do this.

Scrub Vegetables

Have water in the housekeeping area along with kitchen scrub brushes. Have the children scrub carrots, celery, potatoes, radishes, and anything else available in your area. These can then be cut up and used for a tasting party at the end of a story.

Many-Colored Leaf

Tack a many-colored leaf to the easel. Place the same colors in the tempera paint rack with the easel. Make sure that the lighter colors go from right to left for the right-handed child and the opposite for the left-handed child. Have the children blend the colors, paint a leaf, stroke the colors next to each other, or whatever they want to do. Talk about the many colors of the leaf.

Activities for Plants *(cont.)*

Individual Activities *(cont.)*

Leaf Press

Roll out play dough on a table. Press leaves or pine branches into the play dough to get a print.

A Tree Is Nice

On a large piece of butcher paper, draw two lines to form the trunk of a tree. Have available pans of red, yellow, green, and brown tempera paint. Have the children place their hands in paint and put them on the top part of the trunk. When dry, place in a spot where all the parents can see!

Muffin Liner Flowers

Use muffin liners to form the heads of flowers. Glue the bottom of the liner onto paper and make stems, leaves, bugs, worms, ground, and sky with crayons or markers.

Flower Rubbing

Use the pattern for flower rubbing on page 112. Roll tempera paint over the glue pattern. Place paper over the pattern and press with the hands to pick up the print.

Tissue Paper Tint

Place colored tissue paper on a sheet of manila paper. Dribble water from a meat baster on the tissue paper. Allow it to stand for a few minutes and then remove the tissue paper. Allow to dry. When the manila paper is dry, have the children draw around the colors to make flowers. Cut out the flowers.

Group Activities

Rock and Sock Walk

Gather the children together and explain that they are going outside. When outside, cover one spot on the grass with a rock. Explain that every day they are going to check to see if the rock is still there. They are also going to keep a journal of what was done and what the weather was like. In one week, they are going to take off the rock and notice the color of the grass. All will be recorded in the journal. Then they will leave the rock off the spot and keep track of the number of days needed to restore the grass.

The teacher then puts an old sock over his or her shoe. Walk around with the children in mud, water, or anyplace where seeds can be picked up. Take the sock off and return to the building. Place the sock in soil and cover it with more soil and water. Watch to see if the sock sprouts plants.

Growing Things Hunt

Go for a walk and look for twigs, leaves with veins, and needles from evergreens. Bring them back to the room and look through a magnifying glass to see things up close. What is the difference between needles and leaves with veins? Make a rubbing of the leaves or needles by placing them on a solid surface. Place a piece of typing paper over them and use a pencil to rub over the leaves and needles. The key to success in this is to keep the leaves firmly in place. Sometimes a loop of tape placed on the bottom of the leaf makes it stick to the table.

Activities for Plants *(cont.)*

Group Activities *(cont.)*

The Tiny Seed

Show the children a milkweed pod, sunflower, or any plant that has seeds on it. Milkweed pods can be found in some fields in the fall. Sunflower seed heads can be purchased anytime of the year in commercial plant nurseries. Show how the seeds come out of the pod. Ask, "What do you think happens to the seeds if they are left out in the field?" *(Write down the answers.)* "We are going to read a book about the adventures of a tiny seed."

Read *The Tiny Seed*. After reading the book, go through it again and talk about the following things:

- If too close to the sun, seeds are burned up.
- If a seed gets on ice, it cannot grow.
- If a seed falls into the ocean, it drowns and never grows.
- If a seed lands in the desert, it does not grow.
- Sometimes birds and mice eat the seeds.
- Once a seed starts to grow, it could be stepped on or picked.

Ask, "What happened to the tiny seed? Do you think it is easy to be a seed? Why?"

Have students pretend to be seeds. Act out a seed that gets burning hot *(sweating)*, gets icy cold *(shivering)*, lands in the ocean *(swimming strokes)*, waves away birds *(waving hands)*, and avoids being stepped on *(crouching down)*.

Walk to the next area, pretending to be a growing seed.

The Carrot Seed

Place a soup kettle up high. In the kettle have a carrot with a string attached and a package of carrot seeds with a string attached. Have the strings draped over the edge of the kettle. Ask the children if they might know what is attached to the strings. Have them guess. Then have them pull the string that is attached to the package of seeds. Ask children if they have ever planted carrot seeds. Say, "We are going to read a story about a little boy who plants a carrot seed."

Read *The Carrot Seed*. After reading the story, have the children pull the string attached to the carrot. Then have them look at the picture at the end of the book. The little boy's carrot was wheeled away in a large wheelbarrow. Ask, "Do you think that it was the same size as the carrot just pulled out of the soup kettle? Which was bigger and which was smaller?"

The boy worked hard to get the carrot seed to grow. Review what he did first, second, and so on. Use the sequence cards patterns on page 251. See if the children can put in sequence the growing of a carrot. Mix the up cards and see if they can do it again.

Walk to the next area, pretending to dig in the garden.

Activities for Plants *(cont.)*

Group Activities *(cont.)*

The Giving Tree

Ask the children if they have ever given a friend anything special. Talk about what was given. Say, "Today we spent time looking for trees, leaves, and pine branches. Did you ever think of giving a tree a hug? Today we are going to read a story about a tree that gave things to a boy."

Prepare glue rubbings 24 hours earlier. The patterns are on pages 252–256. Place these in a spiral-bound art pad and cover each finished page with newsprint taped to the top. As each section is rubbed, flip to the next page.

Read *The Giving Tree.*

- After reading *"And the boy loved the tree . . . very much. And the tree was happy,"* rub the heart pattern with chalk.
- After reading *"Take my apples, Boy, and sell them in the city. Then you will have money and you will be happy,"* rub the pattern of the apple.
- After reading *"The forest is my house, but you may cut off my branches and build a house. Then you will be happy,"* rub the pattern of the branch.
- After reading *"Cut down my trunk and make a boat, said the tree. Then you can sail away . . . and be happy,"* rub the pattern for the trunk.
- After reading *"Come, Boy, sit down. Sit and rest,"* rub the pattern for the stump.
- Continue to read: *"And the boy did. And the tree was happy."*

Say, "Trees can give up things, and you can give things to your friends, but more important than giving things is how you act. Give hugs, winks, help pick up other's toys, etc. Can you give some other ideas?"

This story is the type that can be used with small youngsters, middle-grade students, teenagers, and even adults. Note that the tree is happy at the beginning and at the end. During the story the tree gave of itself tirelessly to make the boy happy.

Play a descending scale on a piano or autoharp or hum and have the children pretend they are apples falling from the tree. Then have them walk to the next area, each pretending to be a falling apple.

Activities for Plants *(cont.)*

Group Activities *(cont.)*

The Gunnywolf

How many of the children like flowers? Write down the names and then the flowers that they like. The teacher can mention the flower that he or she likes. Say, "Sometimes we like to pick the flowers from our garden, and sometimes we like to buy the flowers from the store. We are going to hear a story about a little girl who wanted to have flowers for her father and went to the woods to pick them. Let's find out what happened to her during her walk."

Read *The Gunnywolf*. After reading, ask who she met during her walk. "Was the wolf a bad wolf? Really, the wolf just wanted to hear the little girl sing 'ABC.'" Practice singing the song with the class. Then divide the class into a group of girls and a group of boys. Have the boys sit in a line perpendicular from the teacher and the line of girls facing the boys. The boys will play the good wolf, and the girls will act out the part of the little girl. The teacher then can either re-read the story or tell the story. When the "ABC" song occurs in the story, have the girls say, "pit-a-pat, pit-a-pat." When the wolf wakes up, have the boys say, "Un-ka-cha, un-ka-cha" as the wolf runs to find the little girl. Both the pit-a-pat and the un-ka-cha sequence work well with the slap-thighs-and-clap-hands patterning.

Games

Falling Acorns

Pretend to fall like an acorn from the tree. Be still on the floor because it is winter. Slowly sprout and then grow into a tree. Stretch as high as possible to reach the sky.

Walter the Walzing Worm by Hap Palmer

"A Tree Fell Down" from *Easy Does It* by Hap Palmer

Pretending

- Stoop down low and pretend to be a seed. Pretend to grow and stretch to the ceiling.
- Pretend to be a flower and pretend that the wind is blowing. Sway from side to side.
- Pretend to be wheat that has just been cut down by a combine. Fall to the floor.

Lid Toss

Get plastic lids from coffee cans or larger cans. In a wide-open outdoor space, toss the plastic lids. Hold them flat with thumb and fingers and flip to open space. Try to make them move flat and sail like Frisbees.

Basketball Hoop

For a basketball hoop, tie a cardboard box to a tree. Instead of a basketball, use a sock which is filled with cotton and knotted on the end. Tie the box at a height appropriate for the children.

Activities for Plants (cont.)

Songs, Action Poems, and Fingerplay

"Do You Know This Little Tree?"

(Tune: "Do You Know the Muffin Man?")

Do you know this little tree, little tree, little tree?

Do you know this little tree, growing from a seed?
(Put hands low to the ground.)

Do you know the gentle rain, gentle rain, gentle rain?

Do you know the gentle rain, nurturing the tree?
(Flutter fingers in the air.)

Do you know the warm bright sun, warm bright sun, warm bright sun?

Do you know the warm bright sun, helping grow the tree?
(Form arms in a circle.)

Do you know the little boy, little boy, little boy?

Do you know the little boy, watching the growing tree?
(Hold hands waist high.)

Do you know the grown-up man, grown-up man, grown-up man?

Do you know the grown-up man, who remembers the little tree?
(Hold hands high up in the air.)

"Baby Seed"

(Traditional)

In a milkweed cradle
(Form a cradle with both hands.)

Snug and warm,

Baby seeds are hiding

Safe from harm.

Open wide the cradle,
(Open hands.)

Hold it high.
(Hold hands up high.)

Come, Mr. Wind,

Help them fly.
(Wave arm above head.)

"I Dig, Dig, Dig"

(Traditional)

I dig, dig, dig,
(Pretend to dig.)

And I plant some seeds.
(Stoop down and pretend to plant seeds.)

I rake, rake, rake,
(Pretend to rake.)

And I pull some weeds.
(Pretend to pull up weeds.)

I wait and watch
(Stoop down and pretend to watch plants grow.)

and soon I know
(Place hands on hips and nod head up and down.)

My garden sprouts
(Raise hands and pretend that plants are growing.)

And starts to grow.

Activities for Plants *(cont.)*

Songs, Action Poems, and Fingerplay *(cont.)*

"Relaxing Flowers"
(Traditional)

Five little flowers,
(Hold up five fingers.)
Standing in the sun;
See their heads nodding,
(Make fingers nod.)
Bowing, one by one.
(Make fingers bow.)
Down, down, down,
(Raise hands, wiggle fingers, and lower arms to act out falling rain.)
Falls the gentle rain,
And the five little flowers
Lift up their heads again!
(Hold up five fingers.)

"Mistress Mary"
(Nursery Rhyme)

Mistress Mary, quite contrary,
How does your garden grow?
With silver bells and cockle shells
And pretty maids all in a row.

Records, Cassettes, and CDs

Palmer, Hap. *Easy Does It.* "A Tree Fell Down." Educational Activities, Inc., 1977.

Patterns for Plants

Bulletin Board for Plants (Background)

Patterns for Plants *(cont.)*

Sequence Cards for *The Carrot Seed*

Patterns for Plants *(cont.)*

Heart Shape for *The Giving Tree*

Tree
+
Me

Patterns for Plants *(cont.)*

Apple Shape for *The Giving Tree*

Patterns for Plants *(cont.)*

Branches Shape for *The Giving Tree*

Patterns for Plants *(cont.)*

Trunk Shape for *The Giving Tree*

Tree
+
Me

Patterns for Plants *(cont.)*

Stump Shape for *The Giving Tree*

Five Plans for Shapes

	Day One ■	Day Two ▲	Day Three ●	Day Four ▭	Day Five ◆
Individual Activities	• Stencils and Easel Paper (cut into square shapes) • Shape Cookies • Overhead Projector Shapes	• Stencils and Easel Paper (cut into triangle shapes) • Parquetry Set • Q-Tip Painting	• Stencils and Easel Paper (cut into circle shapes) • Empty Can Printing • Velcro Match	• Stencils and Easel Paper (cut into rectangle shapes) • Button Sort • Parquetry Set • Sponge Stamp	• Stencils and Easel Paper (cut into diamond shapes) • Block Day
Group Activities	*The Shape of Things*	*The Secret Birthday Message*	*Color Farm*	*The Shapes Game*	*Changes, Changes*
Games	Daily: Find objects in the room which are the shape for the day. Daily: Play Over the River outside. Daily: Use obstacle course inside.				
Songs, Action Poems, Fingerplay	Sing "Go in and out the Window" all week.				
Transitions	Use arms and fingers to make the shape of the day as children move to the next area.	Do the same as day one.	Do the same as day one.	Do the same as day one.	Walk stiff like block people.

Room Preparation for Shapes

Bulletin Board

Use the bulletin board pattern on page 263 for shapes.

Mobile

Use the patterns on page 264 for a mobile. Use the shapes and hang them individually from the ceiling.

Extended Activity

Prepare a matching shape game using a foam board. Cut out two shapes for the children to match. Cut one shape from construction paper and the other from a texture material. Place the construction paper shape on the foam board, attached with Velcro. Fill a box with other shapes and matching shapes made of textured material. Have children reach into the box and, using touch, find the shape matching the one already on the board. Place the matching shape on the board, again using Velcro.

More Extended Activities

Use the following all week long:

1. Name a special shape per day.
2. Have stencils for that shape for each day. Use the patterns on page 265 to cut shapes out of plastic lids from coffee cans or other appropriate lids.
3. Have the easel set up each day. Have the easel paper for that day cut to the shape for the day.

Famous Paintings

- Seurat, Georges Pierre. *Sunday Afternoon on the Island of La Grande Jatte.* 1886.
- Any Pablo Picasso painting from the cubism period

Suggested Literature

Carle, Eric. *The Secret Birthday Message.* Harper and Row, 1986.

Dodds, Dayle Ann. *The Shape of Things.* Candlewick Press, 1994.

Ehlert, Lois. *Color Farm.* Lippincott, 1990.

Hutchins, Pat. *Changes, Changes.* Macmillan, 1971.

Testa, Fulvio. *If You Look Around You.* E. P. Dutton Inc., 1983.

Tucker, Sian. *The Shapes Game.* Henry Holt and Company, 1989.

Materials

- cookie dough
- construction paper
- crayons
- comic strip
- pie tin for paint
- clamp clothespins
- 24" x 24" (61 cm x 61 cm) foam board
- shape cookie cutters
- butcher paper tape
- shaped buttons
- Q-Tips
- thin sponge
- manila paper
- overhead projector
- circular Velcro stick-ons
- parquetry set
- colored tempera paint
- sponge for printing
- several sizes of empty cans

Activities for Shapes

Individual Activities

Shape Cookies

Either mix a standard butter cookie recipe or purchase cookie dough from the store. Roll out the dough and have the children cut round, square, triangle, or any other shapes you may have in the way of cookie cutters. Bake and serve for snack time. Make sure that you talk about the shapes the children are eating.

Overhead Projector Shapes

Place shapes on an overhead projector and focus on a sheet of paper taped low on a wall. Give the children crayons and have them draw over the images they see focused on the paper. Place a title over the class picture, "The Shape of Things."

Parquetry Set

Commercially made parquetry sets are a good way to show different shapes. Most sets come with patterns which are easy for most children to follow.

Q-Tip Painting

Have children look closely at a comic strip. Notice that the pictures are really dots placed very close together to form the shapes and colors. Get out a magnifying glass and show the children. There is a very famous painting done by Georges Seurat many, many years ago called *A Sunday Afternoon on the Island of La Grande Jatte*. If a reproduction of this picture is available from the library or a museum, have the children notice how all the dots form the picture. Use a magnifying glass. Show the children a Q-Tip and say that they can paint the same way as Seurat and make comic strips, too. Give them paper and tempera paint. Make sure that they have a separate Q-Tip for each color.

Empty Can Printing

Place a thin sheet of sponge in a pie tin. Under the sponge sheet, place tempera paint. Have several colors in separate pie pans available for the children. Use the open tops or the bottoms of many sizes of cans to press on the sponge. Then press the cans on a sheet of paper. Use several colors, have shapes overlap, and make designs.

Velcro Match

Use a sheet of foam board about 18" x 24" (46 cm x 61 cm). Place circular Velcro stick-on patches in a row down each side of the sheet. Do not put them too close to the edge since room is needed for the objects to be placed on the stickers. On the left side, place shapes from *The Secret Birthday Message*, using the patterns on page 266. The matching Velcro circle is placed behind each shape so that it will stay on the board. Cut matching shapes and place Velcro circles behind each. Have the children place the two shapes that match across from each other on the board. Use heavy paper to make the shapes, and the activity will last longer.

Activities for Shapes *(cont.)*

Individual Activities *(cont.)*

Button Sort

Sort out buttons according to small round and large round. If other shapes such as square, triangle, and rectangle are available, sort them also. An egg carton is a good container in which to sort buttons.

Sponge Stamp

Cut sponges into the shapes for the week—square, triangle, rectangle, etc. Attach a clamp clothespin to the top of each. Have the children dip them into tempera paint and then stamp them on paper. See how many designs can be made with all the shapes.

Block Day

Have one day where all the blocks are out and ready to be used. Include kindergarten blocks or unit blocks, hollow blocks, Lincoln Logs, Duplo, and any other commercially made blocks. Use blocks that stick together, cardboard blocks, and any block accessories. Take pictures of the creations. Then break down the creations and start again.

Group Activities

The Shape of Things

If the class project The Shape of Things was done before the group time, use this to talk about shapes. Then read the story *The Shape of Things*. Use the last page to see how many shapes the children can find in the picture. Write down and draw the shapes on a piece of paper. Which shape appeared the most?

The Secret Birthday Message

Draw a map of how to come into the building and come to the room. See if the children can follow the map. Say, "Sometimes people draw maps to secret places. That is what people did long ago if they wanted to hide something. But sometimes we could do that if we wanted to hide a secret surprise." Show the cover of the book and explain that "There is a secret message in this book which has to do with a birthday. Let's read a special book about a secret birthday message."

Read *The Secret Birthday Message*. After reading the story, talk about the shapes that lead the way to the surprise present. Using the patterns on page 265, show the different shapes. Read the book again and place the shapes in order as they lead to the surprise. Try rearranging them and see whether the children can get them in the right order again. They may have to use the book again to get the clues.

Activities for Shapes *(cont.)*

Group Activities *(cont.)*

Color Farm

Use the shapes from *The Secret Birthday Message* on an overhead projector and see whether the children can remember the names of the different shapes. Say, "On the farm there are different animals, and their shapes are sometimes like the shapes we saw in *The Secret Birthday Message* story. Let's listen to a story about the animals."

Read *Color Farm* and point out how the pages are cut out to show the children shapes. Since the story is simple and the pages are unique, it may be valuable to re-read the story. Talk about the different animals in the story. Which was the favorite? Act like that animal. Who had another favorite? How did that animal act?

Walk to the next area like a favorite animal.

The Shapes Game

The teacher explains that it is easy to name the shapes if they are separate from everything else. But it is harder to name them when they are part of our house, backyard, rooms in the house, things we wear, and the world around us. Ask the children if they can see a circle just by staying seated and looking around. How about a square? triangle? or rectangle? *The Shapes Game* book shows us where some of the shapes are in our world.

Read *The Shapes Game*. As the teacher reads, point out the word and then show the shape. Stop before going to another shape and have the children stay seated and look around the room. Have them point to that specific shape.

If the children still seem interested, read *If You Look Around You*. This book shows pictures that seem like the world we live in. Ask the children to go home and see whether they can find an item that is the shape for the day. When they come back the next day, ask them to tell everyone what the item of that shape was.

Changes, Changes

Talk about the blocks that were used for building that day. Say, "Do you think that blocks would like to tell stories about all the things they did? Let's look at the pictures in *Changes, Changes*." The children can now make up their own stories.

This story is in video and is very good. If available, use it after the children have made up their own stories.

Ask, "How do block people walk? Do you think they are stiff? Do their arms move freely? Let us walk the way you think the block people walk."

Activities for Shapes *(cont.)*

Games

Obstacle Course

Set up an obstacle course that leads around the room. Mark the floor with triangles that point in the same direction and lead the children around the room. Have them go under tables, over hollow blocks, and other items. The next day, mark the floor with squares that have arrows in the center pointing the direction to go. They may be varied each day with another shape with an arrow in the center pointing the direction to go.

Over the River

If it is possible to go outdoors, mark the pavement with two lines parallel to each other but about three feet (one meter) apart. This will represent "the river." Then place circles, triangles, squares, and rectangles in "the river." Give one child directions to cross from one side to the other by stepping only on the circles. Then tell the next child to cross from one side to the other by stepping only on the squares. Keep on going through the whole class until each has a turn. Keep notes on which shapes any children do not know. Plan future activities to involve those shapes.

Songs, Action Poems, and Fingerplay

"Go in and out the Window"

(Traditional)

Go in and out the window,
Go in and out the window,
Go in and out the window,
As we have done before.

Additional Literature for the Week

Hoban, Tana. *Circles, Triangles, and Squares.* Macmillan Publishing Co., 1979.
Hoban, Tana. *Shapes, Shapes, Shapes.* Greenwillow Press, 1986.

Cassettes and CDs

Millang, Steve and Greg Scelsa. *We All Live Together, Volume 3.*
Palmer, Hap. *Learning Basic Skills Through Music, Volume II.* Activity Records, Inc., 1969.
  "One Shape, Three Shapes"
  "Triangle, Circles, and Squares"
Palmer, Hap. *Sally the Swinging Snake.* Educational Activities, Inc., 1987.
  "Everything Has a Shape"
Stewart, Georgiana Liccione. *Shapes in Action.* Kimbo, 1980.

Video

Changes, Changes. Children's Circle. Weston Woods, 1989.

Patterns for Shapes

Shapes Bulletin Board

Patterns for Shapes *(cont.)*

Shapes Mobile

Cut out and put colored cellophane or plastic wrap in this space.

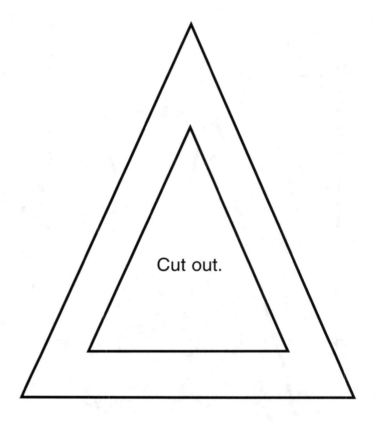

Cut out.

Cut out.

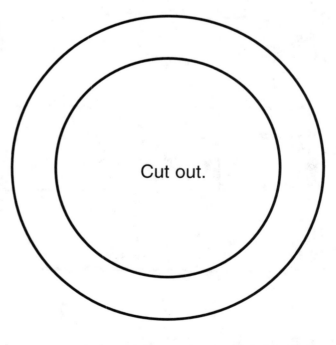

Cut out.

Patterns for Shapes *(cont.)*

Basic Shapes for Overhead Projector, Plastic Shapes, and Velcro

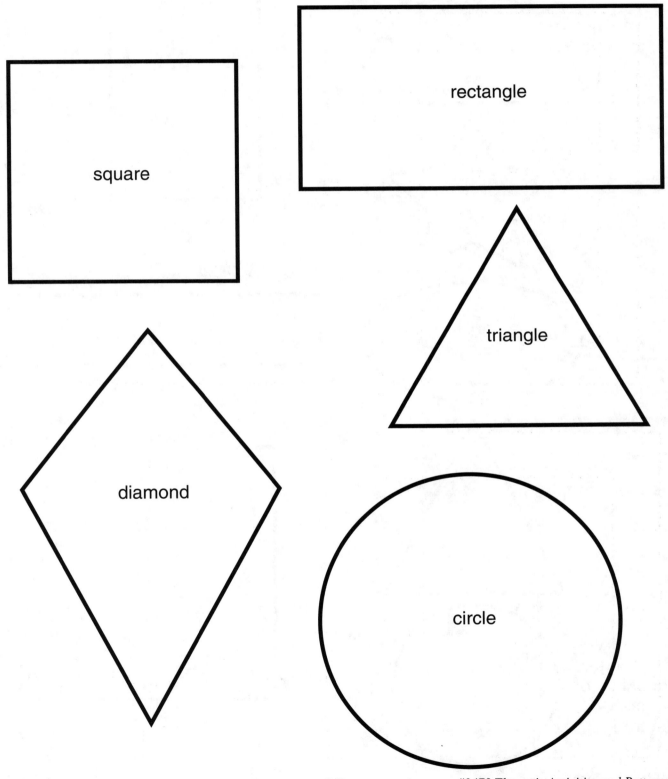

Patterns for Shapes *(cont.)*

Pattern Pieces for *The Secret Birthday Message*

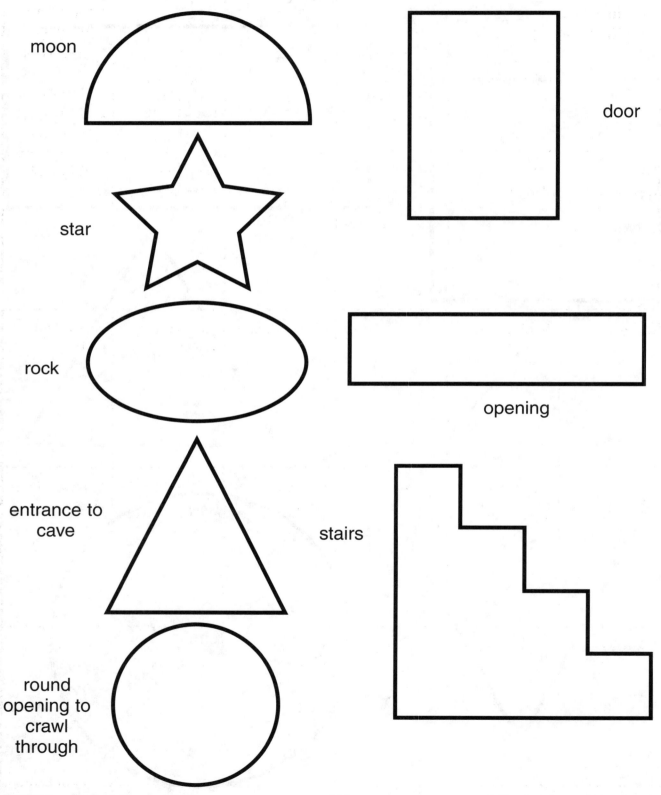

moon

door

star

rock

opening

entrance to cave

stairs

round opening to crawl through

Five Plans for Time/Measurement

	Day One	Day Two	Day Three	Day Four	Day Five
Individual Activities	• Water Table • Sea Bottle • Year Calendar	• Daily Calendar • Housekeeping Area • Print with Beans	• Ladybug • Hour Glass • Clocks	• Cereal Picture • Milk Picture • Go to Bed with Dali	• Paper Tape Measure • Carpenter's Tape Measures • Egg Carton Inchworms
Group Activities	*A House for Hermit Crab*	*Today Is Monday*	*The Grouchy Ladybug*	*Clocks and More Clocks*	*Inch by Inch*
Games	Musical Chairs	Musical Chairs	Musical Chairs	Alarm Clock Hide	Alarm Clock Hide
Songs, Action Poems, Fingerplay	"Hickory, Dickory, Dock"	"Hickory, Dickory, Dock"	• "The Clock" • "If You're Happy and You Know It"	• "The Clock" • "Wee Willie Winkie"	"I Have a Little Watch"
Transitions	Move arms like a clock.	Parade while saying "zoooop."	Walk like a grouchy bug.	Swing hands like the clock.	Crawl like an inchworm.

Room Preparation for Time/Measurement

Teacher Note

Little children have no concept of time as an adult knows time. Their feeling of time is the schedule for the school day and the time for meals at home. But they can be introduced to items that help them know about time. A calendar and a clock are such items. It is important to avoid digital clocks and watches at this time of their lives. Also, to spend energy explaining "half an hour" and similar concepts at this point is wasted energy. The books suggested are meant to pique a child's interest and not to demand understanding of time and measurement.

Bulletin Board

Have the grandfather clock in the center of the bulletin board. Surround it with clocks of different shapes and sizes. Suggested patterns are given on page 274. This pattern should be put on an overhead and enlarged.

Clocks

Have as many broken clocks as available. Allow the children to explore without the fear of breaking any of them. Modern metronomes are somewhat unbreakable. The ticking of the metronome is similar to a clock and can be used with the children if they are supervised. Also have tape measures for the children to experiment with.

Mobile

Hang the clock patterns on page 275 at various spots from the ceiling.

Suggested Famous Painting

Persistence of Memory by Salvadore Dali

Suggested Literature

Carle, Eric. *The Grouchy Ladybug.* Thomas Y. Crowell, 1977.
Carle, Eric. *A House for Hermit Crab.* Picture Books Studio, Ltd., 1987.
Carle, Eric. *Today Is Monday.* Philomel Books, 1993.
Hutchins, Pat. *Clocks and More Clocks.* Simon & Schuster, 1970.
Lionni, Leo. *Inch by Inch.* Astor-Honor, 1960.

Materials

- water table
- food coloring
- daily calendar
- tape measure
- green tempera paint
- green beans
- chalk
- shells
- plastic fish
- hour glass
- pie tin
- red and black construction paper
- cereals
- fiber egg cartons
- 16-oz clear plastic bottle
- yearly calendar
- clocks
- thin sponge sheet
- manila paper
- milk

Activities for Time/Measurement

Individual Activities

Water Table *(A House for Hermit Crab)*

Have many shells for the children to explore—starfish, conch shells, coral, and snail shells.

Sea Bottle *(A House for Hermit Crab)*

Put about 10 ounces of water tinted with blue food coloring in a clear plastic 16-ounce bottle. Add about ¹⁄₃ cup of cooking oil. Hold the bottle on its side and gently rock to create waves.

Year Calendar and Daily Calendar

Have a calendar for the whole year for the children to look through. Talk about the names of the months, circle the children's birthdays, and put their names above the appropriate dates. Have a calendar with the days of the week in a place where the children can see the days. Say, "The days have names just as the months have names."

Housekeeping Area *(Today Is Monday)*

Use plastic food items plus pots and pans for children to pretend they are eating and cooking.

Print with Beans *(Today Is Monday)*

Have a pie tin of green tempera paint with a thin sheet of sponge over it. Have green beans of varying sizes for the children to first place on the tempera paint sponge and then press onto a sheet of 9" x 12" (23 cm x 30 cm) manila paper. Have them cross the prints and make different designs with them.

Ladybug *(The Grouchy Ladybug)*

Have available assorted sizes of circular plastic lids. Have each child pick one out and place it on a piece of red construction paper as a pattern. Then have each one cut out the circle marked on the construction paper and then cut it in half. Glue the two pieces onto black construction paper, allowing space between the two halves. Use white crayon or chalk to draw a half circle above the body for a face. Place two dots on the face for eyes. Then place a fingertip on a stamp pad or into black tempera paint and print this onto the back of the ladybug for her dots.

Hour Glass

Use an hour glass that will not break and let the children watch the sand go to the bottom.

Clocks

Commercially-made flat masonite clocks are designed for preschool classroom use. They do not tell time but have hands so children can move them to form the time. Have this out so that the children can pretend the time. See whether they know numerals and can compare them to the concept of one o'clock, etc.

Cereal Picture *(Clocks and More Clocks)*

Glue different kinds of dry cereal to paper to make patterns.

Activities for Time/Measurement *(cont.)*

Individual Activities *(cont.)*

Milk Picture *(Clocks and More Clocks)*

Paint a coat of milk on manila paper. Draw on this with chalk.

Going to Bed with Dali *(Clocks and More Clocks)*

Have children pretend they are going to bed and that the teacher is going to read a bedtime story. Show Salvador Dali's picture *Persistence of Memory* to the children. Point out the clock drooping and ask, "What does the painting say to you?" Write a story about the painting.

Paper Tape Measures

Pre-cut pieces of green construction paper four inches by one inch (10 cm x 2.5 cm). Fold each narrow end at the one-inch mark. Show children how an inchworm measures by moving along, arching, and then straightening out. Children hold one end of the tape with a finger on one hand and the other end of the tape with a finger on the other hand. Have the children measure items in the room by arching and straightening the paper like an inchworm. Count each arch as "one."

Carpenter's Tape Measures

Have parents donate old tape measures for the children to use. The teacher may have to try out the tape measures ahead of time. Older children can use the kind that snap back automatically, but younger children can hurt themselves on these. The least expensive types that have to be pushed back into the holder are better for the younger children. Most children love to "measure."

Egg Carton Inchworms

Cut a fiber egg carton in half lengthwise. Paint with green tempera paint and put on black dots of paint for the eyes. Have the inchworms crawl around the room once they are dry.

Group Activities

A House for Hermit Crab

Ask the children to tell about the place that they live. Is it small? Is it big? What is it like? Say, "We are going to read a story about a sea creature called a crab." (If the classroom has a plastic crab, show the children the crab.) "But he was a very different kind of crab. He always looked for a place to live and was called a hermit crab. If he grew bigger, just as you grow every day, he had to look for a bigger place to stay. Here is his story."

Read *A House for Hermit Crab*. When finished reading, take out a calendar. Go through the book again and note what the crab did in February until the following January. He added friends to the outside of his shell because he wanted a beautiful house. Write down the months from February to January. Beside each month write down the name of the added sea creature. Then point out the picture of each creature in the book.

Have the children move to the next area, moving their arms like the arms of a clock.

Activities for Time/Measurement *(cont.)*

Group Activities *(cont.)*

Today Is Monday

Show children the calendar for the month. Point out the days of the week. Have them say them with you as you point to the different days. Say, "Let's pretend that today is Monday. What do you think would be a good food for supper?" (*Write down their answers.*) Go through the whole week and write down each item. Then take out *Today Is Monday*. Show the picture of the cat ready to eat.

Read the book with a kind of singsong rhythm. When the teacher gets to Wednesday, "Zoooop" should be stretched out with the o's on a low tone and the voice raised when you get to the letter *p*. Read through again and have the children say "Zoooop" every time it comes in the book. The music for the song is at the end of the book.

After reading the book, have everyone decide what "Zoooop" really is. Have the children parade around the room, one behind the other and clasping each other's waist, saying "Zoooop."

The Grouchy Ladybug

Sing "If You're Happy and You Know It."

> *(Traditional)*

> If you're happy and you know it,
>
> Give a smile.
>
> *(repeat)*
>
> If you're happy and you know it,
>
> Then your face will surely show it.
>
> If you're happy and you know it,
>
> Give a smile.

Say, "Is everyone happy today? Who is not? Why? If you are not happy, how do you feel? Sometimes we get grouchy instead of happy. What is it like to get grouchy? We are going to read about something that got really grouchy about something."

Read *The Grouchy Ladybug*. At the beginning of the book, explain what an aphid is. After reading the book, ask the children what the meaning of grouchy is. Say, "Do you think that the ladybug was really grouchy because she had nothing to eat all day and did not want to share the aphids with the friendly ladybug?" Then go through the book again and point to the clocks on the top of each page. Read where the short hand is pointed. That tells what the hour is. (Most young children do not have the concept of knowing that the long hand has to be on the 12 to give the hour time. It is not beneficial to explain this to them now.)

Walk around the room looking grouchy and pouting.

Activities for Time/Measurement*(cont.)*

Group Activities *(cont.)*

Clocks and More Clocks

Use as many different types of clocks as possible. Mention to the parents at the beginning of this unit that you need many different types of clocks—especially those that are not working anymore. Show the children the different kinds of clocks from wind-up to electric and from alarm to decorative. Also have old wrist watches. Have them talk about the different kinds of clocks they have at home. Say, "We are going to read a story about a man who had clocks in each room. And this is what happened."

Read *Clocks and More Clocks*. After reading the story, ask why the clocks seemed to be telling the man a different time. Who helped the man know that each clock was telling the right time? (He was told to wear a watch.) Use a flat masonite teaching clock to see whether the children can tell the numerals on the clock. Keep the long hand on the 12 but move the short hand to the other numerals. See whether the children can read the numerals.

Walk to the next area, swinging the arms like the hands on the clock.

Inch by Inch

Use a piece of green construction paper 6" x .5" (15 cm x 1.75 cm) to show how the inchworm measures things. The inchworm is in the outdoors and measures many things. Let's find out exactly what it measures.

Read *Inch by Inch*. After reading the book, ask what the inchworm really measured. Go through the pages again and talk about everything that the inchworm measured. Ask, "What was the one thing that the inchworm could not measure? What did the inchworm do to trick the nightingale? Could all the children be inchworms? Could you crawl with your backs arched and then flattened out again? Let's try." Move to the next area, moving like an inchworm.

Games

Musical Chairs

Make one line of chairs. Have them alternate facing the opposite direction. Have one less chair than the number of children in the class. Always leave this many chairs and do not take one away per round. (If the teacher takes them away, there will be a large group of children with nothing to do as they are put out of the game, and most young children cannot stand not being the winner.) Play "Syncopated Clock" by Leroy Anderson and stop it periodically as children try to find a chair.

Alarm Clock Hide

Hide a softly ticking timer. Set it for five minutes. See whether the children can find it. If it is found before the alarm goes off, say "Hip, Hip, Hooray!" for the one who found it.

Activities for Time/Measurement *(cont.)*

Songs, Action Poems, and Fingerplay

"Hickory, Dickory, Dock"

(Nursery Rhyme)

Hickory, dickory, dock!
(Join hands and let arms fall to knees. Sway back and forth.)

The mouse ran up the clock;
(Run fingers up the arm and shoulder.)

The clock struck one,
(Clap hands loudly one time.)

The mouse ran down,
(Run fingers down shoulder and arm.)

Hickory, dickory, dock!
(Sway hands and arms back and forth.)

"The Clock"

(Traditional)

With a tick and a tock,

(Move arm as a pendulum, hand upraised and elbow resting in cupped other hand. Click tongue in time to movement.)

And a tick and a tock,

The clock tells all the day.

We listen while we read a book,

And when it's time to play.

"I Have a Little Watch"

(Traditional)

I have a little watch right here.
(Make a circle with thumb and index finger.)

I hold it near my ear.
(Move circled thumb and finger next to the ear.)

It tells us when our playtime's past.
And when it's time to sleep at last.
(Put hands together and next to face.)

"Wee Willie Winkie"

(Nursery Rhyme)

Wee Willie Winkie runs through the town,

Upstairs and downstairs in his nightgown.

Rapping at the windows, crying through the lock

"Are the children in their beds?

For it's past eight o'clock."

"Ladybug, Ladybug"

(Nursery Rhymes)

Ladybug, ladybug, fly away home!

Your house is on fire; your children are gone,

All but one, and her name is Ann,

And she crept under the pudding pan.

Records, Cassettes, CDs

Hap Palmer. *Learning Basic Skills Through Music, Volume II*. Educational Activities, Inc., 1969.

"Paper Clocks"

"Today Is Monday" song source. Children's Records. Red Cover Records.

Additional Literature

Weisner, David. *Tuesday.* Clarion, 1991.

Patterns for Time/Measurement

Time Bulletin Board

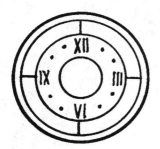

Patterns for Time/Measurement *(cont.)*

Time Mobile

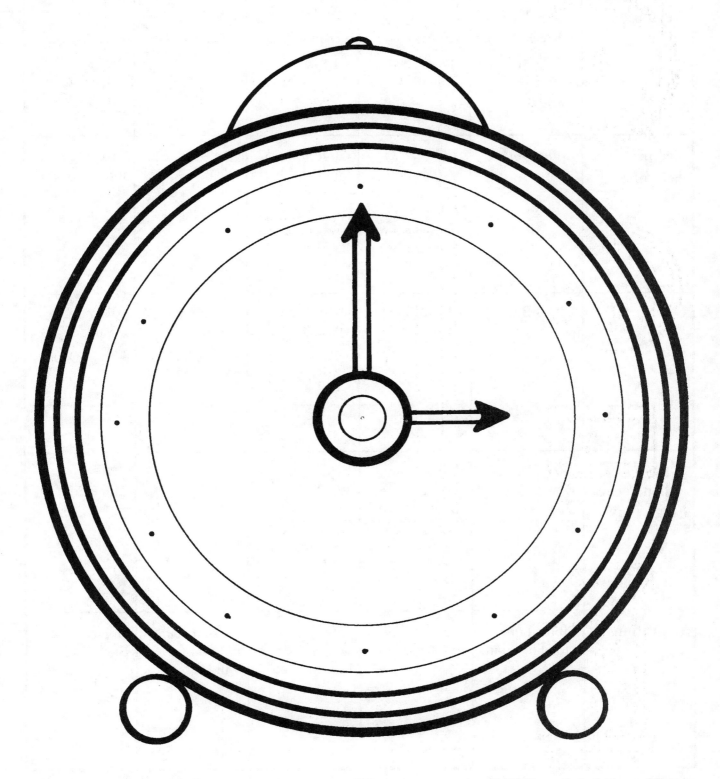

Fifteen Plans for Weather

	Day One	Day Two	Day Three	Day Four	Day Five
Individual Activities	• Foam Sculpture • Bread Clouds • Cotton Clouds	• Make Butter • Milk Carton Blocks • Whey Pictures	• Balloons in Water Table • Windmills • Blow Paint	• Bag Kite • Blow Feathers	• Finger-Paint with Blue • Taste Waters • Wet Chalkboard
Group Activities	*Little Cloud*	*It Looked Like Spilt Milk*	*Gilberto and the Wind*	*The Wind Blew*	*Bringing the Rain to Kapiti Plain*
Games	Cloud Ball	Cloud Ball	• Crepe Paper Wand • Parachute	• Crepe Paper Wand • Parachute	• Rain Tube Parade • Rain Dance
Songs, Action Poems, Fingerplay	"Row, Row, Row Your Boat"	"Row, Row, Row Your Boat"	"This Little Wind"	"This Little Wind"	"This Thunder"
Transitions	Pretend one cloud has rain.	Pretend one cloud has rain.	A very strong wind is blowing you.	Make a sound of strong wind.	Hop on one foot.

Fifteen Plans for Weather *(cont.)*

	Day Six	Day Seven	Day Eight	Day Nine	Day Ten
Individual Activities	• Sock Bottom Butterfly • Paper Towel Butterfly	• Spaghetti Art • Textured Finger Paint	• Print Turtle • Magic Umbrella	• Paint with Colored Tissue • Paint with Ice • Bubbles in Water	• Marble Roll • Chalk Rainbow • Prism • Animal Pairs
Group Activities	*Where Does the Butterfly Go When It Rains?*	*Cloudy with a Chance of Meatballs*	*Turtle Tale*	*A Rainbow of My Own*	*Noah's Ark*
Games	Caterpillar to Butterfly	Nylon Paddle	"Little Raindrops"	Dance with Crepe Paper	Row Boat
Songs, Action Poems, Fingerplay	"It's Raining, It's Pouring"	"It's Raining, It's Pouring"	"Rain, Rain, Go Away"	"Row, Row, Row Your Boat"	"Rain, Rain, Go Away"
Transitions	Make a hand butterfly and flap the wings.	Pretend to row a boat.	Move slowly like a turtle.	Follow the rainbow.	Pretend to row a boat.

Fifteen Plans for Weather *(cont.)*

	Day Eleven	**Day Twelve**	**Day Thirteen**	**Day Fourteen**	**Day Fifteen**
Individual Activities	• Bottle Scoop • Clean Mud • Goop • Outside Artist	• Freezer Wrap Painting • Ice in Water Table	• String on Brayer • Mitten Stencil • Icicle Paint	• Popcorn Snow • Newspaper Snowball Fight • Spray Paint Snow • Colored Popcorn	• Wind-Blown Feather Maze • Finding Home File Folder Game
Group Activities	*Mud Puddle*	*Happy Day*	*The Mitten*	*The Snowy Day*	Teacher's Hat
Games	Mud Puddle	"Little Raindrops"	• Mitten Bells • Mitten Match	Popcorn Popper	
Songs, Action Poems, Fingerplay		"The North Wind Doth Blow"	"The North Wind Doth Blow"	"The North Wind Doth Blow"	(any for this unit)
Transitions	Carry soap to the next area.	Dance to the next area.	Pretend to sneeze.	Make snow angels.	Follow the hat.

Room Preparation for Weather

Bulletin Board

Use the patterns on page 295. The page contains drawings for the four seasons. Enlarge or use overhead transparencies to make them larger. Seasons can be spread out on the bulletin board. Sun, stars, clouds, raindrops, and wind can be put in between.

Wind Chimes

Use a wire hanger. Using string or thread to hang nails, screws, bolts, and metal washers so that they touch each other. When moved by air, they will become wind chimes.

Suggested Background Music

- Grofé, Ferde. *Grand Canyon Suite*
- Handel, George. *Water Music*

Suggested Famous Paintings

- Caillebotte, Gustave. *Paris Street*: *Rainy Day*
- El Greco. *View of Toledo*
- Glackens, William. *Central Park, Winter*

Housekeeping Area

Put out sponges, basters, eyedroppers, squeeze bottles, measuring cups, and plastic tubing along with the water table. Place prisms in the science area.

Extended Activities

See the "Clean Mud" recipe in the plants unit on page 242.

Rain Tube

Use a large cardboard tube such as that usually found in the center of wrapping paper. Put large headed nails into the tube about an inch apart. Alternate areas down the tube. Place rice and beans in the tube and tape the top and bottom so that these do not fall out. Gently tilt the tube so that the beans and rice fall to the bottom. Turn over and let them fall again. It will sound like falling rain.

Tornado

Tornado Tubes can be purchased at science stores or educational suppliers. The activity requires two 2-liter, 1-liter, or 16-oz. plastic soda bottles. Fill one bottle ⅔ full of water and screw the Tornado Tube on that bottle. Then attach the empty bottle to the other end of the Tornado Tube. Place the full bottle on the top. Shake the upper bottle briefly in a circular motion, and a tornado will result as the liquid goes to the bottom bottle.

Rain Gauge

Attach a jar to a heavy stick or a tree near the window. Mark the jar at one-inch intervals with nail polish. When it rains, look out and see how much rain has come down.

Room Preparation for Weather *(cont.)*

Suggested Literature for Weather

Aardema, Verna. *Bringing the Rain to Kapiti Plain*. Scholastic, 1981.

Asch, Frank. *Turtle Tale*. Scholastic, 1978.

Barrett, Judi. *Cloudy with a Chance of Meatballs*. Simon & Schuster, 1978.

Brett, Jan. *The Mitten*. Putnam, 1989.

Carle, Eric. *Little Cloud*. Philomel Books, 1996.

Ets, Marie. *Gilberto and the Wind*. Penguin Books, 1969.

Freeman, Don. *A Rainbow of My Own*. Puffin Books, 1978.

Garelick, May. *Where Does the Butterfly Go When It Rains?* Mondo Publishing, 1997.

Hutchins, Pat. *The Wind Blew*. Puffins Books, 1978.

Keats, Ezra Jack. *The Snowy Day*. Penguin Books, 1962.

Krauss, Ruth. *Happy Day*. Harper and Row, 1949.

Munsch, Robert. *Mud Puddle*. Annick Press, 1982.

Shaw, Charles Green. *It Looked Like Spilt Milk*. HarperCollins, 1948. (also available through Scholastic Books)

Spier, Peter. *Noah's Ark*. Doubleday, 1977.

Materials

- foam pieces
- white bread
- manila paper
- chalk
- balloons
- finger-paint paper
- ribbons
- distilled water
- seltzer water
- crayons
- spaghetti
- rice
- popcorn
- spray bottles
- tempera paint
- glue
- cornstarch
- toothbrush

- toothpicks
- cream cheese
- milk cartons
- blue construction paper
- 1/4" diameter straws
- blue finger paint
- string
- soda water
- paper or electric fan
- paper toweling
- cornmeal
- colored tissue paper
- newspaper
- freezer paper
- lace
- icicles
- ice cubes
- hairbrush

- egg cartons
- cotton
- whipping cream
- white chalk
- brass fasteners
- large paper bag
- feathers
- tap water
- colored markers
- clamp clothespins
- dried coffee
- animal pairs
- food coloring
- paint brayer
- rickrack
- powdered tempera
- scrub brush
- eyedropper

Activities for Weather

Individual Activities

Foam Sculpture

Use a Styrofoam egg carton as the basis for this sculpture. With toothpicks, add different shapes of Styrofoam. Peanut shapes, rounds, cones, squares, and large shapes can be broken to form cloud shapes. Pretend they are clouds in the sky.

Bread Clouds

Give each child a piece of white bread. Have them tear off the crust edges and make a cloud shape. Spread with very soft cream cheese and let them eat the cloud.

Cotton Clouds

Use cotton balls, rolls of cotton, or cotton batting. Put out dark-blue construction paper, glue, and white chalk. Have the children tear the large pieces of cotton into cloud shapes. Add the cotton balls for the smaller clouds. Complete the picture with the white chalk, adding stars, lightning, wind, and tornadoes.

Make Butter

Use an electric beater to whip heavy cream. Whip until the cream separates into butter and whey. Use a spoon to press the butter against the bowl and force all the liquid from the butter. If sweet butter is desired, put on crackers and taste. Sometimes the children may prefer a little salt added to the butter and then placed on crackers.

Whey Pictures

Use liquid from the butter to coat a sheet of manila paper. Draw on this with colored chalk. Notice how bright the colors are.

Milk Carton Blocks

Have the children bring in empty half-gallon milk cartons. Tape at the top. Stack them up and see how tall they can be built. Lay them flat and make the outline of a house, boat, or city.

Balloons in Water Table

Inflate small balloons and place them in the water table. Have the children blow or fan them, causing them to move. Sometimes a little water in the balloons makes them stay in the water easier.

Windmills *(Gilberto and the Wind)*

Use the pattern for the windmills on page 297. Color with crayons. Cut on the solid line. Punch holes at the dots. Place the corners with the dots together to form a windmill. Place a small brass fastener through the holes. Punch a hole in a $1/4$-inch wide plastic straw. Put the fastener through the straw hole and bend the ends to hold in place. The key to allowing the windmill to move is allowing enough space between the windmill and the bend of the fastener.

Activities for Weather *(cont.)*

Individual Activities *(cont.)*

Blow Paint

Use the glossy side of the finger-paint paper. Moisten paper with water. Spoon on thinned tempera paint. Have the children lean close to the edge of the table and blow the paint around. Switch the paper and blow in another direction. You may want to have just one child at a table to allow enough space to blow.

Blow Feathers

Supply different sizes of feathers. Have children try to keep them in the air by blowing at them.

Bag Kite

Use a large grocery bag and attach one strand of ribbon on each side of the bag. Decorate with colored markers or crayons. Use crepe paper, string, and construction paper or fabric for the tail. Have the children run and catch the wind in the bag. Younger children may need a smaller bag.

Finger-Paint with Blue

Coat finger-paint paper with water and add blue finger paint. Have the children finger-paint with background music from the storm portion of the *Grand Canyon Suite*. Let their creations be dictated by the sound of the music. Let them pretend that their hands are the storm and they can make swirls or streaks.

Taste Different Waters

Provide water from the area, seltzer water, bottled spring water, soda water, mineral water, and any other specialized water that your area has. Have these in marked pitchers. Have children pour into paper cups and sample. Which one is their favorite?

Wet Chalkboard

Moisten the chalkboard and use an electric fan, paper fan, or hair dryer to see how long it will take to dry. Make sure that the fan and the cords are not hazardous to the children.

Sock Bottom Butterfly *(Where Does the Butterfly Go When It Rains?)*

Stand on paper and outline the bottom of the feet, either with or without shoes. Cut out and decorate like the wings of a butterfly. Make a circle of tape or use double-sided tape and attach one side to the butterfly wing and the other side to the bottom of the feet. Sit on the floor and put feet forward in front of a mirror which is on the floor. Put the feet together and have the butterfly move as the feet wiggle.

Paper Towel Butterfly *(Where Does the Butterfly Go When It Rains?)*

Use white paper toweling and decorate with colored markers. Pinch the center of the paper together and flair out the ends to form a butterfly shape. Hold the center together with a clamp or regular clothespin.

Activities for Weather *(cont.)*

Individual Activities *(cont.)*

Spaghetti Art

Boil spaghetti until soft. Drain but do not rinse. Have children arrange the strands of spaghetti on a piece of cardboard to make a design. The starch in the spaghetti will serve as glue to the cardboard. Make sure the children make a design and do not put globs of spaghetti in one spot. It will not adhere if there are too many pieces in one spot.

Textured Finger Paint

Place a coating of water on the finger-paint paper. Use any color of finger paint. Make texture with the addition of cornmeal, dried coffee grounds, or rice.

Print Turtle *(Turtle Tale)*

Start with a piece of wood which the children can hold and stamp with. Use Styrofoam meat trays and cut out a large half circle for the body and a small half circle for the head. Cut four rectangles for the legs. Glue pieces on the wood to form a turtle. Stamp in a tempera paint pan which has a thin sponge covering the paint. This will serve as a good stamp pad.

Magic Umbrella

The teacher and a child sit under the umbrella, one child at a time. The child tells the teacher what his or her secret wish is. The teacher writes it down and puts it in a secret wish box. At the end of the year, open the box and see if the wish came true.

Paint with Colored Tissue

Use colored tissue paper. Cut in small squares. Have all the colors of the rainbow available. Give children a bowl of water and a sheet of manila paper. Have them crumple up the tissue, dab it in the water, and "print" it on the paper. Try to get all the colors of the rainbow on the paper.

Paint with Ice

Mix tempera paint with a little water. Put it in small paper cups, place a craft stick in the center, and put it in the freezer. When frozen, tear the paper cup off the colored ice cube. Make many colors using this technique. Have children rub the frozen tempera on the manila paper and create a medley of colors.

Activities for Weather *(cont.)*

Individual Activities *(cont.)*

Bubbles in Water

In a small bowl, have the children blow bubbles through a straw. The bubble mixture can be made of dish soap and a little colored water. Gently place a piece of white paper over the bubbles and pick up the colors. Turn over and dry flat.

Marble Roll *(Noah's Ark)*

In a metal 9" x 13" (23 cm x 33 cm) cake pan, place a sheet of manila paper. Have several containers of marbles rolling around in tempera paint. Take one color at a time and put the marbles in the pan. Roll them around in the pan. Take them out. Then put another color in the pan, roll it around, and take it out. Stop when you feel the design is complete or pleasing.

Chalk Rainbow

Moisten manila paper with water. If it is raining outside, place the paper out in the rain to get wet. Bring it in and draw a rainbow on the paper with colored chalk.

Prism

Have the children experiment with the prism. The teacher may have to angle the prism so that the sun rays are picked up, and the rainbow is seen in the room.

Animal Pairs *(Noah's Ark)*

Put out pairs of every animal. Build a block boat and have the animals walk to the boat.

Bottle Scoop

Cut the bottle according to the diagram here. Use it to scoop up clean mud or dirty mud.

Goop

Mix three parts cornstarch to one part water. Mix together and let it sit. Have the children try to pick it up when it feels hard and watch their amazement as it turns to liquid and runs through their fingers.

Outside Artist

Use mud to paint outside on the sidewalk. Use a scrub brush, hairbrush, vegetable scrubber, and a toothbrush. The "painting" can be washed off easily. If you want to do this inside, use corrugated cardboard instead of the sidewalk.

Freezer Wrap Painting

Use markers to make a design on freezer paper. When the design is completed, place a sheet of manila paper over the design and gently rub. Since the design is on a waxed surface, it will not soak in and is easily transferred to the manila paper.

Ice in Water Table

Place ice cubes in the water table and have the boats float around the ice cubes.

Activities for Weather *(cont.)*

Individual Activities *(cont.)*

String on Brayer *(The Mitten)*

Wind yarn around a paint brayer in a random pattern. Roll in tempera paint and then roll on a contrasting color of paper.

Mitten Stencil *(The Mitten)*

Use the pattern on page 298 for the mitten story to make a cardboard stencil. Have children draw around the stencil. Then decorate the mitten with markers, crayons, lace, yarn, etc.

Icicle Paint

Find icicles. Break them off (and also break off any sharp points). Have the children put on their mittens. Sprinkle powdered tempera on manila paper and have the children spread it around with their mitten-held icicle.

Popcorn Snow

If you live in an area where there is no snow or if it is the time of the year when there is no snow, try popcorn snow. Place a large sheet on the floor. In the center place the popcorn popper. Tape down the cord. Put popcorn in the popper but do not use oil. Put the cover on. When the popcorn starts to pop, take the cover off and have the children enjoy the popcorn spreading all over the sheet.

Newspaper Snowball Fight

In the block area, set up two walls. Behind them roll up balls of newspaper as snowballs. Throw snowballs at each other.

Spray Paint Snow

If you do have snow, fill a spray bottle with food coloring and water. Have the children go outside and make designs in the snow.

Colored Popcorn

Use the popcorn made for popcorn snow and put in food-colored water. Take out the popcorn and let it dry. Have the children glue it on manila paper or colored construction paper, making designs or shapes.

Wind-Blown Feather Maze

Use the pattern on page 301 to have the children trace the path of the feather as blown by the wind.

Finding Home File Folder Game

Use the patterns on pages 302 and 303. The file folder game recalls some of the stories in the unit as the child finds home through all kinds of weather.

Activities for Weather *(cont.)*

Group Activities

Little Cloud

Ask children whether they know how a cloud becomes a cloud. Then show them how it really is formed.

1. Pour about one inch (2.5 cm) of boiling hot water in a glass jar.
2. Put a metal tray of ice cubes over the top of the jar.
3. Darken the room and shine a flashlight toward the middle of the jar. Watch a small cloud begin to form in the jar.

Cut three sizes of cloud shapes. Put them on the overhead projector. Have the children tell the teacher how to arrange them so they are big to small. Turn off the projector, rearrange, and have the children repeat the process. Explain that the little cloud has a story to tell.

Read *Little Cloud.* After reading the story, have the children lie on the floor and look at the ceiling. Let them imagine that they are looking at the sky and seeing clouds. What shapes do they see? What sizes? Where are they going? Are there any rain clouds?

Move to the next area, pretending that one of the "ceiling clouds" starts to rain.

It Looked Like Spilt Milk

Pre-make flannelboard pieces for the tray. Use the patterns on page 296. Explain that clouds have all kinds of shapes. Sometimes the sky looks as if someone spilled some milk. Pour some milk on a piece of construction paper. Say "What kind of shape does it have? Does it look like a cloud? Let's read a story and find out about the cloud shapes."

Read *It Looked Like Spilt Milk.* As the story is read, put the shapes up on the flannelboard. After reading the story, ask, "Did the spilt milk cloud in the book look like our spilt milk cloud? Look at some of the shapes on the flannelboard. What do they look like?" Leave the flannelboard and cloud pieces out most of the week so the children can retell the story.

Gilberto and the Wind

Have objects on a tray such as a blade of grass, paper kite, apple, leaf, feather, string, straw, napkin, hammer, nail, piece of wood, and inflated balloon. Have the children guess which ones the wind would blow away. Write down the items that the children think will blow away. If the weather is nice, take the children outside and put the tray on a bench or table. Hopefully, the wind will blow away the lightweight items. If the weather is bad, use a paper or electric fan inside to show how some items will blow away. Say, "Sometimes the wind blows things, and sometimes the wind is very quiet. Be very quiet like the wind is sometimes and listen to the story."

Read *Gilberto and the Wind.* After reading the story, ask the children what some of the things were that the wind blew for Gilberto. Go through the list made before the story. Then go through each page of the story to compare the things that Gilberto's wind blew and our wind blew. Were they the same? Were some of our things different? Which were they?

Move to the next area, pretending that a very strong wind is blowing at you.

Activities for Weather *(cont.)*

Group Activities *(cont.)*

The Wind Blew

Show children a hair dryer. Show how it blows the hair dry. Then show how it blows feathers. Say, "It is like a wind but smaller. The wind can blow big things, too. Can you think of anything that you have seen the wind blow? Have the things been big or little? We have a story about a wind that blew little things and then decided to blow big things."

Read *The Wind Blew.* Ask what the little things were that the wind blew. Then ask what the big thing was that it blew out to sea. Use a parachute or sheet to be the sail of the boat. Have the children take hold all around the parachute. Swirl it up and let it rest down. Put whiffle balls in the center and have them pop up. Then use one of the parachute records to do other activities.

Make whooshing sounds of a strong wind as children move to the next area.

Bringing the Rain to Kapiti Plain

Ask children to pretend with the teacher that it is a very hot day. Wipe sweat from the forehead, loosen the neck button, roll up the sleeves, etc. Say, "There is a story that happened a long, long time ago. The people needed rain so much. And this is what happened."

Read *Bringing the Rain to Kapiti Plain.* Have the children repeat these lines with you:

> To green-up the grass,
> all brown and dead,
> That needed the rain
> from the cloud overhead—
> The big, black cloud,
> All heavy with rain,
> That shadowed the ground
> on Kapiti Plain.

Read the story with a deliberate voice. When the rain comes, speed up the pace.

For younger children, obtain the video produced by *Reading Rainbow* and read by James Earl Jones.

After reading the story, notice that Ki-pat stands on one foot. See if children can stand on one foot like Ki-pat. Then hop to the next area on one foot.

Activities for Weather (cont.)

Group Activities (cont.)

Where Does the Butterfly Go When It Rains?

Have children cross wrists with the palms facing them. Interlink the thumbs. They now have a butterfly.

Have them wiggle the butterfly. Ask whether they have ever watched a butterfly. Ask, "Where is its home? Does it have a mommy or a daddy? What do you think happens to it when it rains?

Read *Where Does the Butterfly Go When It Rains?* Did the story tell what happens to the butterfly in the rain? Have your hand butterfly fly around and see if there is a spot in the room where it can hide. If the weather permits, have the children go outside. Have their hand butterflies try to find a spot where a butterfly can go in the rain.

Cloudy with a Chance of Meatballs (for older children)

Have a pan of water and slowly dribble some down from the teacher's raised hand. Say, "What is the water like? Is it clear? Is it clean? Would you drink it? What would you do if every time it rained, there was some food in the rain? At first it would be really neat, but after awhile it would not be fun anymore. We are going to read a story about a whole town that had constant rain with food. You listen and see what they did about it."

Read *Cloudy with a Chance of Meatballs.* After reading the story, ask the children what the town did about the constant rain with food. Have the children sit on a large rug and pretend they are the town rowing on the stale bread to another place. While they are rowing, pretend to point to a place you think would be a good place to land. Get off the boat of stale bread and shout, "Hooray! We won't have food rain!"

Then walk to the next area, pretending to row a boat.

Turtle Tale

Have an eyedropper. Have the children count the drops as the teacher squeezes the rubber top. Try again. Say, "How many this time? We know that if there is water in the eyedropper, it will come out. We also know that if there is a dark cloud and thunder, there will be rain. What would you do if you had to walk from your house to another house in the rain? Do you have an umbrella? Does a turtle have an umbrella? He has a built-in umbrella! Let's see how he uses it."

Read *Turtle Tale.* Ask, "Did the turtle know when to use his 'umbrella'? What was the wise thing for him to do with his head? 'Out in the sun and in when it rains.' Is this a wise saying for children? Our heads should be out in the sun or good weather and in when it rains."

Activities for Weather *(cont.)*

Group Activities *(cont.)*

A Rainbow of My Own

Use a prism to show children a rainbow from sunlight or a lightbulb. Practice first to make sure the angle is right to catch the rays. Ask, "How would you like to have a rainbow of your own?"

Read *A Rainbow of My Own*. Ask, "Where did the rainbow of his own come from? *(fish bowl)* But where else was his rainbow? *(in the garden of flowers)*" Cut a paper plate in half. Attach crepe paper streamers the colors of the rainbow on the curved section. Use your hand to hold the straight edge. Swirl the "rainbow" and lead the children around the room. Have them walk, hop, jump, and gallop, following the rainbow. Have the rainbow lead them to the next area.

Noah's Ark

Ask children if they have ever been on a boat. "How big was it? Was it fun? What did you do?" Show the picture of the very big boat or ark on the cover of the book. This is a wordless book, so have the children tell the story from the pictures. If the videotape is available, play that. After the video is seen or the children tell the story from the pictures, explain that the story tells of the very first rainbow. The rainbow is a promise that there will never be a flood covering the entire earth again. Ask children, "Everytime you see a rainbow, what does it promise?"

Use the "rainbow" made from crepe paper in *Rainbow of My Own* to lead the children to the next area.

Mud Puddle

Have a bucket of brown circles with paper clips fastened to them. Have the circles numbered from one to nine. Either have the teacher or a child pretend to fish out the circles with a long dowel and attached string with a magnet. Pull them out and ask what the numeral on the circle is. Then take all the circles out and count them. Say, "There were nine puddles in the bucket! Do you think they will behave if we put them off into the corner?" Say, "I know a very bad puddle, and this is that puddle's story."

Read *Mud Puddle*. As you read, notice these lines:

> She washed out her ears.
> She washed out her eyes.
> She even washed out her mouth.
> Everytime Julie Ann was put into the tub, another thing had to be scrubbed.

Ask the children how Julie Ann got rid of the puddle. Show children a bar of soap. Have everyone smell the soap. Take out the puddles used at the beginning of the group activity. Put them on a cookie sheet with the numerals up. Put a towel over them and remove one. Now remove the towel and see if the children can identify the missing numeral. Show the missing puddle and rub soap over it so that it won't reappear. Continue the process until all the puddles are gone.

Have one child carry the soap and lead the others to the next area.

Activities for Weather *(cont.)*

Group Activities *(cont.)*

Happy Day

Bring a cardboard box to the story area. Have in it Styrofoam pieces. At the very bottom, have a yellow plastic flower. Have the children guess what is at the bottom of the box. Write down their answers. Then explain that all the animals in the forest had a very happy day. Ask whether the children had a happy day. What happened to make them happy? Say, "Let's read *Happy Day* and see why all the animals were happy."

Read *Happy Day* up to the point before finding the flower in the snow. Open the cardboard box and show the children the flower at the bottom. Say, "Oh, this makes me so happy!" Then read the last page of the book and show how flowers at the end of winter make people happy and animals happy too. Why?

Make up a "Happy Day Box." Have the children take turns taking it home and bringing something back that makes them happy about spring (or any season). Keep a record of the items each child brings, the date, and the child's name.

Then have the children pretend to be animals. First they are sleeping, then they open their eyes, and then they sniff, get up, laugh, run, and dance. Let them dance to the next area.

The Mitten

Cut two pieces of white felt mitten, using the pattern on page 298. Place Velcro pieces on the edges to keep them together. The patterns for the animals on page 299 can be cut from paper or traced through the pattern onto heavy Pellon. If made from Pellon, it will last longer.

Ask children what kinds of clothes they wear in the winter. When they mention mittens, ask what colors their mittens are. "Does anyone have white mittens? What color is the snow? If you lost a white mitten in the snow, would it be easy to find? We are going to read a story about a white mitten that got lost in the snow, and it had quite an adventure."

Read *The Mitten*. After reading the story, tell it again. This time, show the white felt mitten. As the story is told, place the animals in the mitten. When the mouse enters the mitten, have all the children say, "Aaaaaa-aaaaa-aaaaaa-ca-chew!" Pull the mitten apart and have all the animals scatter.

Have a regular pair of mittens. Quietly place a small item such as a button, marble, stick of gum, or safety pin in the mitten and slip it over the hand. Have the children feel the mitten and smell the mittten and see whether they can tell what is in the mitten. Have the children close their eyes while the teacher takes out that item and replaces it with another one. Let the children open their eyes and guess what is now in the mitten on the teacher's hand.

Walk around the room while pretending to sneeze. But always cover the mouth with the hands.

290

Activities for Weather *(cont.)*

Group Activities *(cont.)*

The Snowy Day

Have ice cubes on a warming tray and some on a table. As the children gather, have them watch the ice cubes melt. Ask, "Which do you think will become water first?" While waiting to see which will melt first, have them sing the following song to the tune of "I'm a Little Teapot."

> We are little ice cubes short and fat,
>
> One on a warm spot,
>
> And one just sat.
>
> When we get all warmed up, then we shout,
>
> Wipe up the water and throw us out!

Have the teacher tell the children that it has to be very cold out to have ice and snow. If it is warm, then the ice will melt and we will have rain instead of snow. Ask children what they do on a snowy day. Have they ever made angels in the snow?

Read *Snowy Day*. Say, "Peter did a lot of things in the snow. What were they? Peter also made angels in the snow. How do you do that?" Have all the children lie down on the floor, pretend they are in the snow, and make angels.

Then walk to the next area waving arms and still making angels.

Teacher's Hat

Wear a wide-brimmed hat. At the outer edge of the hat, have items hanging from string that represent any story used in this unit. From construction paper cut shapes of clouds, paper, windmills, raindrops, butterflies, turtles, spaghetti, rainbows, Noah's ark, puddles, and snowflakes. If plastic shapes cannot be found in craft stores, use the patterns on page 300. Have the children point to the shapes they like the best. See if they remember the story that goes with the item hanging from the hat. Can they tell the story? Go around the hat and see if they can name the stories or just tell what they remember.

Then have them "follow the hat" to the next area.

Games

Cloud Ball

Divide the class into groups of twos. Have the two children hold a ball between them at their tummies. Refer to it as their cloud. Move around and see if the ball can stay without falling down. If it falls, pick it up quickly before the cloud turns to rain!

Crepe Paper Wand

Attach crepe paper to a six-inch (15 cm) dowel. Have children wave these around to music. Use any of the records or cassettes listed at the end of the unit.

Activities for Weather *(cont.)*

Games *(cont.)*

Nylon Paddle

Make a paddle of an old nylon stocking pulled over a wire hanger bent and pulled into a diamond shape. Attach the nylon to the hanger with a rubber band. Use this paddle to bat around balloons and pretend to be the wind.

Parachute

Any of the parachute records or cassettes work well with wind. However, if you do not have a parachute, a large sheet will do. It is more fun if you have whiffle balls to toss in the sheet. They look like snow or popcorn.

Rain Dance

Make a circle and pass around the rain tube. Let each child take a turn to make up a rain dance, starting with one foot. Keep the sound of rain going, using the rain tube.

Caterpillar to Butterfly

Have children crawl around like caterpillars. Then let them bend down and roll into tight balls as if in a cocoon. Then have them unfold, stretch, and flutter around as butterflies. The teacher announces that the rain is coming, and all the children try to find a place to hide. The teacher says, "The sun is out now." All the children return to the group and start again as caterpillars.

Outside Spray

Spray a hose up in the air. As the water falls, notice the rainbow.

Popcorn Popper

Use Hula-Hoops for the popcorn poppers. Have about two or three children sit inside each Hula-Hoop. The children pretend to be kernels that crouch down and pop up when teacher says "Ready." Then pretend to eat the popcorn.

Mitten Match

Have children make a pile of all their mittens. They are then to walk back and wait for a signal. When teacher says, "Get your mittens," have everyone run to the pile and put on their mittens.

Mitten Bells

Sew bells to mittens or have the children hold bells with mitten hands. Shake them to any of the listed records or cassettes.

Mud Puddle

Mark off a one-yard (one-meter) circle on the playground surface. Tell the children that it is a mud puddle. See how many can jump across without stepping in the mud.

(See "Muddy Water Puddles" from *Sally the Singing Snake.*)

Activities for Weather *(cont.)*

Songs, Action Poems, and Fingerplay

"Little Raindrops"
(Traditional)

(Children act out the poem with one sun, one cloud, several raindrops, and several flowers crouched down on the floor.)

This is the sun, high up in the sky.
(One child pretends to be the sun with arms circular and high.)

A dark cloud suddenly comes sailing by.
(Another cloud child steps in front of the sun.)

These are the raindrops,
Pitter, pattering down,
(Several children pretend to sprinkle raindrops on the crouched-down flowers.)

Watering the flowers,
Growing on the ground.
(Children who are the flowers stretch and reach high.)

"This Little Wind"
(Traditional)

This little wind blows silver rain.
(Hold up five fingers starting with the thumb. Bend each down as the verse progresses.)
This little wind drifts snow.
This little wind sings a whistled tune.
This little wind hums low.
And this little wind rocks baby birds,
Tenderly to and fro.
(Put hands together and rock.)

"Thunder"
(Tune: Brother John)

I hear thunder, I hear thunder.
Hark, don't you? Hark, don't you?
Pitter, patter raindrops, pitter, patter raindrops,
I'm wet through.
So are you.

"The North Wind Doth Blow"
(Nursery Rhyme)

The North Wind doth blow,
And we shall have snow.
And what will the robin do then, poor thing?
He will sit in the barn and keep himself warm,
With his little head tucked under his wing, poor thing!

"It's Raining, It's Pouring"
(Nursery Rhyme)

It's raining, it's pouring.
The old man is snoring.
He went to bed with a pain in his head,
And didn't get up until morning.

Activities for Weather (cont.)

Songs, Action Poems, and Fingerplay (cont.)

"Rain, Rain, Go Away"
(Nursery Rhyme)

Rain, rain, go away.

Come again some other day.

"Row, Row, Row Your Boat"
(Traditional)

Row, row, row your boat,

Gently down the stream.

Merrily, merrily, merrily, merrily,

Life is but a dream.

Records, Cassettes, and CD's

Jenkins, Ella. *I Know the Colors in the Rainbow.* Activity Records, Inc., 1981.

"I Know the Colors in the Rainbow"

"It Won't Rain, It Won't Rain"

Palmer, Hap. *Sally the Singing Snake.* Educational Activities, Inc., 1987.

"Muddy Water Puddles"

Strickland, Willy and James Earle. *There's Music in the Colors.* Kimbo, 1976.

"Black Can Be a Closet"

Videos

Bringing the Rain to Kapiti Plain. Reading Rainbow. Narrated by James Earl Jones.

Noah's Ark. Stories to Remember. Distributed by Media Home Entertainment, Inc., Heron Communications, Inc., 1989.

Snowy Day. Children's Circle. Weston Woods, 1983.

Patterns for Weather

Weather Bulletin Board

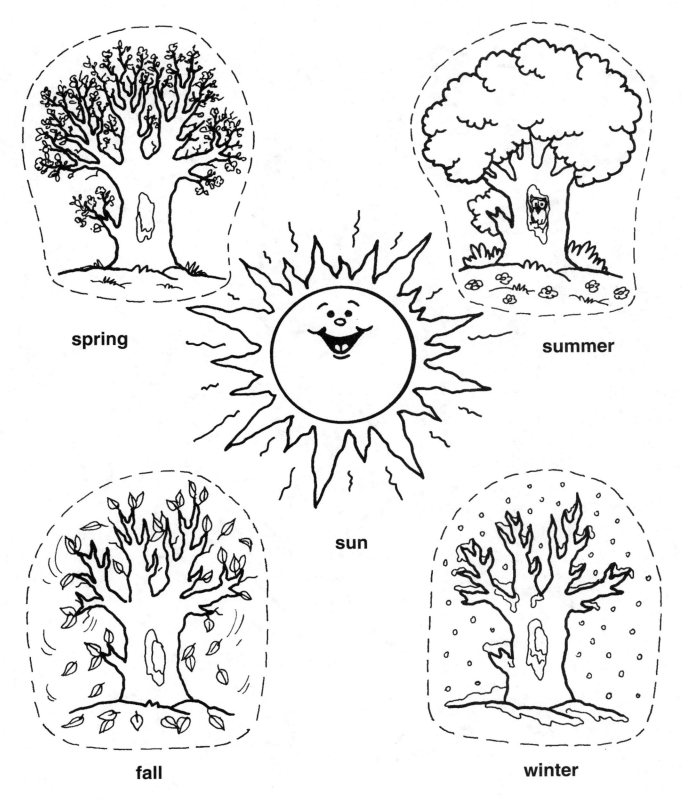

spring

summer

sun

fall

winter

Patterns for Weather (cont.)

Flannelboard Pieces for *It Looked Like Spilt Milk*

Patterns for Weather *(cont.)*

Windmill Pattern

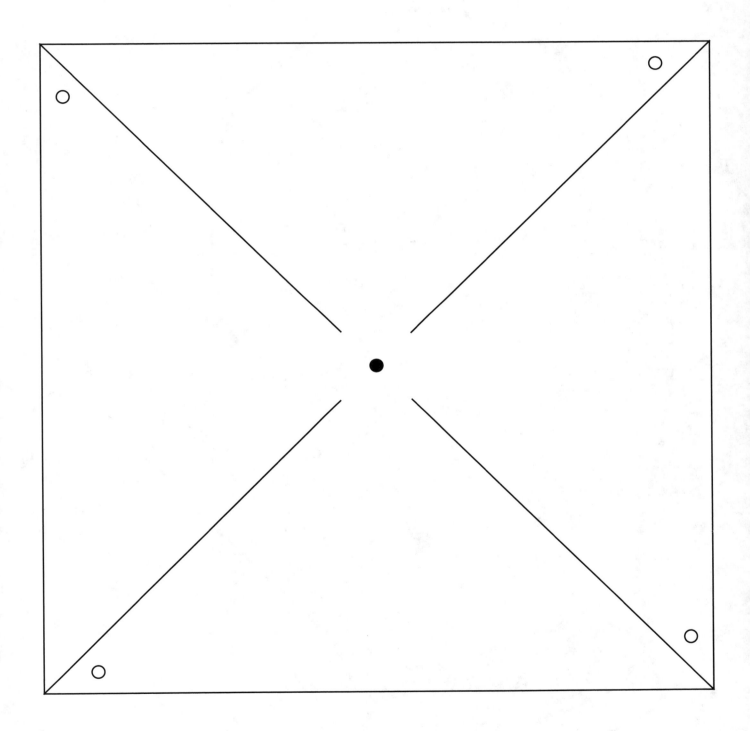

Patterns for Weather *(cont.)*

Pattern for *The Mitten*

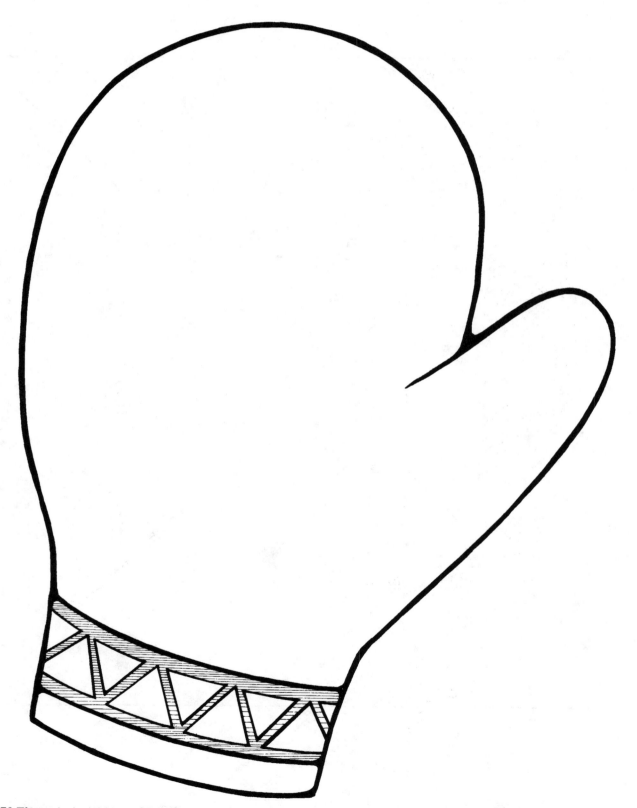

298

Patterns for Weather (cont.)

Patterns for Animal Pieces for *The Mitten*

Patterns for Weather (cont.)

Shapes to Hang from Hat

Patterns for Weather *(cont.)*

Wind-Blown Feather Maze

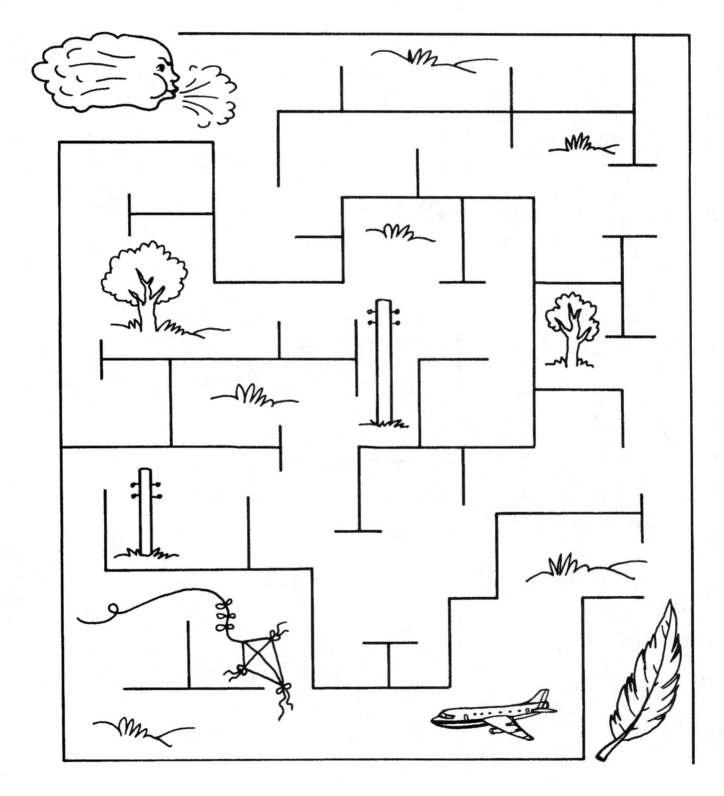

Patterns for Weather *(cont.)*

Finding Home Through the Weather File Folder Game

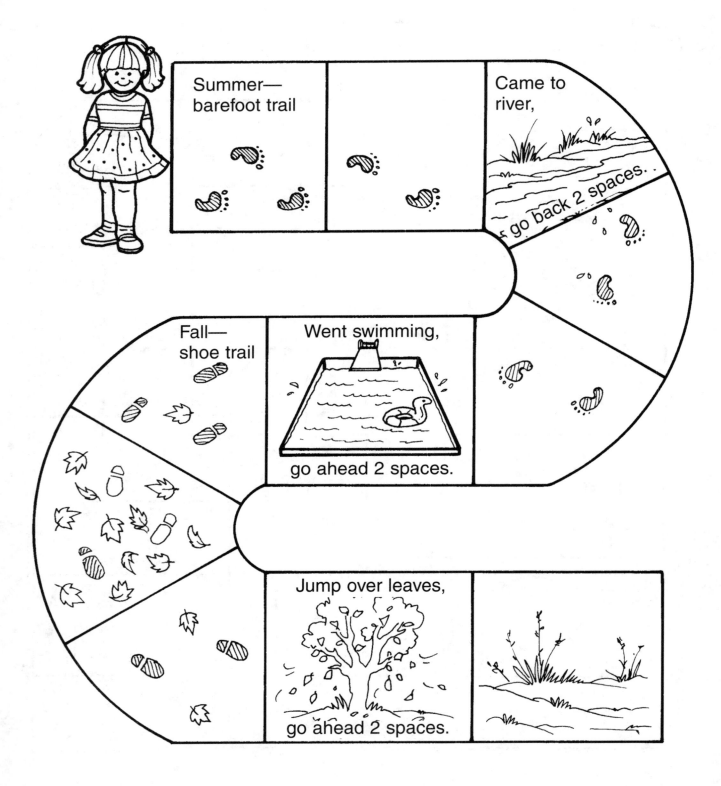

Summer— barefoot trail

Came to river, go back 2 spaces.

Fall— shoe trail

Went swimming, go ahead 2 spaces.

Jump over leaves, go ahead 2 spaces.

Patterns for Weather *(cont.)*

Finding Home Through the Weather File Folder Game *(cont.)*

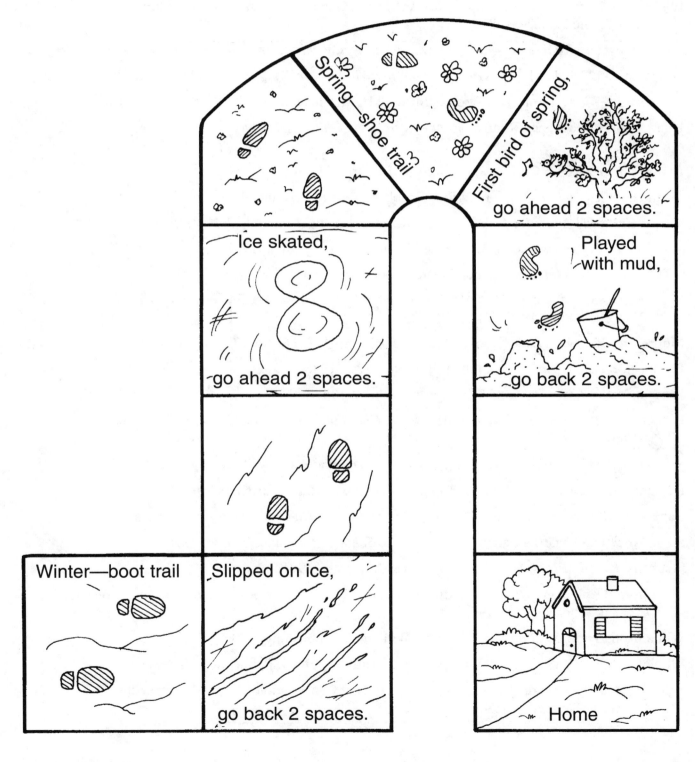

Bibliography

Carratello, John and Patty. *Eric Carle—Across the Curriculum with Favorite Authors*. Teacher Created Materials, Inc., 1992.

Fabion, Bobbie. *Twinkle, Twinkle—An Animal Loves Mother Goose*. Dutton Children's Books, 1996.

Faggella, Kathy. *Crayons, Crafts, and Concepts*. First Teacher Press, 1985.

Flint Public Library. *Ring a Ring o' Roses* (Stories, Games, and Fingerplays for Preschool Children) Flint Public Library, 1981.

Forte, Imogene. *Rainy Day Magic for Wonderful Wet Weather*. Incentive Publications, Inc., 1983.

Fox, Dan and Claude Marks. *Go in and out the Window for Young People*. Henry Holt and Co., 1987.

Gingerbread Man. (Storytime Books, Illustrated) McClanahan Books, 1996.

Hunt, Tamara and Nancy Renfro. *Puppetry in Early Childhood Education*. Nancy Renfro Studios, 1982.

Irving, Jan and Robin Currie. *Mudluscious*. Libraries Unlimited, 1986.

Jasmine, Grace. *Circle Time Activities*. Teacher Created Materials, Inc., 1997.

———*Everyday Activities for Preschool*. Teacher Created Materials, Inc., 1995.

———*Preschool Arts & Crafts*. Teacher Created Materials, Inc., 1997.

———*Preschool Games*. Teacher Created Materials, Inc., 1997.

Kohl, Mary. *Scribble Cookies and Other Independent Creative Art Experiences for Children*. Bright Ring Publishing, 1985.

Moore, Jo Ellen and Leslie Tryon. *Bears, Bears, Bears*. Evan-Moor Corp., 1988.

Pagnucci, Susan. *I Can!* (folk tales) Bur Oak Press, 1986.

Patrick, Jennett. *Gingerbread Kids*. Partners Press, 1987.

Pecuch, Patricia. *Ezra Jack Keats—Across the Curriculum with Favorite Authors*. Teacher Created Materials, 1995.

Rockwell, Ann. *Games and How to Play Them*. Thomas Y. Crowell Co., 1973.

Rojankovsky, Feodor. *The Tall Book of Mother Goose*. Harper Brothers Pub., 1942.

Silberstein-Storfer, Muriel and Mablen Jones. *Doing Art Together*. Harry N. Abrams, Inc., 1997.

Stein, Arleen and Martha Lane. *Teddy Bears at School*. Humanics Limited, 1986.

Stephens, Karen. *Block Adventures*. First Teacher Press, 1991.

Thompson, Debbie and Darlene Hardwick. *Early Childhood Themes Through the Year*. Teacher Created Materials, Inc., 1993.

Williamson, Sarah A. *Stop, Look, Listen*. Williamson Publishing, 1996.

Wilmes, Liz and Dick. *Paint Without Brushes*. Building Block Publications, 1993.

Zeitlein, Stacy A. "Finding Fascinating Projects That Can Promote Boy/Girl Partnerships." *Young Children*. September 1997.